WITHDRAWAL

THE LEARNING SCIENCES IN EDUCATIONAL ASSESSMENT

There is mounting hope in the United States that federal legislation in the form of No Child Left Behind and the Race to the Top fund will improve educational outcomes. As titanic as the challenge appears to be, however, the solution could be at our fingertips. This volume identifies visual types of cognitive models in reading, science, and mathematics for researchers, test developers, school administrators, policy makers, and teachers. In the process of identifying these cognitive models, the book also explores methodological or translation issues to consider as decisions are made about how to generate psychologically informative and psychometrically viable large-scale assessments based on the learning sciences. Initiatives to overhaul educational systems in disrepair may begin with national policies, but the success of these policies will hinge on how well stakeholders begin to rethink what is possible with a keystone of the educational system: large-scale assessment.

Jacqueline P. Leighton is Professor of Educational Psychology and Director of the Centre for Research in Applied Measurement and Evaluation at the University of Alberta. She is also registered as a psychologist by the College of Alberta Psychologists. Her specialization is educational assessment and cognitive psychology, with an emphasis on test development and validity analysis. Dr. Leighton's current research is on identifying and evaluating methods for generating cognitive models for educational-assessment practice. Her research has been funded by the Natural Sciences and Engineering Research Council of Canada and the Canadian Education Statistics Council and is currently funded by the Social Sciences and Humanities Research Council of Canada.

Mark J. Gierl is Professor of Educational Psychology at the University of Alberta. His specialization is educational and psychological testing, with an emphasis on the application of cognitive principles to assessment practices. Dr. Gierl's current research is focused on differential item and bundle functioning, cognitive diagnostic assessment, and assessment engineering. His research is funded by both the College Board and the Social Sciences and Humanities Research Council of Canada. He holds the Canada Research Chair in Educational Measurement.

The Learning Sciences in Educational Assessment

THE ROLE OF COGNITIVE MODELS

Jacqueline P. Leighton
University of Alberta

Mark J. Gierl
University of Alberta

CAMBRIDGE
UNIVERSITY PRESS

CAMBRIDGE UNIVERSITY PRESS
Cambridge, New York, Melbourne, Madrid, Cape Town,
Singapore, São Paulo, Delhi, Tokyo, Mexico City

Cambridge University Press
32 Avenue of the Americas, New York, NY 10013-2473, USA

www.cambridge.org
Information on this title: www.cambridge.org/9780521194112

© Jacqueline P. Leighton and Mark J. Gierl 2011

First published 2011

Printed in the United States of America

A catalog record for this publication is available from the British Library.

Library of Congress Cataloging in Publication data
Leighton, Jacqueline P.
  The learning sciences in educational assessment: the role of cognitive models/
Jacqueline P. Leighton, Mark J. Gierl.
    p. cm.
  Includes index.
  ISBN 978-0-521-19411-2 (hardback)
  1. Educational tests and measurements. 2. Educational psychology.
  3. Cognition. I. Gierl, Mark J. II. Title.
  LB3051.L425 2011
  371.260973–dc22   2011004251

ISBN 978-0-521-19411-2 Hardback

CONTENTS

v

1

The Learning Sciences in Educational Assessment: An Introduction

Victor Hugo is credited with stating that "There is nothing more powerful than an idea whose time has come." In educational achievement testing,[1] a multi-billion-dollar activity with profound implications for individuals, governments, and countries, the idea whose time has come, it seems, is that *large-scale achievement tests must be designed according to the science of human learning*. Why this idea, and why now? To begin to set a context for this idea and this question, a litany of research studies and public policy reports can be cited to make the simple point that students in the United States and abroad are performing relatively poorly in relation to expected standards and projected economic growth requirements (e.g., American Association for the Advancement of Science, 1993; Chen, Gorin, Thompson, & Tatsuoka, 2008; Grigg, Lauko, & Brockway, 2006; Hanushek, 2003, 2009; Kilpatrick, Swafford, & Findell, 2001; Kirsch, Braun, & Yamamoto, 2007; Manski & Wise, 1983; Murnane, Willet, Dulhaldeborde, & Tyler, 2000; National Commission on Excellence in Education, 1983; National Mathematics Advisory Panel, 2008; National Research Council, 2005, 2007, 2009; Newcombe et al., 2009; Phillips, 2007; Provasnik, Gonzales, & Miller, 2009). According to a 2007 article in the *New York Times*, Gary Phillips, chief scientist at the American Institutes for Research, was quoted as saying, "our Asian

---

[1] The terms "testing" and "assessment" are used interchangeably in the present volume to denote formal measurement techniques and evaluation procedures.

economic competitors are winning the race to prepare students in math and science." Phillips made this comment in relation to a report equating the standardized large-scale test scores of grade-eight students in each of the fifty U.S. states with those of their peers in forty-five countries. Underlying the sentiment in this quote is the supposition that test scores reveal valuable information about the quality of student learning and achievement[2] for feeding future innovation and economic growth. If test scores reveal that U.S. students are underperforming relative to their peers in other countries, then learning is likely being compromised, and innovation and economic growth may also falter.

To change this potentially grim outcome, there are at least three options: Change the educational system, change the large-scale tests,[3] or change both. In the balance of this book, we focus on the second option – changing the large-scale tests. This decision does not indicate that the first and third options lack merit. In fact, the third option is ideal. However, in this first chapter, we present a rationale for why it makes sense to focus on changing tests, that is, to design and develop large-scale educational assessments based on the learning sciences. To start, we discuss the relatively poor test performance of many U.S. students as an impetus for the growing motivation in North America to enhance the information large-scale educational

---

[2] Although we recognize that learning and achievement sometimes connote different ideas (e.g., learning might be used in relation to the processes involved in the acquisition of knowledge and skills, and achievement might be used in relation to demonstrations of those knowledge and skills), learning and achievement are used interchangeably in this volume. The goal of most educational initiatives and institutions is to have learning and achievement overlap significantly. In addition, developers of achievement tests strive to design measures that are sensitive to progressions in learning.

[3] The focus is on large-scale educational testing because testing companies and assessment branches of government agencies have the human and financial capital to consistently develop, refine, and administrate standardized, psychometrically sound assessments based on scientific cognitive learning models for large numbers of students. Although classroom tests could also be developed from findings in the learning sciences, these are less likely to be developed according to the same models due to a lack of resources.

assessments currently provide about student learning. Next, we present well-accepted knowledge from the learning sciences about the nature of thinking, learning, and performance to help determine the types of knowledge and skill components that may be required for measurement as large-scale educational assessments are designed and developed. After that, illustrative empirical studies in the field of educational measurement are reviewed to demonstrate the nature of the attempts to design and develop assessments based on the learning sciences (also commonly referred to as *cognitive diagnostic assessments* [CDA] or *cognitively based tests*; see Leighton & Gierl, 2007). Then, we offer a view on what is needed in the field of educational assessment to incorporate and systematically evaluate cognitive models in the design and development of large-scale assessments. Finally, we present a conclusion and roadmap for the present volume that outlines the rationale and content of the next six chapters, including what may be needed to change large-scale tests and ensure they provide the information about student learning and achievement many stakeholders seek.

THE IMPETUS FOR CHANGE: LOW ACHIEVEMENT TEST RESULTS

The U.S. Department of Education (2008) posted the following summary of the results achieved by fifteen-year-old American students in reading, science, and mathematics on the Programme for International Student Assessment (PISA™) administered by the Organization for Economic Cooperation and Development (OECD, 2007, 2009; see also U.S. results on Third International Mathematics and Science Study [TIMSS], Hanushek, 2009):

1. In the 2003 PISA administration, which focused on reading literacy, U.S. students received an average score just higher than the OECD average of approximately 500 (i.e., 495 versus 494, respectively; see OECD, 2003) but lower than seventeen

OECD jurisdictions. Reading literacy scores were not compiled for U.S. students in 2006 due to an administrative problem with the test booklets.

2. In the 2006 PISA administration, which focused on science literacy, U.S. students received lower scores relative to their peers in sixteen of the other twenty-nine OECD jurisdictions and in six of the twenty-seven non-OECD jurisdictions; in two specific types of scientific literacy (i.e., explaining phenomena scientifically and using scientific evidence), U.S. students received lower scores than the OECD average (i.e., 486 versus 500, and 489 versus 499, respectively).

3. In the 2006 PISA administration, which also measured mathematical literacy, U.S. students received an average score (i.e., 474) that was lower than the OECD average of 498, and lower than twenty-three OECD jurisdictions and eight non-OECD jurisdictions.

As an introduction to this section on the impetus for change, we focus on the PISA results posted by the U.S. Department of Education for three reasons: First, as a psychometrically sound assessment, PISA results are noteworthy; second, PISA provides a broad view of how well students can apply what they are learning to novel tasks, because the assessment measures *literacy* in reading, science, and mathematics as opposed to measuring knowledge of a specific curriculum (e.g., see de Lange, 2007, for a discussion of the Third International Mathematics and Science Study [TIMSS] in relation to specific curricula); and third, forty-one countries participated in the 2003 administration of PISA (fifty-seven countries participated in 2006), and the sheer size of this endeavor renders the assessment results relevant to many stakeholders who can initiate substantial change in education policies and practices, especially in the United States.

Although the United States may be the most notable country struggling with the literacy performance of its adolescents, it is not the only one. Students in countries such as Australia, Canada, Japan, and the United Kingdom may be performing better than American students on PISA, but there is still substantial room for improvement (OECD, 2007). For example, in the domain of scientific literacy, an average of only 1.3 percent of students across OECD countries were classified into the top category of science proficiency (i.e., level 6 on the PISA 2006 proficiency scale; see OECD, 2007, p. 14). Finland and New Zealand had 3.9 percent of their students classified into this top category, whereas countries such as Australia, Canada, Japan, and the United Kingdom only had between 2 and 3 percent of their students meet this high level of performance (OECD, 2007). By including level 5, the next highest category of science proficiency, the percentage of students considered to be high performers across OECD countries rose to an average of 9 percent. Again Finland and New Zealand had the highest percentage of students classified into categories 5 or 6 (21 and 18 percent, respectively). Countries such as Australia, Canada, and Japan had between 14 and 16 percent of students classified into one of these top two categories. Twenty-five countries had less than 5 percent of their students reaching the highest categories (levels 5 and 6) of science proficiency, and fifteen had less than 1 percent.

There are many incentives for wanting students to be classified into the highest level of proficiency in core academic domains (see Hanushek, 2005). For example, in science, the classification of students into the highest category provided by PISA is assumed to mean that students are able to engage the types of higher-order thinking skills that will be necessary for many twenty-first-century jobs (Hanushek, 2009). These higher-order thinking skills include (a) identifying, explaining, and applying scientific knowledge in a variety of multifaceted life situations; (b) connecting distinct sources of information and explanations, and making use of evidence from those sources to defend decisions; (c) demonstrating advanced thinking and reasoning, and using scientific understanding to justify solutions to novel scientific and technological situations; and (d) using scientific knowledge and developing arguments in support of recommendations and decisions that focus on personal, social, or global situations. A student classified into one of the top categories of science performance is arguably better prepared than a student classified into the lowest level for tackling science in the classroom and ultimately contributing and pursuing scientific innovation in the labor market. At the lowest level of proficiency, students know and can do few things. According to the OECD (2007, p. 14), "At Level 1, students have such a limited scientific knowledge that it can only be applied to a few, familiar situations. They can present scientific explanations that are obvious and that follow explicitly from given evidence." When countries are ranked by the percentages of fifteen-year-olds classified above the lowest level of 1 (i.e., levels 2, 3, 4, 5, and 6) on the PISA proficiency scale, Finland is ranked first, Canada is ranked fourth, and the United States is ranked thirty-sixth of fifty-seven countries (OECD, 2007, p. 20, table 1).

Policy makers recognize that large-scale educational testing for students in kindergarten through grade twelve can be a powerful measure of accountability and a driver of educational reform and improvement. There is also mounting hope in the United States that federal legislation, in the form of the No Child Left Behind Act (NCLB, 2002; see also Race to the Top Fund), can improve educational outcomes by mandating states that accept Title 1 funds to administer annual large-scale educational testing in at least seven grade levels (Koretz & Hamilton, 2006, p. 531). On the one hand, the mandate of NCLB makes sense given that results from national (and international) large-scale educational assessments provide a snapshot of student achievement and the success of educational systems for attaining specific outcomes. At a minimum, the results from these assessments allow us to generate conclusions about whether students are performing as expected (i.e., being classified into projected categories of proficiency) or whether performance could be improved. On the other hand, it seems reasonable to ask whether these test results will provide additional information about student learning aside from their performance at a single point in time, including partial knowledge and skills, misconceptions, and areas of genuine cognitive strength. For example, could these test results shed light on why U.S. students are struggling with explaining phenomena scientifically and using scientific evidence (see OECD, 2009)? Given the cost and time spent on designing, developing, and administering these large-scale educational assessments, it seems wasteful not to have them provide at least some information about the possible sources of students' learning impasses and incorrect responses. In fact, these tests do not even provide unequivocal information about the quality of higher-order thinking students possess, because the items are not typically evaluated for whether they elicit in students the appropriate thinking skills of interest (Schmeiser & Welch, 2006). In short, many of these large-scale educational tests have not been designed to provide information on the quality of students' thinking and learning. Consequently, a poor or good test result conveys little information about how students think, reason, or problem-solve with the knowledge and skills presented in test items. Hence, little information can be gleaned from many large-scale test results about possible student misconceptions or other pedagogically based reasons students may struggle with core academic concepts and skills.

Billions of dollars are spent every year on education, but these expenditures do not translate to superior test results for American students (Hanushek, 2005). In fact, there appears to be little association between educational expenditures and large-scale achievement test scores (see Hanushek, 2009, p. 49). The cost for public elementary and secondary education in the United States was estimated at approximately $543 billion for the 2009–2010 school year (Hussar & Bailey, 2008), and the national average current expenditure per student was estimated at around $10,844 for 2009–2010, which rose from $9,683 in 2006–2007 (Zhou, 2009). These figures are startling not because the United States spends too little or too much, but rather because one would expect a significant, positive correlation to exist between amounts spent on education and educational outcomes. Moreover, the United States is a leader in research and innovation, and one would expect that children educated in one of the richest and most resourceful countries in the world would perform better than children in countries who do not have the same financial or human intellectual capital.

The absence of a relationship between educational expenditures and large-scale educational test scores might lead one to conclude that infusing money into teacher professional development or other initiatives to boost instruction is wasteful because it does not translate into higher test scores. Alternatively, one could conclude that money spent on professional development or other initiatives is working, but we do not have the appropriate tools to measure their benefits (see Polikoff, 2010). For example, suppose we tried to use large-scale achievement tests to measure the learning outcomes derived from newly funded and innovative instructional programs. Suppose further that the learning goals driving these innovative instructional programs were focused on the quality of students' thinking processes, such as the nature of their representations and search strategies for problem solving, the depth and breadth of the inter-relations among their networks of knowledge and skills, novel frames of reference, and their combinatorial mechanisms to use analogy and metaphor. If this were the case, then learning strides could be occurring but would be missed with large-scale testing (see Hanushek, 2005), because current large-scale tests have not been designed to measure these thinking processes. Students taught to engage specific thinking processes might find few outlets in traditional[4] constructed-response and multiple-choice items to show off their newfound competencies. If the tests students took failed to measure what teachers were trying to teach, then it would not be surprising to find relatively poor test results. Pumping money into schools to

---

[4] The term "traditional tests" is used in the present chapter to denote test-item design and development that is not formally based on learning scientific research and commonly based on historical practice, such as the use of Bloom's taxonomy to develop test items of varying difficulty levels. Most operational large-scale educational tests are traditional (Ferrara & DeMauro, 2006).

enhance instruction without a concomitant effort to change or revise large-scale educational achievement testing might even be viewed as a setup to fail – as missing the boat in detecting any gains or improvements achieved in student learning and thinking (see Hanushek, 2009; Mislevy, 1993).

In sum, the large-scale educational assessments that proved effective decades ago may no longer be sufficient to measure twenty-first-century knowledge and skills. We now live in a time when most students are digitally prodigious, engaging multiple modes of electronic communication, and cultivating informal networks of expression, discussion, and collaboration outside of the classroom more often than inside the classroom (Collins, Halverson, & Brown, 2009; see also Russell, 2005; Shute et al., 2010; Thomas, Li, Knott, & Zhongxiao, 2008). Undoubtedly students are using sophisticated thinking processes to learn and navigate through these complex systems of communication, most of which are underwritten by technological gadgets. The rate at which technology changes and the scale of students' ability to learn and pick up new tools suggest that complex problem solving is occurring. Our task is to figure out how to assess it (NRC, 2005; Pashler, Rohrer, Cepeda, & Carpenter, 2007). As titanic as the challenge of educational reform appears to be, however, there is optimism that inroads may take place with the design and development of large-scale educational tests based on advances in the learning sciences. These new types of tests might even inform us about the knowledge and skills that characterize adaptability, innovation, and higher-order thinking for job and economic growth in the twenty-first century. This is the idea whose time has come.

THE LEARNING SCIENCES

The learning sciences are an inter-disciplinary domain of study. Although its foundations can be traced back to educational technology, socio-cultural studies, computing science, anthropology, and cognitive science, the main focus is consistently on what is needed to make human learning more successful. To maximize learning, the mechanisms that enhance or hinder learning are identified and investigated. In this respect, cognitive science has played a particularly pivotal role. Its influence can be traced back to Piaget's *constructivism* (Piaget & Inhelder, 1967), which emphasized the qualitatively different structure of children's knowledge and thinking in relation to adult knowledge and thinking, as well as the instructional importance of recognizing these differences as new knowledge is introduced to learners (e.g., Siegler, 2005). Sawyer (2006, p. 2) emphasized this point:

> [B]eginning in the 1970s, a new science of learning was born – based in research emerging from psychology, computer science, philosophy, sociology, and other scientific disciplines. As they closely studied children's learning, scientists discovered that instruction was deeply flawed. By the 1990s, after about twenty years of research, learning scientists had reached a consensus on the following basic facts about learning – a consensus that was published by the United States National Research Council. (see Bransford, Brown, & Cocking, 2000)

According to Sawyer, the five basic facts about learning are the following:

1. *Deep conceptual understanding is needed to apply knowledge.* Knowledge about facts and procedures will not transfer to novel settings and will therefore be relatively useless unless students also know the situations for when these facts and procedures can be applied (see Kilpatrick et al., 2001; Kuhn, 2001). Helping students gain conceptual understanding involves helping them to recognize the structural features of problem-solving situations and not just their surface-level characteristics (Chi, Feltovich, & Glaser, 1981; Slotta & Chi, 2006).
2. *Learning, not just teaching, must be a focus.* The science of human learning emphasizes that individuals develop deep conceptual

understanding by actively participating in the learning process by co-creating meaning and not simply by listening to teacher instruction. Individuals are viewed as active and interactive recipients of new knowledge and skills insofar as they have an essential role in shaping their learning environments and interpreting the information they receive in meaningful ways.

3. *Learning environments must be created.* Individuals learn within environments that can either enable or disable knowledge and skills. Learning scientists have identified variables within environments (e.g., use of feedback, modeling strategic thinking, reciprocal teaching, cognitive apprenticeships) that promote intended learning outcomes and help build inter-connected networks of knowledge and skills that permit students to demonstrate conceptual understanding and higher levels of thought and performance within subject domains.

4. *Knowledge builds on itself.* Students come to school with ideas about the way the world works. Some of this knowledge and these skills may be accurate, and some may reflect misconceptions or alternative conceptions about the mechanisms of the external environment. Successful instructors recognize the importance of students' existing knowledge and skills in their attempts to facilitate the acquisition of new knowledge and skills. Learning environments that build on students' existing knowledge and skills by engaging discussion of empirical evidence and challenging misconceptions (or alternative conceptions) can exemplify to students the appropriate methods to use for seeking accurate and consistent knowledge.

5. *Reflection.* Students learn more deeply when they are able to ponder and explain their newly acquired knowledge and skills than when they do not. Reflection allows students to think about the inter-connections between new and existing knowledge and skills and their implications for problem solving.

In addition to these five facts, an important focus is placed on the process and quality of thinking as it occurs in particular domains of knowledge. For example, in the domains of medicine, music, mathematics, science, and art, higher-order thinking is exemplified by complex networks of inter-related, domain-specific declarative knowledge and procedural skills that need to be nurtured and allowed to flourish over time with sustained practice (Anderson, 2007; Chomsky, 1959; Ericsson, 2009; Ericsson, Charness, Feltovich, & Hoffman, 2006; Ericsson & Simon, 1993). As a function of deliberate practice and experience, the organizational and substantive content of this knowledge and these skills changes and grows in efficiency. For example, in contrast to novices, experts have rich and complex networks of knowledge and skills in their domains of expertise to support sophisticated mental representations of task information as well as strategic and adaptive problem solving. Furthermore, they adjust their knowledge and skills accordingly as task demands vary, and show a discerning awareness and understanding of their problem-solving processes, including their particular strengths and weaknesses. Higher-order thinking is also dependent on self-awareness and a learner's meta-cognitive skills (e.g., Baron, 2000; Stanovich, 2009) to appropriately regulate the quality of task encodings, decodings, and interpretations of environmental variables, as well as the selection, application, and execution of rules and strategies to solve well-defined and ill-defined tasks (e.g., Newell & Simon, 1972).

To develop large-scale educational assessments based on the learning sciences, the five facts outlined by Sawyer need to be incorporated into test-item design. Frameworks or methods must be developed to illustrate how to systematically design test items, for example, to evaluate conceptual understanding and application of knowledge (see Sawyer's first fact mentioned previously). Moreover, the processes and overall quality of thinking must be measured. The question of how this is to be done has yet to be answered.

Traditional large-scale educational items are currently designed and developed according to test blueprints that show the required content and skill specifications for a domain of interest (Downing & Haladyna, 2006; Gierl, 1997; Leighton, in press; Schmeiser & Welch, 2006). In particular, Bloom's taxonomy of educational objectives (Bloom et al., 1956; see also Anderson et al., 2001, for a revised version of Bloom's taxonomy) is a general framework often used by content experts and test developers to specify the level of thinking at which items will be designed (Downing & Haladyna, 2006; Gierl, 1997; Leighton, in press; Schmeiser & Welch, 2006). According to Bloom et al. (1956), cognitive skills can be represented along a continuum. As shown in Figure 1.1, *knowledge* represents the most basic level of thinking because it simply indicates a student's ability to recall or remember facts. Following this most basic level, more advanced levels include *comprehension, application, analysis, synthesis,* and *evaluation*. The most sophisticated level of thinking, *evaluation,* means that the student can make judgments about the value of ideas, solutions, or material. Inherent to this ordering of knowledge and skills is the assumption that human thinking is hierarchical and that the attainment of more sophisticated levels of thinking presumes the mastery of lower levels of thinking.

Although Bloom's (1956) taxonomy reflects a simple quasi-model of thinking that can be applied across content domains to design and develop test items, it is not based in learning scientific theory. Moreover, the taxonomy has not been empirically corroborated or validated as a tool leading to the development of items that reliably elicit particular thinking skills (Schmeiser & Welch, 2006). Consequently, it cannot function as an exemplar of how learning scientific theory is translated into an empirically based framework or method for designing and developing educational test items to measure knowledge and thinking skills. To answer the question of how the learning sciences can be used to design and develop test items, we need to directly consult learning scientific data and theory. In particular, we need to identify domains of knowledge (i.e., reading, science, and mathematics) and the processes of thinking within these domains that characterize

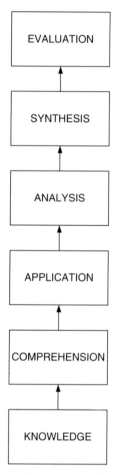

FIGURE 1.1. A diagrammatic representation of Bloom's taxonomy.

skilled performance. Learning scientists often build cognitive models, situated within content domains, to illustrate knowledge and skills of interest that characterize higher-order versus lower-order forms of thinking and performance. The challenge then is to identify cognitive models in reading, science, and mathematics that illustrate the knowledge and skills we seek to measure with large-scale educational assessments.

THE EMPEROR'S NEW CLOTHES: DESIGNING AND DEVELOPING LARGE-SCALE EDUCATIONAL ASSESSMENTS

The Danish poet and author Hans Christian Andersen wrote a story about an emperor who loved to dress in beautiful clothes. One day two swindlers persuaded him to consider an invisible frock. The swindlers convinced the emperor the invisible clothes were real by saying that only the noblest of minds could appreciate the exquisiteness of the garments. The emperor and his men pretended to see these new clothes, hoping their beauty might marvel the townspeople. On a clear afternoon the emperor wore his new clothes as he walked through the town until a young boy cried out, "The emperor is naked! He has no clothes!" The crowd screamed with laughter and the emperor ran in humiliation. As he hid, he cursed both the swindlers and his vanity. This children's story reminds us that trends require scrutiny. As researchers and practitioners, we must be especially wary of the evidence available for new academic claims or educational trends, lest we be sold invisible new "clothes."

In the past two decades, educational measurement researchers and practitioners have observed the intensification of the claim that the learning sciences should be integrated into the design and development of large-scale achievement tests. This claim is made based on the expectation that these new tests will provide better information than current traditional tests about student achievement and learning. However, although the claim sounds reasonable, there is still no systematic evidence to validate the claim. Snow and Lohman (1989) wrote about the sensibility of mining the learning sciences for information on how to enhance the design and development of educational measures more than two decades ago:

> First, the cognitive psychology of problem solving is a central concern for educational measurement because all mental tests are, in some sense, problem-solving tasks. Hence, existing or proposed

test designs ought to be evaluated as such. . . . Second, the two most
general purposes of educational measurement, the assessment of
student aptitudes and achievements, would appear to cut across
the matrix of cognitive psychology in different ways. . . . Thus,
different slices across the field of cognitive psychology might be
needed to inform test design and evaluation. (Snow & Lohman,
1989, p. 265)

Although Snow and Lohman (1989) refer specifically to "cognitive
psychology" in their writings, the spirit of their words is understood to mean that any discipline – not just cognitive psychology –
that sheds light on how students engage in problem-solving tasks
should be integrated into the design of educational tests. Although
the learning sciences offer a wealth of data and theories about the
structure and acquisition of knowledge and skills, empirically based
cognitive frameworks for guiding the design of test items do not
exist (Schmeiser & Welch, 2006). Even Evidence-Centered Design
(ECD; see Mislevy, Steinberg, & Almond, 2003), which is arguably
one of the most sophisticated frameworks for specifying an evidentiary argument of an assessment, is relatively silent on the learning
scientific basis of the models employed. For example, although ECD
provides a framework for "developing assessment tasks that elicit
evidence (scores) that bears directly on the claims that one wants
to make about what a student knows and can do" (Shute, Hansen, &
Russell, 2008, p. 294), it is also the case that ECD has been described
as "simply [formalizing] the kind of thinking ordinarily done by
expert assessment developers" (Shute et al., 2008, p. 294) and not
necessarily modernizing this thinking to explicitly include advances
in the learning sciences.

There is every reason, in principle, to suspect that such cognitive
frameworks could be developed. However, there are no current tem-
plates of how such a framework might be developed, which requires
the translation of data and theory from the learning sciences and
subsequently putting it into practice. In other words, we are aware of

no published frameworks or methods for summarizing and mapping the learning scientific facts presented in the previous section onto a set of guidelines for the design and development of educational test items measuring student achievement and learning. Although publications originating from the National Research Council such as *Knowing What Students Know* (2001) and *Taking Science to School* (2007) provide selective surveys and illustrative examples of cognitive research, there is no systematic organization of this research into sets of cognitive models within particular content domains to guide educational test-item development. Furthermore, although we recognize that there are innovative studies examining the design of test items based on the learning sciences (e.g., Bennett & Gitomer, 2008; Shute et al., 2008), we are aware of no published empirical studies designed to investigate whether test items designed from learning science theory are more successful at eliciting expected knowledge and skills in students in relation to traditional large-scale tests. Therefore, there is much work to be done to demonstrate that the marriage between the learning sciences with educational measurement is feasible and, importantly, yields better student information and test-based inferences than current, traditional large-scale educational tests.

Challenges in Translation

As an example of the challenge associated with translating learning scientific theory into guidelines for test-item design, consider Figure 1.2. This is a cognitive model (or hierarchy) of the attributes required to reason about a type of logical task, namely, categorical syllogisms (see Leighton, Gierl, & Hunka, 2004). The hierarchy shown in this figure is similar in structure to other types of cognitive models in the learning sciences (e.g., Chi, 1997; Klahr & Dunbar, 1988; Kintsch, 1998; Kuhn, 2005; Shrager & Siegler, 1998). This example illustrates a series of attributes (i.e., knowledge, thinking skills) and their associated

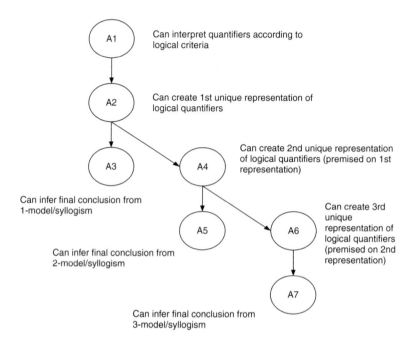

FIGURE 1.2. Attribute hierarchy of Johnson-Laird's (1983) theory of mental models. Reproduced from Leighton, J. P., Gierl, M. J., & Hunka, S. (2004). The attribute hierarchy method for cognitive assessment: A Variation on Tatsuoka's rule-space approach. *Journal of Educational Measurement, 41,* 205–236 with permission from John Wiley and Sons.

dependencies. A series of questions must be considered in relation to using Figure 1.2 for test-item design. For example, how specific are the attributes? Do they represent knowledge and skills that are instructionally relevant? Do we measure all individual attributes in a test of the knowledge and skills shown in the model? Do we measure all individual attributes and all their possible dependencies? Are all attribute dependencies measurable? To complicate matters further, the hierarchy in Figure 1.2 was not found as-is in the research literature on logical reasoning. Rather, it was developed by reading, sifting, and interpreting the research on mental models, much of which was developed in the content domain of logical reasoning (see also Johnson-Laird & Bara, 1984; Johnson-Laird, 2004; Leighton & Sternberg, 2003). Translating learning scientific research to create cognitive models or cognitive frameworks for test-item design is therefore challenging on two fronts. First, if existing models are not found in the literature and must be created from a synthesis of the research literature, the potential for error or bias in the process of synthesis must be recognized and then minimized. Second, if existing models are found in the learning scientific literature, the component attributes – or knowledge and skills – must be summarized and represented in some acceptable form and be considered relevant for testing, otherwise models may be dismissed and go unused by assessment specialists for the design and development of large-scale educational tests.

Designing and developing large-scale tests based on the science of human learning has considerable appeal among researchers and practitioners (e.g., Baxter & Glaser, 1998; Borsboom, 2005; Cronbach, 1957; Embretson & Daniel, 2008; Greeno, 2003; Gorin, 2006, 2009; Gorin & Embretson, 2006; Irvine & Kyllonen, 2002; Leighton & Gierl, 2007; Lohman & Nichols, 2006; Mislevy, 2006; Mislevy & Haertel, 2006; Mislevy et al., 2010; Pellegrino, Baxter, & Glaser, 1999; Rupp, 2007). However, as many advocates recognize, it is not sufficient to simply adopt the goal without a systematic plan for how this goal will be addressed. Scientific evidence must be produced to show that the integration of the learning sciences with educational measurement practice is useful, feasible, and most importantly for educators and policy makers, that this integration affords superior information about test takers. In the end, this integration must lead to better tests and better inferences about students' knowledge and skills relative to what traditional tests – which are not based on the learning sciences – can offer. Moreover, the operational aspects of designing and developing educational tests based on the learning sciences cannot be excessively laborious and expensive so as to effectively disqualify this avenue of growth.

Examples of Integrative Educational Measurement Studies

Researchers in educational measurement are actively investigating the processes by which large-scale educational test items can be designed and developed from learning scientific models of cognition (e.g., Baxter & Glaser, 1998; Briggs, Alonzo, Schwab & Wilson, 2006; Chi, 1997; Chen et al., 2008; Embretson, 1998; Gierl et al., 2009; Gierl, Zheng, & Cui, 2008; Leighton, Cui, & Cor, 2009; Mislevy et al., 2003; Rupp & Templin, 2008; Wilson & Sloane, 2000). These studies can be classified according to the three types of research methods commonly used: qualitative, quantitative, and mixed methods.

Qualitative studies frequently include data in the form of verbal reports collected from student interviews or teacher or expert judgments about the knowledge and skills required to respond to and/or solve educational test items (e.g., Baxter & Glaser, 1998; Briggs et al., 2006; Chi, 1997; Wilson & Sloane, 2000). To illustrate an investigation where the source of data is largely qualitative, consider a now classic study by Baxter and Glaser (1998). The objective of Baxter and Glaser's (1998) study was to introduce a learning scientific framework, the *cognitive components of competence*, as a tool to develop and evaluate science assessments. The cognitive components of competence were compiled from research on expertise and skilled-knowledge acquisition (see Chi, 1997; Chi, Glaser, & Farr, 1988; Ericsson & Smith, 1991; Gobbo & Chi, 1986) and included, for example, the problem representations used by learners to guide "planning and anticipation of alternative outcomes, goal-directed strategies that influence problem solution, self-monitoring activities that control and regulate thinking and reasoning, and the explanation of principles underlying performance that facilitates learning and problem solving" (Baxter & Glaser, 1998, p. 37). Baxter and Glaser applied this analytical framework to students' verbal reports to evaluate the extent to which students' thinking on performance test items in science matched or mismatched test specifications.

Baxter and Glaser (1998) collected, analyzed, and compared students' problem-solving verbal reports against the content and skill specifications of the items under study. For example, in the first empirical demonstration, twenty-three grade-eight students were interviewed as they solved an item in which they needed to examine the process by which rock layers fold and twist. Following the interviews, students' verbal reports were coded and analyzed according to Baxter and Glaser's cognitive components of competence framework. From this analysis, they concluded that there was a mismatch between the content and skills assumed to be measured by the item and the quality of students' knowledge and thinking skills. In particular, they found that the item could not be used to discriminate between students who had studied earthquakes in school (and demonstrated appropriate knowledge and thinking skills) from those who had not or those who were simply following rote procedures algorithmically. In another empirical demonstration, twelve high school students were interviewed as they solved a task in which they were asked to "describe the possible forms of energy and types of material involved in the digestion of a piece of bread and explain fully how they are related" (p. 41). Once again, Baxter and Glaser found a mismatch between the content knowledge and skills assumed to be elicited by the item and the quality of knowledge and thinking exhibited by students.

Additional empirical data were presented by Baxter and Glaser to evaluate the correspondence between students' cognitive activities with their measured science performance scores. For example, in a study where twenty grade-five students provided verbal reports as they solved the *Critter Museum task*, Baxter and Glaser found that the problem-solving components of high-scoring students could not be distinguished from the problem-solving components of low-scoring students; that is, students who scored a 0 or a 1 on a scale ranging from 0 to 4 were just as likely as students who scored a 4 to demonstrate relevant cognitive activities such as knowledge of insects, classification system skills, or an understanding of the evolutionary origins of shared features. Baxter and Glaser concluded from these empirical demonstrations that, in some cases, performance item scores matched the quality of cognitive activities exemplified during problem solving, and in other cases they did not.

In addition to qualitative studies, quantitative studies have been conducted to investigate the integration of the learning sciences with educational measurement. The main source of data in *quantitative studies* is actual or simulated test scores obtained from traditional large-scale educational assessments (e.g., Birenbaum, Tatsuoka, & Yamada, 2004; Chen et al., 2008; Embretson, 1998; Gierl et al., 2008; Mislevy et al., 2003; Rupp & Templin, 2008). Consider an illustrative study conducted by Chen et al. (2008). Chen et al. (2008) used a previously developed cognitive model (see Corter & Tatsuoka, 2002; Gonzalez & Miles, 2001; Tatsuoka, Corter, & Guerrero, 2004; see also Tatsuoka, 2009) to describe the knowledge and skills required for successful mathematics performance among Taiwanese grade-eight students on the Trends in International Mathematics and Science Study (TIMSS)-1999.

The cognitive model used by Chen et al. (2008) had been originally developed with data from American students' performance on the TIMSS. To supplement this cognitive model, reviews of multiple documents in relation to TIMSS were also conducted. These documents included content frameworks associated with previous versions of TIMSS, past cognitive modeling research with mathematics items from the SAT™ and the Graduate Record Examination (GRE™), and written descriptions or protocols from domain experts who evaluated the types of knowledge and skills required to respond to similar types of items (Corter & Tatsuoka, 2002; Gonzalez & Miles, 2001; Tatsuoka et al., 2004). As a check on the authenticity of the knowledge and skills included in the final version of the cognitive model, interviews with students and high school mathematics teachers were conducted, in addition to a statistical evaluation of the model components with other samples of students (see Corter & Tatsuoka, 2002; Tatsuoka et al., 2004; Tatsuoka, Corter, & Tatsuoka, 2004). Using Tatsuoka's (1983, 1985, 1995) rule-space methodology, Chen et al. (2008) converted student item responses into *attribute mastery* probabilities, where an attribute was defined as a knowledge structure or skill included in the cognitive model and was expected to underlie successful item performance. The results of these analyses indicated that the cognitive model used to account for American performance on the TIMSS was also useful in classifying Taiwanese student performance. Almost all Taiwanese students were successfully classified into one of the pre-determined attribute mastery patterns, with classification rates ranging from 99.3 to 99.9 percent.

A third type of research can be classified as *mixed-methods studies*, where data sources include verbal reports (or some other type of student interview data) and traditional large-scale educational test scores (e.g., Leighton et al., 2009; Leighton et al., in press). The studies included in this third category frequently combine both qualitative and quantitative approaches to summarize student performance according to classes of mastered knowledge and skills. For example, in an effort to evaluate the usefulness of cognitive models in accounting for examinees' large-scale test scores, Leighton et al. (2009) developed two cognitive models of the knowledge and skills examinees might use to respond to twenty-one algebra items sampled from the March 2005 administration of the SAT. The first cognitive model was developed from expert analysis; that is, an expert in mathematics and statistics reviewed the items and sketched a comprehensive model of knowledge and skills required to respond to the items. The second cognitive model was developed from the verbal reports provided by twenty-one students as they responded to the set of SAT algebra items. These students were recruited from New York City schools, had taken the PSAT in grade ten, and were en route to take the SAT.

Leighton et al. (2009) found that, depending on the ability level of the students sampled, both cognitive models could adequately account for students' test performance on the March 2005 administration of the SAT. In particular, compared to the model developed by expert analysis, the cognitive model developed from students' verbal reports provided a better account of higher-ability students' performance on the SAT items. In contrast, compared to the model developed from students' verbal reports, the cognitive model developed by expert analysis provided a better account of average-ability students' performance on the SAT items.

A Research Gap: What is Needed to Facilitate the Use of Cognitive Models in Large-Scale Assessment?

Controlled Comparative Studies

Despite the growing attempts to integrate learning scientific research into the design and development of large-scale educational test items, there are noteworthy research gaps. For example, none of the studies mentioned in the previous section (see Examples of Integrative Educational Measurement Studies) compared the results and inferences obtained from applying cognitive models to traditional tests to the results and inferences that are obtained from these traditional tests in the absence of applying *cognitive models*. Although Baxter and Glaser (1998) used the cognitive components of competence framework to evaluate students' knowledge and thinking skills on performance items in science and compared the results to the items' specifications, we do not know how these results ultimately impacted test-based inferences. By how much did inferences change depending on the criteria used to evaluate test performance? Likewise, how well would test items developed from the cognitive components of competence framework compare with items developed from Bloom's taxonomy in eliciting expected knowledge and skills in students? Answers to these questions would help us evaluate claims about how much information is gained, relative to current traditional tests, when cognitive frameworks or models are applied to the design and development of test items. Qualitative studies of the knowledge and skills students use to answer test items are pedagogically rich, but evidence is still lacking on whether the results from these studies can provide guidelines for the design of more informative large-scale test items that lead to enhanced test-based inferences.

The research conducted by Chen et al. (2008) is also illustrative of the need for additional evidence. Using cognitive models to summarize and account for performance on traditional large-scale educational tests reflects attempts to *retrofit*. Retrofitting can be described as the application of a new psychometric or statistical model to examinees' item-response data collected from an existing traditional test. Retrofitting often works because the knowledge and skills indentified in the cognitive model are incorporated into a psychometric model, for example, via an incidence matrix (i.e., the Q-matrix in Tatsuoka's 1983 rule-space methodology; for additional methods to incorporate cognitive variables in psychometric models, see Embretson & Daniel, 2008). This matrix identifies the points of association between successful test-item performance and the mastery of knowledge and skills in the model. Such cognitively based statistical models permit the underlying latent structure of test scores to be evaluated against a hypothesized cognitive model of student-response processes (sees Rupp, 2007; see also Chapter 7 of this volume).

The technical sophistication of cognitively based statistical models is impressive, and yet there is little, if any, empirical evidence that the information (including test-based inferences) derived from such test analyses is any more defensible or useful to stakeholders than the information derived from traditional large-scale educational tests. If the knowledge and skills or attributes included in cognitively based statistical models simply reflect finer-grained content specifications, then one would expect the information provided by these models to be as useful as traditional test results and not provide additional insight into students' cognitive activities. It is important to note that with few exceptions (e.g., Embretson & Wetzel, 1987; Gorin & Embretson,

2006; see also Mislevy, 2006, for evidence-centered design) this is often the case. Even if the cognitive models were developed directly from learning scientific research and used to design and develop items, the question of whether these cognitively based tests are any more informative than traditional tests is warranted in order to adequately evaluate claims about the utility of generating these new tests. This same critique can be levied to the mixed-method studies described in the previous section.

In sum, evidence is needed to show that large-scale educational tests based on the learning sciences are more sensitive measures of knowledge and skill acquisition than tests designed from traditional specifications. For example, two tests, one designed and developed from findings in the learning sciences (i.e., a cognitively based test) and another designed and developed from traditional specifications, could be created. The two tests could then be administered in a counterbalanced order to students, randomly assigned to either a traditional instructional environment or an innovative learning environment. If the cognitively based test were a more sensitive measure of learning and achievement than the traditional test, then we would expect the innovative learning group to perform better on the cognitively based test than on the traditional test. The control group might perform equally well on both tests. Additional evidence could include data on criterion measures of learning such as students' performance in subsequent programs. For example, students' performance in subsequent learning programs would be expected to correlate more strongly with scores on the cognitively based test than with scores on the traditional test. The effectiveness of remediation based on items or questions missed on the cognitively based test could also be investigated.

Understanding How Cognitive Models Fit within
Validity Arguments
Incorporating cognitive models into test design and development is required because it promises to fortify validity arguments for

test-based inferences. At the time this chapter was written, validity theorists recommend that test-based inferences must be defended on two fronts – with an interpretive argument and a validity argument (see Kane, 2006, p. 23). The *interpretative argument* is formulated first, and it is designed to specify "the proposed interpretations and uses of test results by laying out the network of inferences and assumptions leading from the observed performances [scores] to the conclusions and decisions [inferences] based on the performances." After the interpretative argument is specified, the *validity argument* is made, that is, "an evaluation of the interpretative argument" (Kane, 2006, p. 23). The validity argument is designed to scrutinize the interpretative argument with results from statistical analyses, content analyses, and empirical analyses that can inform the scientific integrity of the interpretative argument. To this end, cognitive models have a potentially important role to play in providing a line of evidence in validity arguments for the assumptions made in the interpretative argument. Cognitive models can be used to support the identification and relationship among the knowledge, skills, and competencies that are the focus of testing, and lend support for test-item content, test-item formats, and ultimately inferences about students' mastery of the knowledge and skills laid out in the interpretative argument.

Unfortunately, cognitive models are not used in validity arguments for large-scale assessments (Ferrara & DeMauro, 2006). In their comprehensive review of standardized assessment of individual achievement in K–12, Ferrara and DeMauro state that many of the validity reports compiled by companies designing large-scale assessments "do not suggest that test designs are intended to support inferences about student achievement in relation to models of cognition and learning" (p. 613). Instead, the validation efforts currently in place focus on listing content standards and the alignment of test items to specific standards. "Alignment" in these reports is usually defined, rather loosely, as a panel of experts agreeing that an item's content characteristics match a given content strand in the knowledge and skills measured. Empirically based alignment studies, where the knowledge and skills students actually use to solve items are evaluated, are not normally initiated or included (see Ferrara & DeMauro, 2006, p. 613). We propose that one reason why testing specialists may not include cognitive models to form interpretative arguments and/or validity arguments for large-scale achievement tests is because cognitive models are (a) difficult to identify among all available learning scientific research, and (b) not obviously adaptable or translatable into interpretative and/or validity arguments. Cognitive models, as will be illustrated in Chapters 3, 4, and 5, often include knowledge and skills articulated at a level of grain size that is finer in detail than test blueprints or specifications. Given the incongruence in grain size, testing specialists may need assistance finding appropriate cognitive models and translating cognitive models into interpretative and/or validity arguments.

Diagrammatic Representations

There are probably many reasons why research is lacking on the use and efficacy of cognitive models in the design and development of large-scale tests. One clear obstacle to this research being conducted is that we do not have sufficient ready-to-use learning scientific information to help us generate testable hypotheses about how people demonstrate their learning, including knowledge and skills, on tests. This is to be expected given that, as Sawyer (2006, p. 14) points out, "learning sciences research is complex and difficult. A typical learning sciences research project takes a minimum of a year.... after the years of observation are complete, the hard work just begins ..." In other words, although learning scientists are conducting research at the front lines of how students learn, assessment specialists are waiting for the results of this research. Meanwhile, the practice of large-scale educational testing must go on. It is doubtful that the administration of any large-scale educational assessment can be halted as we wait for learning scientific research results. Alternatively, even when we do receive the results from learning scientific research, it may not be immediately obvious how to best represent and use these results to improve the design of testing products or generate new ones. Learning sciences theory is often ahead of practice, and principles learned from research projects in one content domain may not be simply represented and, therefore, not be easily translated and applicable to another (Carver, 2006). For large-scale achievement tests, many of which can be high stakes, the question that arises is how best to represent research from the learning sciences such that translating this research into testing products is facilitated and productive. Before determining whether new tests developed from cognitive models will be informative and as psychometrically rigorous as tests developed using more traditional methods, cognitive models must first be represented in some form and then made available for translation into testing products.

In order to contribute to this effort, it would be useful to have a more systematic documentation of the types of learning scientific cognitive models that are available in the academic domains of reading, science, and mathematics. Moreover, in light of the need for a more systematic documentation, it is necessary to ask what might be the best presentation of cognitive models for assessment specialists. This question is pertinent because Bloom's taxonomy is a simple quasi-cognitive model that is often represented as a straightforward hierarchy of knowledge and skills (see Figure 1.1). Possibly as a consequence of this simplicity, Bloom's taxonomy or some variant of it is often used in the design and development of almost all large-scale educational assessments (Schmeiser & Welch, 2006). Therefore, in an effort to provide the most constructive documentation of cognitive models and promote their consideration for the design and development of large-scale educational assessments, we must be sensitive to representations that facilitate the conceptualization and use of models. Toward this end, *diagrammatic* representations of cognitive models might serve as a functional summary of the information the learning sciences have to offer assessment specialists. In support of diagrams, Larkin and Simon (1987; see also Greeno, 1983; and Koedinger & Anderson, 1990) found that in domains such as economics, geometry, and physics, where problems often have a spatial component, problem solving is facilitated when task-related information is represented in a diagram. Resnick (1983) adds that in mathematics, educators "have developed an extensive repertoire of concrete and pictorial representations of mathematical concepts" (p. 31). More recently, Tubau (2008; see also Ainsworth & Loizou, 2003; Tversky, 2002; see also Mislevy et al., 2010, for external representations used in assessments) concluded from analyses of empirical research that visual representations or diagrams were most useful for summarizing causal and spatial relationships, including associations between categories, and were less useful for summarizing discrete, abstract, or hypothetical elements such as relative frequencies. In short, diagrams appear to alleviate demands on working memory, reduce the amount of task-related search activities, and promote perceptual, implicit, and explicit causal inferences related to problem solving.

Designing and developing large-scale educational assessments based on cognitive models is a problem-solving endeavor that may benefit from diagrammatic representations. Although some might argue that test design and development do not require the visualization of knowledge and skills (i.e., a spatial component) and therefore diagrammatic representations are unnecessary, it is important to recognize that cognitive components such as knowledge and skills share causal inter-dependencies that could be fruitfully described diagrammatically (Tubau, 2008). Many problem-solving endeavors profit from a diversity of tools, and diagrammatic representations of cognitive models are worthwhile to explore. Presenting knowledge and skills in a diagram may assist assessment specialists in recognizing the most important model-based components to measure and the relations that implicitly hold among components. Although a comprehensive catalog of cognitive models cannot be produced in this single volume, at a minimum, it is useful to offer a guide of the most influential, currently available cognitive models in diagrammatic form that can be found in the learning sciences. Such a guide could promote further research into their applicability in test design and development, and ultimately help us collect systematic evidence to answer the question of whether large-scale educational tests based on the learning sciences lead to more information and better test-based inferences about students than traditional large-scale educational tests.

CONCLUSION AND OVERVIEW FOR THE BOOK

The idea of integrating the learning sciences with educational measurement, especially large-scale tests, is enticing. Yet without proof that it can lead to better testing products, it would be foolhardy to recommend changes to operational testing programs. Experimental design is the hallmark of the scientific method. Educational researchers and practitioners who enthusiastically hypothesize that better tests can be created by basing them on the learning sciences must demonstrate using controlled studies that these types of tests lead to better information and, thus, better inferences about students than traditional assessments. To get us onto this research program, there needs to be (a) documentation of the learning or cognitive models that can be translated into test-item design; and once this documentation is made available, there needs to be (b) a systematic investigation of whether students randomly assigned to take a "cognitively based test" versus a "traditional control test" have distinct profiles of test-based inferences.

It is reasonable to question whether existing large-scale educational achievement tests are able to adequately measure innovative changes in instruction and student learning and, if not, whether new forms of achievement tests need to be designed and developed. Hanushek (2005, 2009; see also Bishop, 1989, 1991) explicitly recognizes the importance of measuring cognitive skills and alludes to the issue of whether current large-scale educational tests, namely PISA, are appropriate measures of the types of knowledge and skills we want to cultivate in students as they prepare for the jobs of the twenty-first century:

> Much of the discussion of school quality – in part related to new efforts to provide better accountability – has identified cognitive skills as the important dimension. And, while there is ongoing debate about the testing and measurement of these skills, most parents and policy makers alike accept the notion that cognitive skills are a key dimension of schooling outcomes.

Given that funds spent on educational reform are not leading to expected improvements in test scores (see Hanushek, 2009), it seems we have nothing to lose and everything to gain from questioning the very measures designed to assess scholastic achievement and learning. However, the claim that redesigned large-scale educational tests (i.e., cognitively based tests) are superior measures of student achievement and learning must be scientifically evaluated with systematic evidence. Otherwise, there is danger of buying into an idea too soon. The evidence must be presented, sifted, and scrutinized for its accuracy and practicality. Initiatives to overhaul educational systems in disrepair must begin with ideas, but the success of any idea or policy will hinge on how well policy makers, educators, and researchers evaluate the evidence in support of whether it resolves the questions we seek to answer. Large-scale educational testing has the potential to become the gold standard in the assessment of meaningful learning by providing a credible measuring stick with which to systematically evaluate students' academic achievements and learning progressions over time. However, for large-scale educational tests to become a gold standard in the measurement of achievement and learning, they need to be modified and refined. The readjustment is expected to reflect the type of learning that scientists define as real and meaningful – that is, conceptual, reflective, and adaptive. A skeptic would query whether such an innovative measurement tool is needed to assess achievement and learning or whether such a tool can even be designed from what is known about the science of learning. These are legitimate empirical questions deserving of research and analysis.

Although there is interest in designing and developing, and even validating large-scale educational tests based on the science of learning, there are no published studies that do this and then compare the results with those obtained from traditional large-scale assessments. This absence is partly due, we believe, to the relatively sparse documentation of the *learning scientific cognitive models* that can guide researchers in the design and development of educational tests. Even the widely cited book *Knowing What Students Know* provides only a small section devoted to exemplars of cognitive models. The absence of such documentation is notable because it suggests that the identification of cognitive models may not be straightforward. This may occur because the components of cognitive models are embedded within and across multiple research programs and papers; alternatively, it is not clear which models apply to the work of test developers and psychometricians. Whatever the case may be, the initial first step, we believe, is to begin to explore fruitful avenues for identifying, representing, and evaluating cognitive models from the learning scientific research literature. There is a general consensus that cognitive models should reflect the knowledge and skills students require or need to acquire in order to master educational outcomes. Although there are slightly varying definitions of what constitutes a cognitive model (see, for example, a definition provided by the NRC in the 2001 publication *Knowing What Students Know*, p. 179), the definition of a cognitive model used here is borrowed from Leighton and Gierl's (2007, p. 6) description of a cognitive model, which is a "simplified description of human problem solving on standardized educational tasks, which helps to characterize the knowledge and skills students at different levels of learning have acquired and to facilitate the explanation and prediction of students' performance."

The purpose of this book, then, is to organize in one volume a targeted presentation of the most promising and relevant diagrammatic cognitive models in the domains of reading, science, and mathematics for helping to inform research into the design, development, and even validation of large-scale achievement tests in education. Through this presentation, it is also our intention to explore a potential set of guidelines for how to identify and evaluate cognitive models for testing purposes. Needless to say, it is beyond the scope of this book to comprehensively outline the entire space of cognitive models available in the learning sciences and categorize them within a table or other organizational scheme. Not only is it unfeasible to accomplish such a goal within the confines of a monograph such as this, but it would also be premature. We, in the educational measurement community, are still in the early stages of knowing how to best consider cognitive models, including the identification and use of these models in educational testing. It is therefore prudent, we believe, first to initiate a presentation of the types of cognitive models that may be worthy of identification for educational testing specialists, given their representational formats; and second, to begin to consider possible ways to evaluate such models. As more research is undertaken to identify and evaluate cognitive models, the end goal may ultimately be a comprehensive categorization of models for testing specialists to use in their testing programs. However, to begin with such a scheme would bypass and possibly even gloss over the intellectual scrutiny required to create such a scheme.

The roadmap for the balance of this book is as follows. Chapter 2 provides a description and illustration of the kinds of cognitive models currently used in assessment, and also presents a set of characteristics – granularity, measurability, and instructional relevance – that will be used as our criteria to evaluate cognitive models in reading, science, and mathematics for the purpose of designing and developing large-scale educational tests. Chapters 3, 4, and 5 present targeted reviews of diagrammatic cognitive models in reading, science, and mathematics that have received substantial attention and empirical verification in the learning sciences to merit discussion and analysis.

As we introduce these models of reading, science, and mathematics, we begin each chapter by discussing relevant large-scale achievement test results that indicate the relative standing of U.S. students in reading, science, and mathematics, respectively. We use these results only as a way to contextualize the need for cognitive models; that is, to provide a rationale for using and integrating cognitive models in the design and development of large-scale assessments. The purpose of beginning each chapter with a discussion of these large-scale test results is not to anchor any of the cognitive models presented to traditional tests (it would be inappropriate to do so given that these tests have not been developed in line with these models), but simply to provide illustrations that students are generally not performing as well as they could be in core academic domains and that changes to large-scale assessments are needed. It is for this reason that a variety of large-scale assessment results are high-lighted, and in some cases only in cursory form. Chapter 6 summarizes the information presented in the preceding chapters with recommendations for research, and Chapter 7 – our technical appendix – outlines the cognitively based statistical methods that could be used to incorporate the knowledge and skills identified in the cognitive models in previous chapters. In particular, Chapter 7 provides a review of some popular cognitively based statistical methods. It further presents recent application of these methods in the areas of reading comprehension, (computing) science, and mathematics that highlights both the strengths and weaknesses of the applications as they relate to the inferences we can make about students' knowledge and skills.

REFERENCES

Ainsworth, S. & Loizou, A. (2003). The effects of self-explaining when learning with text or diagrams. *Cognitive Science, 27,* 669–681.

American Association for the Advancement of Science. (1993). *Benchmarks for science literacy.* New York: Oxford University Press.

Anderson, L.W., Krathwohl, D.R., Airasian, P.W., Cruikshank, K.A., Mayer, R.E., Pintrich, P.R., Raths, J., & Wittrock, C. (Eds.). (2001). *A taxonomy for learning, teaching, and assessing – a revision of Bloom's Taxonomy of Educational Objectives.* New York: Addison Wesley Longman.

Anderson, J.R. (2007) *How can the human mind occur in the physical universe?* New York: Oxford University Press.

Baron, J. (2000). *Thinking and deciding* (3rd ed.). New York: Cambridge University Press.

Baxter, G. & Glaser, R. (1998). Investigating the cognitive complexity of science assessments. *Educational Measurement: Issues and Practices, 17,* 37–45.

Bennett, R.E. & Gitomer, D.H. (2008). Transforming K-12 assessment: Integrating accountability testing, formative assessment, and professional support. *ETS Research Memorandum-08-13,* 1–30. Princeton, NJ: Educational Testing Service.

Birenbaum, M., Tatsuoka, C., & Yamada, T. (2004). Diagnostic assessment in TIMSS-R: Between countries and within-country comparisons of eighth graders' mathematics performance. *Studies in Educational Evaluation, 30,* 151–173.

Bishop, J. (1989). Is the test score decline responsible for the productivity growth decline? *American Economic Review, 79,* 178–97.

Bishop, J.H. (1991). Achievement, test scores, and relative wages. In M. H. Kosters (Ed.), *Workers and their wages* (pp. 146–186). Washington, DC: The AEI Press.

Bloom, B., Englehart, M. Furst, E., Hill, W., & Krathwohl, D. (1956). *Taxonomy of educational objectives: The classification of educational goals. Handbook I: Cognitive domain.* New York: Longmans, Green.

Borsboom, D. (2005). *Measuring the mind: Conceptual issues in contemporary psychometrics.* New York: Cambridge University Press.

Bransford, J.D., Brown, A.L., & Cocking, R.R. (2000). *How people learn: Brain, mind, experience, and school: Expanded edition.* Washington, DC: National Academy Press.

Briggs, D.C., Alonzo, A. C., Schwab, C., & Wilson, M. (2006). Diagnostic assessment with ordered multiple-choice items. *Educational Assessment, 11*(1), 33–63.

Carver, S.M. (2006). Assessing for deep understanding. In R.K. Sawyer (Ed.), *The Cambridge handbook of the learning sciences* (pp. 205–221). New York: Cambridge University Press.

Chen, Y.-H., Gorin, J.S., Thompson, M.S. & Tatsuoka, K.K. (2008). Cross-cultural validity of the TIMSS-1999 mathematics test: Verification of a cognitive model. *International Journal of Testing, 8,* 251–271.

Chi, M.T.H. (1997). Quantifying qualitative analyses of verbal data: A practical guide. *The Journal of the Learning Sciences, 6,* 271–315.

Chi, M., Feltovich, P., & Glaser, R. (1981). Categorization and representation of physics problems by experts and novices. *Cognitive Science, 5*, 121–152.

Chi, M.T.H., Glaser, R., & Farr, M. (Eds.). (1988). *The nature of expertise.* Hillsdale, NJ: Erlbaum.

Chomsky, N. (1959). Review of Skinner's verbal behavior. *Language, 35*, 26–58.

Collins, A., Halverson, R., & Brown, J.S. (2009). *Rethinking Education in the Age of Technology.* New York, NY: Teachers College Press.

Corter, J.E. & Tatsuoka, K.K. (2002). Cognitive and measurement foundations of diagnostic assessments in mathematics. College Board Technical Report. New York: Teachers College, Columbia University.

Cronbach, L.J. (1957). The two disciplines of scientific psychology. *American Psychologist, 12*, 671–684.

de Lange, J. (2007). Large-scale assessment of mathematics education. In F.K. Lester Jr. (Ed.), *National Council of Teachers of Mathematics: Second handbook of research on mathematics teaching and learning* (pp. 1111–1142). Charlotte, NC: Information Age Publishing.

Downing, S.M. & Haladyna, T.M. (Eds.). (2006). *Handbook of test development.* Mahwah, NJ: Erlbaum.

Embretson, S.E. (1998). A cognitive design system approach to generating valid tests: Application to abstract reasoning. *Psychological Methods, 3*, 380–396.

Embretson, S.E. & Daniel, R.S. (2008). Understanding and quantifying cognitive complexity level in mathematical problem solving items. *Psychology Science, 50*, 328–344.

Embretson, S.E. & Wetzel, C.D. (1987). Component latent trait models for paragraph comprehension. *Applied Psychological Measurement, 11*, 175–193.

Ericsson, K.A. (2009). (Ed.). *Development of professional expertise: Toward measurement of expert performance and design of optimal learning environments.* New York, New York: Cambridge University Press.

Ericsson, K.A., Charness, N., Feltovich, P.J., & Hoffman, R.R. (Eds.). (2006). *The Cambridge handbook of expertise and expert performance.* Cambridge, UK: Cambridge University Press.

Ericsson, K.A. & Simon, H.A. (1993). *Protocol analysis: Verbal reports as data.* Cambridge, MA: The MIT Press.

Ericsson, K.A. & Smith, J. (Eds.). (1991). *Toward a general theory of expertise: Prospects and limits.* New York: Cambridge Press.

Ferrara, S. & DeMauro, G.E. (2006). Standardized assessment of individual achievement in K-12. In R. L. Brennan (Ed.), *Educational measurement* (4th ed., pp. 579–621). Westport, CT: National Council on Measurement in Education and American Council on Education.

Gierl, M.J. (1997). Comparing the cognitive representations of test developers and students on a mathematics achievement test using Bloom's taxonomy. *Journal of Educational Research, 91,* 26–32.

Gierl, M.J., Leighton, J.P., Wang, C., Zhou, J., Gokiert, R., & Tan, A. (2009). *Validating cognitive models of task performance in algebra on the SAT®.* College Board Research Report No. 2009-3. New York: The College Board.

Gierl, M.J., Zheng, Y., & Cui, Y. (2008). Using the attribute hierarchy method to identify and interpret cognitive skills that produce group differences. *Journal of Educational Measurement, 45,* 65–89.

Gobbo, C. & Chi, M.T.H. (1986). How knowledge is structured and used by expert and novice children. *Cognitive Development, 1,* 221–237.

Gonzalez, E.J. & Miles, J.A. (2001). *TIMSS 1999 user guide for the international database: IEA's repeat of the third international mathematics and science study at the eighth grade.* Chestnut Hill, MA: TIMSS International Study Center, Boston College.

Gorin, J.S. (2009). Diagnostic Classification Models: Are they Necessary? *Measurement: Interdisciplinary Research and Perspectives, 7*(1), 30–33.

(2006). Test Design with cognition in mind. *Educational Measurement: Issues and Practice, 25*(4), 21–35.

Gorin, J.S. & Embretson, S.E. (2006). Item difficulty modeling of paragraph comprehension items. *Applied Psychological Measurement, 30,* 394–411.

Greeno, J.G. (1983). Forms of understanding in mathematical problem solving. In S.G. Paris, G.M. Olson, H.W. Stevenson (Eds.), *Learning and motivation in the classroom* (pp. 83–111). Hillsdale, NJ: Erlbaum.

(2003). Measurement, trust, and meaning. *Measurement: Interdisciplinary, Research, and Perspectives, 1,* 260–263.

Grigg, W., Lauko, M., & Brockway, D. (2006). *The nation's report card: Science 2005* (NCES 2006-466). U.S. Department of Education, National Center for Education Statistics. Washington, D.C.:U.S. Government Printing Office.

Hanushek, E.A. (2003). The failure of input-based schooling policies. *The Economic Journal, 113,* 64–98.

(2005). The economics of school quality. *German Economic Review, 6,* 269–286.

(2009). The economic value of education and cognitive skills. In G. Sykes, B. Schneider & D. N. Plank (Eds.), *Handbook of education policy research* (pp. 39–56). New York: Routledge.

Hussar, W.J. & Bailey, T.M. (2008). *Projections of Education Statistics to 2017* (NCES 2008-078). National Center for Education Statistics, Institute of Education Sciences, U.S. Department of Education. Washington, DC.

Irvine, S.H. & Kyllonen, P.C. (2002). Item generation for test development. Mahwah, NJ: Lawrence Erlbaum.

Johnson-Laird, P.N. (1983). *Mental models. Towards a cognitive science of language, inference, and consciousness.* Cambridge, MA: Harvard University Press.

Johnson-Laird, P.N. & Bara, B.G. (1984). Syllogistic inference. *Cognition, 16*, 1–61.

Johnson-Laird, P.N. (2004). Mental models and reasoning. In J.P. Leighton & R.J. Sternberg's (Eds.), *Nature of reasoning* (pp. 169–204). Cambridge University Press.

Kane, M. (2006). Validation. In R. L. Brennan (Ed.), *Educational measurement* (4th ed., pp. 17–64). Westport, CT: National Council on Measurement in Education and American Council on Education.

Kilpatrick, J., Swafford, J. & Findell, B. (Ed.). (2001). *Adding It Up: Helping Children Learn Mathematics.* Washington, DC, USA: National Academies Press.

Kintsch, W. (1998). *Comprehension: A paradigm for cognition.* Cambridge, UK: Cambridge University Press.

Kirsch, I., Braun, H., & Yamamoto, K. (2007). *America's perfect storm: Three forces changing our nation's future.* ETS Policy Information Report. Educational Testing Service.

Klahr, D. & Dunbar, K. (1988). Dual search space during scientific reasoning. *Cognitive Science, 12*, 1–48.

Koedinger, K.R. & Anderson, J.R. (1990). Abstract planning and perceptual chunks: Elements of expertise in geometry. *Cognitive Science, 14*, 511–550.

Koretz, D.M. & Hamilton, L.S. (2006). Testing for accountability in K-12. In R. Brennan (Ed.), *Educational Measurement* (4th ed., pp. 531–578). Washington, DC: American Council on Education.

Kuhn, D. (2001). How do people know? *Psychological Science, 12*, 1–8.

(2005). *Education for thinking.* Cambridge, MA: Harvard University Press.

Larkin, J. & Simon, H. (1987). Why a diagram is (sometimes) worth 10,000 words. *Cognitive Science, 11*, 65–99.

Leighton, J.P. (in press). A Cognitive Model for the Assessment of Higher Order Thinking in Students. To appear in G. Schraw (Ed.), *Current perspectives on cognition, learning, and instruction: Assessment of higher order thinking skills. Information Age Publishing.*

Leighton, J.P., Cui, Y., & Cor, M.K. (2009). Testing expert-based and student-based cognitive models: An application of the attribute hierarchy method and hierarchical consistency index. *Applied Measurement in Education, 22*, 1–26.

Leighton, J.P., Gierl, M.J., & Hunka, S. (2004). The attribute hierarchy method for cognitive assessment: A Variation on Tatsuoka's rule-space approach. *Journal of Educational Measurement, 41*, 205–236.

Leighton, J.P. & Gierl, M.J. (2007). Defining and evaluating models of cognition used in educational measurement to make inferences about examinees' thinking processes. *Educational Measurement: Issues and Practice, 26,* 3–16.

Leighton, J.P., Heffernan, C., Cor, M.K., Gokiert, R., & Cui, Y. (in press). An experimental test of student verbal reports and teacher evaluations as a source of validity evidence for test development. *Applied Measurement in Education.*

Leighton, J.P. & Sternberg, R.J. (2003). Reasoning and problem solving. In A.F. Healy & R.W. Proctor (Volume Eds.), *Experimental psychology* (pp. 623–648). Volume 4 in I. B. Weiner (Editor-in-Chief) *Handbook of psychology.* New York: Wiley.

Lohman, D.F. & Nichols, P. (2006). Meeting the NRC panel's recommendations: Commentary on the papers by Mislevy and Haertel, Gorin, and Abedi and Gandara. *Educational Measurement: Issues and Practice, 25,* 58–64.

Manski, C.F. & Wise, D.A. (1983). *College choice in America.* Cambridge, MA: Harvard University Press.

Mislevy, R.J. (1993). Foundations of a new test theory. In N. Frederiksen, R.J. Mislevy, & I.I. Bejar (Eds.), *Test theory for a new generation of tests* (pp. 19–39). Hillsdale, NJ: Lawrence Erlbaum.

(2006). Cognitive psychology and educational assessment. In R. L. Brennan (Ed.), *Educational measurement* (4th ed., pp. 257–305). Westport, CT: National Council on Measurement in Education and American Council on Education.

Mislevy, R.J. & Behrens, J.T., Bennett, R.E., Demark, S.F., Frezzo, D.C., Levy, R., Robinson, D.H., Rutstein, D.W., Shute, V.J., Stanley, K., & Winters, F.I. (2010). On the roles of external knowledge representations in assessment design. *Journal of Technology, Learning, and Assessment, 8*(2). http://escholarship.bc.edu/jtla/vol8/2.

Mislevy, R.J. & Haertel, G. (2006). Implications for evidence-centered design for educational assessment. *Educational Measurement: Issues and Practice, 25,* 6–20.

Mislevy, R.J., Steinberg, L.S., & Almond, R.G. (2003). On the structure of educational assessments. *Measurement: Interdisciplinary Research and Perspectives, 1,* 3–67.

Murnane, R.J., Willett, J.B., Duhaldeborde, Y. & Tyler, J.H. (2000). How important are the cognitive skills of teenagers in predicting subsequent earnings? *Journal of Policy Analysis and Management, 19,* 547–68.

National Commission on Excellence in Education. (1983). *A nation at risk: The imperative for educational reform.* Washington, DC: U.S. Government Printing Office.

National Mathematics Advisory Panel. (2008). *Foundations for Success: The Final Report of the National Mathematics Advisory Panel.* U.S. Department of Education: Washington, DC.

National Research Council (2001). *Knowing what students know: The science and design of educational assessment.* Committee on the Foundations of Assessment. J. Pellegrino, N. Chudowsky, and R. Glaser (Eds.). Board on Testing and Assessment, Center for Education. Washington, DC: National Academy Press.

National Research Council (2005). *How Students Learn: History, Mathematics, and Science in the Classroom.* In M.S. Donovan & J.D. Bransford (Eds.), Division of Behavioral and Social Sciences and Education. Washington, DC: The National Academies Press.

National Research Council (2007). *Taking science to school: Learning and teaching science in grades K-8.* Arlington, VA: National Science Foundation.

National Research Council (2009). *Mathematics Learning in Early Childhood: Paths Toward Excellence and Equity.* Committee on Early Childhood Mathematics, Christopher T. Cross, Taniesha A. Woods, and Heidi Schweingruber, Editors. Center for Education, Division of Behavioral and Social Sciences and Education. Washington, DC: The National Academies Press.

Newcombe, N.S., Ambady, N., Eccles, J., Gomez, L., Klahr, D., Linn, M., Miller, K., & Mix, K. (2009). Psychology's role in mathematics and science education. *American Psychologist, 64,* 538–550.

Newell, A. & Simon, H. A. (1972). *Human problem solving.* NJ: Prentice Hall.

New York Times (Nov. 14, 2007), *Study compares states' math and science scores with other countries'.*

No Child Left Behind Act of 2002, Pub Law No. 107–110 (2002, January). Retrieved April 11, 2009 from http://www.ed.gov/policy/elsec/leg/esea02/107-110.pdf

Organization for Economic Cooperation and Development (2003). *Program for International Student Assessment (PISA).* Author.

Organization for Economic Cooperation and Development (2007). *PISA 2006: Science Competencies for Tomorrow's World Executive Summary.* Author. Accessed from world wide web on March 26, 2010, at http://www.oecd.org/dataoecd/15/13/39725224.pdf.

Organization for Economic Cooperation and Development (2009). *Education today: The OECD perspective.* Author.

Pashler, H., Rohrer, D., Cepeda, N. & Carpenter, S. (2007). Enhancing learning and retarding forgetting: Choices and consequences. *Psychonomic Bulletin & Review, 14,* 187–193.

Pellegrino J.W., Baxter G.P., & Glaser R., (1999). Addressing the "Two Disciplines" problem: linking theories of cognition and learning with assessment and instructional practice. *Review of Research in Education*, 24, 307–352.

Piaget, J. & Inhelder, B. (1967). *The child's conception of space*. New York: W. W. Norton &Co.

Phillips, G.W. (2007). *Expressing international educational achievement in terms of U.S. performance standards: Linking NAEP achievement levels to TIMSS*. Washington, DC: American Institutes for Research.

Polikoff, M. (2010). Instructional sensitivity as a psychometric property of assessments. *Educational Measurement: Issues and Practice*, 29, 3–14.

Provasnik, S., Gonzales, P., & Miller, D. (2009). *U.S. Performance Across International Assessments of Student Achievement: Special Supplement to The Condition of Education 2009* (NCES 2009–083). National Center for Education Statistics, Institute of Education Sciences, U.S. Department of Education. Washington, DC.

Resnick, L.B. (1983). Toward a cognitive theory of instruction. In S.G. Paris, G.M. Olson, H.W. Stevenson (Eds.), *Learning and motivation in the classroom* (pp. 5–38). Hillsdale, NJ: Erlbaum.

Russell, J.F. (2005). Evidence related to awareness, adoption, and implementation of the standards for technological literacy: Content for the study of technology. *The Journal of Technology Studies*, 31, 30–38.

Rupp, A.A. (2007). The answer is in the question: A guide for describing and investigating the conceptual foundations and statistical properties of cognitive psychometric models. *International Journal of Testing*, 7, 95–125.

Rupp, A.A. & Templin, J.L. (2008). Unique characteristics of diagnostic classification models: A comprehensive review of the current state-of-the-art. *Measurement*, 2, 219–262.

Sawyer, R.K. (Ed.). (2006). *The Cambridge handbook of the learning sciences*. New York: Cambridge University Press.

Shute, V.J., Hansen, E.G., & Almond, R.G. (2008). You can't fatten a hog by weighing it – or can you? Evaluating an assessment for learning system called ACED. *International Journal of Artificial Intelligence in Education*, 18, 289–316.

Shute, V.J., Masduki, I., Donmez, O., Kim, Y.J., Dennen, V.P., Jeong, A.C., & Wang, C-Y. (2010). Modeling, assessing, and supporting key competencies within game environments. In D. Ifenthaler, P. Pirnay-Dummer, & N.M. Seel (Eds.), *Computer-based diagnostics and systematic analysis of knowledge* (pp. 281–310). New York, NY: Springer.

Siegler, R.S. (2005). Children's learning. *American Psychologist*, 60, 769–778.

Schmeiser, C.B. & Welch, C.J. (2006). Test development. In R. L. Brennan (Ed.), *Educational measurement* (4th ed., pp. 307–353). Westport,

CT: National Council on Measurement in Education and American Council on Education.

Shrager, J. & Siegler, R.S. (1998). SCADS: A model of children's strategy choices and strategy discoveries. *Psychological Science, 9*, 405–410.

Slotta, J.D. & Chi, M.T.H. (2006). Helping students understand challenging topics in science through ontology training. *Cognition and Instruction, 24*, 261–289.

Snow, R.E. & Lohman, D.F. (1989). Implications of cognitive psychology for educational measurement. In R. L. Linn (Ed.), *Educational measurement* (3rd ed., pp. 263–331). New York: American Council on Education, Macmillan.

Stanovich, K.E. (2009). *What intelligence tests miss: The psychology of rational thought*. New Haven, CT: Yale University Press.

Tatsuoka, K.K. (1983). Rule space: An approach for dealing with misconceptions based on item response theory. *Journal of Educational Measurement, 20*, 345–354.

(1985). A probabilistic model for diagnostic misconceptions in the pattern classification approach. *Journal of Educational Statistics, 10*, 55–73.

(1995). Architecture of knowledge structures and cognitive diagnosis: A statistical pattern recognition and classification approach. In P. D. Nichols, S. F. Chipman., & R. L. Brennan (Eds.), *Cognitively diagnostic assessment* (pp. 327–359). Hillsdale, NJ: Lawrence Erlbaum Associates.

(2009). *Cognitive assessment. An introduction to the rule space method*. New York City, New York: Routledge, Taylor & Francis.

Tatsuoka, K.K., Corter, J.E., & Guerrero, A. (2004). *Coding manual for identifying involvement of content, skill, and process subskills for the TIMSS-R 8th grade and 12th grade general mathematics test items* (Technical Report). New York: Department of Human Development, Teachers College, Columbia University.

Tatsuoka, K.K., Corter, J.E., & Tatsuoka, C. (2004). Patterns of diagnosed mathematical content and process skills in TIMSS-R across a sample of 20 countries. *American Educational Research Journal, 41*, 901–926.

Thomas, D., Li, Q., Knott, L., & Zhongxiao, L. (2008). The structure of student dialogue in web-assisted mathematics courses. *Journal of Educational Technology Systems, 36*, 415–431.

Tubau, E. (2008). Enhancing probabilistic reasoning: The role of causal graphs, statistical format and numerical skills. *Learning and Individual Differences, 18*, 187–196.

Tversky, B. (2002). Some ways that graphics communicate. In N. Allen (Editor), *Words and images: New steps in an old dance*, (pp. 57–74). Westport, CT: Ablex.

U.S. Department of Education, National Center for Education Statistics (2008). *Digest of education statistics, 2008*, Chapter 6 (NCES 2008–022).

Wilson, M. & Sloane, K. (2000). From principles to practice: An embedded assessment system. *Applied Measurement in Education, 13*, 181–208.

Zhou, L. (2009). *Revenues and Expenditures for Public Elementary and Secondary Education: School Year 2006–07 (Fiscal Year 2007)*. (NCES 2009–337). National Center for Education Statistics, Institute of Education Sciences, U.S. Department of Education.

2

Evaluating Cognitive Models in Large-Scale Educational Assessments

In educational assessment, an idea whose time has come is that tests can be designed according to advances in the learning sciences. Currently, researchers and practitioners are studying how learning science outcomes can inform the design, development, and use of large-scale educational assessments. To date, however, there are few examples of large-scale educational tests designed from a learning science perspective and, hence, few empirical studies exist to evaluate the strengths and weaknesses of this approach. Moreover, developing the first generation of assessments using outcomes from the learning sciences is hampered by the limited information available on the types of cognitive models that can facilitate the design, validation, and administration of educational tests. Yet the role of cognitive models is paramount to the success of this endeavor. The National Research Council (NRC, 2001) asserted in their seminal publication, *Knowing What Students Know: The Science and Design of Educational Assessments*, that cognitive models have a foundational role in educational assessment that is currently poorly developed and under-valued:

> A model of cognition and learning, or a description of how people represent knowledge and develop competence in a subject domain, is a cornerstone of the assessment development enterprise. Unfortunately, the model of learning is not made explicit in most assessment development efforts, is not empirically derived, and/or is impoverished relative to what it could be. (p. 176)

45

Because educational assessments are based on cognitive problem-solving tasks (Snow & Lohman, 1989), these models can be used to specify the most important cognitive components for student achievement and to identify tasks for measuring these components. However, there is little information or guidance in the literature on creating these models and, hence, few studies on the application of these models to assessment design, development, or use. To begin to address this gap in the literature, two main ideas are developed in this chapter. First, we present a general description of the term "cognitive model," and we illustrate how cognitive models are currently used in educational assessment. Second, we identify three defining characteristics of these models and describe why these characteristics may help link research from the learning sciences with practices in educational assessment. These characteristics will serve as the criteria used in Chapters 3, 4, and 5 to evaluate current cognitive models in the domains of reading, science, and mathematics, respectively, from the perspective of assessment design.

COGNITIVE MODELS AND EDUCATIONAL ASSESSMENT

The term *cognitive model*, which first appeared in the field of computer science, refers to the mathematical or computational representation of a process, device, or system designed to simulate human problem solving. A similar description is used in cognitive psychology – a cognitive model refers to a mathematical or computational representation that characterizes how the brain executes a complex task by outlining both the basic processes involved and how these processes interact to account for human problem solving. Cognitive modeling is now pervasive in psychology. For example, Busemeyer and Diederich (2010) reported that over 80 percent of the papers published in cognitive science journals included cognitive modeling in some form. These models, although diverse and varied, share a common purpose, which is to explain or account for a psychological phenomenon by mimicking some aspect or characteristic of the phenomenon. Relative to the actual psychological phenomenon under investigation, the model representation is more simplistic, easier to manipulate, and more readily understandable. Hence, the model provides a lens for studying complex cognition by mapping onto some, but not all, of the phenomenon's properties.

Cognitive models are useful in the study of cognition because they provide a representation of the phenomenon that either may not currently exist or, if it does exist, may not be practical or even possible to study without further simplification. Because the model permits a simplified form of representation, learning scientific theories can be more readily evaluated by testing the predictive validity of the models. Hence, one important benefit of cognitive modeling is that it provides a method for generating and evaluating predictions about theories. Yet other advantages also exist (Dawson, 2004). For example, model specification can lead to clearer theories because the process of transforming informal thoughts, statements, and assumptions about a psychological phenomenon into more formal terms and representations requires both precision of ideas and economy of expression. This level of formality, precision, and expression can help identify both hidden and new assumptions, thereby leading to an elaborated and thus more complete model. The specification process can also hint at possible research methods and approaches for studying the model.

Cognitive models also allow us to study complex phenomenon by focusing initially on a small but key set of issues required to understand the phenomenon or by predicting a small but specific set of outcomes. These issues or predictions in turn can lead to new knowledge and a better understanding of the phenomenon. Then, the issues can be refined and the predictions modified in an iterative manner, eventually leading to a new level of understanding and a better specified and hence more complete model. Busemeyer and Diederich (2010) illustrate this iterative process by providing the following five-step description for cognitive modeling:

1. A conceptual and/or theoretical framework is formulated into a more rigorous mathematical or computer language description where basic cognitive principles are used to construct the model. [MODEL SPECIFICATION][1]

2. Because the conceptual framework is often incomplete for model specification, additional assumptions or new details are added to complete the model. [IDENTIFY ASSUMPTIONS]

3. The characteristics or features in the model are estimated using observable data to generate empirical evidence. [METHODS FOR STUDYING MODEL]

4. The empirical evidence generated for the model is then compared with competing models to determine the model's predictive validity and utility. The goal of the analyses in this step is to determine which representation provides better prediction, and hence explanation, for the psychological phenomenon under investigation. [PREDICTIVE VALIDITY OF MODEL]

5. The conceptual theoretical framework is reformulated to construct new models of the phenomenon, given feedback obtained from the empirical results. [MODEL REFINEMENT]

Model specification can also enhance our understanding of cognition because the development and application of these models

---

[1] Model specification can occur at three different levels (Marr, 1982). The *computational* level of analysis outlines the particular information-processing problem (i.e., psychological phenomenon or outcome) the model is designed to explain. The *algorithmic* level of analysis identifies the processing steps, normally articulated with the specificity of a computer program, required to solve the problem that gives rise to a particular psychological phenomenon. The algorithmic level is often termed the "functional architecture" of the cognitive system, and it represents the "programming language of the mind" (Dawson, 1998, p. 12). The *implementation* level of analysis specifies the types of biological or electronic machinery that could be used to physically and in real-time instantiate the information-processing problem being solved.

sometimes yield unexpected results. These results in turn may provide new insights into the phenomenon. That is, by specifying a rigorous model and studying its complexity, new and unexpected properties of the model – and hence new phenomena – may be identified.

In educational assessment, the term cognitive model is applied broadly to characterize the knowledge and skills examinees require to solve items on assessments. Leighton and Gierl (2007a) claim that a cognitive model in educational measurement refers to a "simplified description of human problem solving on standardized educational tasks, which help to characterize the knowledge and skills students at different levels of learning have acquired and to facilitate the explanation and prediction of students' performance" (p. 6).

Educational assessments are based on cognitive problem-solving tasks. Hence, cognitive modeling, in some form, is required to design the assessment, develop tasks to elicit specific problem-solving skills, and interpret task results (i.e., test scores). Because examinees' thinking and problem solving cannot be observed directly, these models can be used when researchers and practitioners want to identify and evaluate the knowledge and skills required for correct task performance. Careful study of this performance may in turn lead to a better understanding of the knowledge and skills used by examinees during problem solving and of the inferences that examinees' test scores can support. The use of cognitive models in educational assessment may also allow us to enhance the teaching-learning cycle. Instructional decisions are guided by students' ability to think and solve problems. Thus, instructors develop methods for making students' thinking overt, so feedback and remediation can focus on overcoming problem-solving weaknesses. Cognitive models provide one method for representing thought in educational assessments. Because these models specify the knowledge and skills required to respond to test items, they can also be used to enhance test score interpretations and to guide instruction when the knowledge and skills specified in the model are used to identify and interpret students' cognitive skill profiles.

COGNITIVE MODEL OF TEST SPECIFICATIONS

Educational assessments are all based on some type of cognitive model, even if this model is only used implicitly to design and develop the assessment. Currently, most large-scale educational assessments are developed from a *cognitive model of test specifications* (Leighton & Gierl, 2007a). These specifications are often generated by content experts as a two-way matrix, where the rows represent content areas and the columns represent cognitive skills (Schmeiser & Welch, 2006). The most widely used taxonomy for identifying the cognitive skills used by examinees to solve test items is Bloom's *Taxonomy of Educational Objectives: Cognitive Domain* (Bloom et al., 1956). The taxonomy provides a systematic outline of the different levels of thinking that were considered by Bloom and his colleagues to be the goals of classroom instruction. The taxonomy ranges from the simplest level, *knowledge* (i.e., recall of specific information), to the most complex level, *evaluation* (i.e., the ability to judge the value of materials and methods for given purposes). The taxonomy is represented as a simple and straightforward hierarchy of knowledge and skills (see Chapter 1, Figure 1.1). Because content experts have extensive knowledge and experience with the examinees, curriculum, and learning environment, they develop items for each cell in the test specifications by anticipating the cognitive skills that examinees will use to answer items correctly in each content area. These judgments serve as the foundation for the cognitive model of test specifications. This model, however, is not based on learning scientific research (see Chapter 1, this volume), but rather serves as the content experts' representation of cognition. This representation, which may or may not be a plausible set of beliefs about problem solving, contributes to the design and development process because it alerts item writers to the potential knowledge and skills that examinees *may use* when solving items in specific content areas. Unfortunately, cognitive models of test specifications, which serve as sophisticated *theories of mind*

(Leighton & Gierl, 2007a; Lohman & Nichols, 1990; Wellman & Lagattuta, 2004), typically remain empirically unsubstantiated. Cognitive models of test specifications often receive little experimental scrutiny, support, or refinement based on the learning sciences. Schmeiser and Welch (2006), in their review of test development for the influential text *Educational Measurement* (4th Edition), maintain that developers should continue to classify items according to cognitive skills, despite the fact that no current cognitive-skill-classification taxonomy is supported by documented validity evidence (p. 316). They also provide this cautionary note:

> But we must also remember that examinees do not reveal the cognitive skills they used to answer a test item, and we cannot presume to know what skills they used because we don't know their instructional history. Because of this, we must infer the cognitive skill path to a response and classify the item accordingly. In reality, we have no direct knowledge that this is the cognitive path invoked by the item, even by a majority of the test takers. Thus, this type of classification of test items is not merely logical and empirical in nature, it is also inferred by the test developer. (p. 316)

In other words, the knowledge and skills outlined in test specifications reflect *cognitive intentions* that may or may not be an accurate representation and description of the knowledge and skills that examinees actually use when solving items. If we consider the five-step description for cognitive modeling offered by Busemeyer and Diederich (2010), test specifications allow the developer to implement the first two steps by specifying the model and identifying assumptions, but not the remaining three steps of studying the model, generating empirical predictions, or refining it.

Illustrative examples of tests developed from cognitive models of test specifications can be found in the subject-specific achievement tests used in most large-scale educational testing programs. The test specifications administered at grade three in mathematics by the Ministry of Education in the province of Alberta in Canada is presented in Figure 2.1. These specifications were created using the content, knowledge, and skills specified in the provincial curriculum, which in Canada is common for the four western provinces of British Columbia, Alberta, Saskatchewan, and Manitoba and the three northern territories, the Yukon, the Northwest Territories, and Nunavut. The mathematics curriculum from kindergarten to grade nine is described in *The Alberta K-9 Mathematics Program of Studies with Achievement Indicators* (2007). The program of studies identifies assumption about mathematical thinking and learning, general outcomes, specific outcomes, and achievement indicators agreed on by the seven provinces and territories. Learning outcomes in the program of studies for K–9 are organized into four content areas: Number, Patterns and Relations, Shape and Space, and Statistics and Probability. By reviewing the program of studies and drawing on the knowledge, beliefs, and experiences of content experts, Alberta Education develops their cognitive model of test specifications (where Figure 2.1 serves as one example). Then, items are developed from the specifications by soliciting the help of teachers throughout the province who work with Alberta Education staff to develop, review, and revise items.

The grade-three Mathematics Provincial Achievement Test is designed to measure students' knowledge and skills in the curriculum-specific content areas of Number, Patterns and Relations, Shape and Space, and Statistics and Probability. Test specifications highlight the content area by cognitive-skill interactions that are expected to occur when students solve test items. In Figure 2.1, for instance, the content area "Patterns and Relations" is crossed with the cognitive skill "Knowledge" to produce two test items. These two knowledge items measure a student's ability to "recall facts, concepts, and terminology, know number facts, recognize place value, know procedures for computations, know procedures for constructing and measuring, know how to use a calculator/computer, and know mental computations and

Content Area	Cognitive Skill		Number of Items
	Knowledge	Skills	
Number • Develop a number sense for whole numbers 0 to 1000, and explore fractions (fifths and tenths) • Apply an arithmetic operation (addition, subtraction, multiplication, or division) on whole numbers, and illustrate its use in creating and solving problems • Use and justify an appropriate calculation strategy or technology to solve problems	5	9	14
Patterns and Relations • Investigate, establish and communicate rules for numerical and non-numerical patterns, including those found in the home, and use these rules to make predictions	2	4	6
Shape and space • Estimate, measure and compare, using whole numbers and primarily standard units of measure • Describe, classify, construct and relate 3-D objects and 2-D shapes • Use numbers and direction words to describe the relative positions of objects in one dimension, using everyday contexts	4	8	12
Statistics and Probability • Collect first- and second-hand data, display the results in more than one way, and interpret the data to make predictions • Use simple probability experiments, designed by others, to explain outcomes	3	5	8
Number of Questions	14	26	40

FIGURE 2.1. The test specifications used for a grade-three Mathematics Achievement Test. Adapted from Alberta Education (2008). *Alberta Provincial Achievement Testing, Subject Bulletin 2008–2009: Grade 3 Mathematics*. Edmonton, AB: Alberta Education.

estimation strategies"[2] (Alberta Education, 2008, p. 1). These knowledge components are expected to be related to the content area of Patterns and Relations; that is, content involving the capacity to "investigate,

---

[2] Similarly, content experts describe "skills" as being characterized by a student's ability to represent basic mathematical concepts in concrete, pictorial, and/ or symbolic models; apply a math concept in both familiar and new situations; create new problem situations that exemplify a concept; justify answers; judge reasonableness of answers; communicate why and when certain strategies are appropriate; demonstrate and apply relationships among numbers, operations, forms, and models; explain relationships among geometric forms; and use a variety of problem-solving strategies.

establish, and communicate rules for numerical and non-numerical patterns, including those found in the home, and use [of] these rules to make predictions" (Alberta Education, 2008, p. 1). These specifications are beneficial in test design because they can be generated, refined, and validated by content experts, which in turn can be used to develop test items by practicing teachers in relatively short order.

However, there are also some drawbacks when using these specifications for measuring complex problem-solving skills. The cognitive skills are not defined explicitly, meaning that the mapping of the content-by-skill interaction in the specifications onto the actual test items in each cell is vague. For example, a variety of items could, in principle, be created to measure knowledge for Patterns and Relations. The variety of items that could be generated is then exacerbated by the fact that most cells contain only a small number of items. The specifications also force the test user (e.g., teachers, administrators) to assume that the content-by-skill interaction is consistent for all students, regardless of their achievement level, instructional sequencing, or gender, and that there is little or no cognitive-response variability in how students solve the items in each cell of the test specifications. This assumption is required because one specification is applied to the entire test-taking population. However, perhaps the most important limitation stems from the fact that no empirical evidence is available to support the content area by cognitive-skill interactions, meaning that the knowledge and skills that examinees are expected to use may not, in fact, be used during problem solving (Brown & Burton, 1978; Gierl, 1997; Leighton & Gokiert, 2008; Norris, Leighton, & Phillips, 2004; Poggio et al., 2005). The possible discrepancy, and hence inaccuracy, between the intended performance outlined in the cognitive model of test specifications and actual performance of examinees cannot be evaluated, because the model is not validated with human studies. The end result is that test score inferences about complex cognition are weak, coarse, and largely unsubstantiated when a cognitive model of test specifications is used to study complex cognition.

COGNITIVE MODELS OF TASK PERFORMANCE

An alternative to test specifications is a *cognitive model of task performance* (Leighton & Gierl, 2007a). This model specifies in detail the thinking processes that underlie test performance. Typically, it is developed by studying examinees as they solve items or tasks in a specific content area, and by identifying the knowledge and skills required to solve tasks using basic cognitive principles. One method for creating this type of model is to administer tasks to a sample of examinees, use think-aloud methods, and then conduct protocol and/ or verbal analysis on the response data (Chi, 1997; Ericsson & Simon, 1993; Leighton, 2004; Leighton & Gierl, 2007b; Newell & Simon, 1972; Taylor & Dionne, 2000). These methods yield the psychological evidence and empirical support required to substantiate the cognitive model. As a result, cognitive models of task performance can be used to make specific, empirically based inferences about examinees' knowledge and skills. The main drawback of using a cognitive model of task performance in educational assessments stems from the fact that there is little information currently available on the knowledge and skills that characterize student performance in most testing situations. That is, few cognitive models exist to help guide the design of educational assessments. Moreover, developing cognitive models of task performance is labor intensive, because cognitive models require substantiation with some form of experimental or quasi-experimental investigation.

Although few cognitive models exist to help guide the design of assessments, the *Number Knowledge Test* (Okamoto & Case, 1996) serves as one example of an assessment developed from a cognitive model of task performance. Researchers who study the development of mathematical cognition have identified a *central conceptual structure* that affects how students learn key mathematical concepts in elementary school (Case, 1992; Case & Griffin, 1990; Griffin, Case, & Sandieson, 1992). A central conceptual structure is a network of

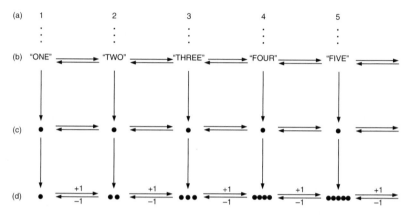

FIGURE 2.2. Diagrammatic overview of the central conceptual structure in the form of a "mental counting line" cognitive model. The model outlines the knowledge structures and processing skills that underlie learning whole numbers in mathematics. Adapted from Case, R. (1996). Reconceptualizing the nature of children's conceptual structures and their development in middle childhood. *Monographs of the Society for Research in Child Development, 61* (1–26), Serial 246.

semantic nodes that help students organize domain-specific information to solve a broad array of math problems. Over time, this structure also provides the foundation for developing new learning and problem-solving skills. According to Case (1996), the structure is central in three ways: It forms the conceptual center for how students understand ideas related to specific topics; it is the foundation upon which more complex networks can be created; and it is produced from students' information-processing and problem-solving activities.

Case and his colleagues (e.g., Case, 1996; Case & Griffin, 1990; Okamoto & Case, 1996) proposed a diagrammatic representation of the central conceptual structure, which serves as a cognitive model of task performance for the knowledge and skills underlying the learning of whole numbers in mathematics. Their "mental counting" line cognitive model is presented in Figure 2.2. The first row of the model (labeled [a] in Figure 2.2) provides a representation that indicates students can recognize written numerals. This primary skill is foundational and it is in turn mapped onto subsequent rows in the model. The second row (labeled [b]), described as the "verbal labeling" line, indicates that students can recognize and generate the number words, such as one, two, three, and so on. The third row (labeled [c]), the "mental action" line, is used by students to associate groups of objects (e.g., dots, blocks, marbles) with numbers that represent those groups. Initially, this association may require the student to transform the representation, such as translating the number of physical objects to a set of mental objects, but over time the association becomes linked within the mind of the student. The fourth row (labeled [d]), the "conceptual interpretation" line, illustrates the formation of more complex associations such as linking specific numbers of objects to representations (e.g., fingers can be used to present number sets) as well as introducing the concepts of addition and subtraction to the number set. Each line is also linked by horizontal and vertical arrows indicating "transformations" that allow students to move between the rows and columns. The cognitive model in Figure 2.2 is conceptualized as a relatively simple structure containing numbers ranging from 1 to 10. But, through instruction and development, more complex structures are formed that may involve two or more mental counting lines with a larger range of whole numbers.

In an effort to generate tasks that measure the knowledge and skills identified in the mental counting line cognitive model, Okamoto and Case (1996) developed the *Number Knowledge Test*. This test was created to assess students' informal knowledge of whole numbers as well as the knowledge and skills associated with whole-number concepts. Sample items are presented in Table 2.1. Item 1 states "What number comes right after 7?" whereas item 2 states "What number comes two numbers after 7?" Okamoto and Case claim that these two items measure the skill of knowing what number comes after another number, also shown by the *next* arrow connecting the number nodes in the second row (labeled [b]) of Figure 2.2. This skill is critical to the concept of whole numbers, according to Okamoto and Case, because it measures whether students have acquired the explicit representation

TABLE 2.1. *Sample items from the number knowledge test (Okamoto & Case, 1996)*

Item 1. What number comes right after 7?

Item 2: What number comes two numbers after 7?

Item 3: [Show student the numbers, 8, 5, 2, 6, and then ask:] When you are counting, which of these numbers do you say first?

Item 4: [Show student the numbers, 8, 5, 2, 6, and then ask:] When you are counting, which of these numbers do you say last?

Item 5: Which of these two numbers is bigger, 5 or 4?

Item 6: Which of these two numbers is bigger, 7 or 9?

---

of what number comes after another number. In items 3 and 4, students are presented with four numbers and asked, "When you are counting, which of these numbers do you say first?" and "Which of these numbers do you say last?" Okamoto and Case claim that students must go through the counting sequence mentally while monitoring visually the display of the numbers. These skills – recognizing written numerals and verbal labeling – are specified in the first two rows (labeled [a] and [b]) of Figure 2.2. Hence, these items measure two unique skills in the cognitive model. In items 5 and 6, students are asked, respectively, "Which of these two numbers is bigger, 5 or 4"? and "Which of these two numbers is bigger, 7 or 9?" These items evaluate a student's ability to use the ordinal information in the second row (labeled [b]) to make cardinal decisions required in the fourth row (labeled [d]) of Figure 2.2. As a result, they measure two unique skills in the cognitive model.

The mental counting line cognitive model, which is based on central conceptual structure theory, has been empirically tested with students, and it can be used to measure components of the model. The model also accounts for problem-solving performance on tasks specific to thinking and problem solving in mathematics. For instance, Okamoto and Case (1996) reported that their tasks on the *Number Knowledge Test* produced proportion-correct scores that were ordered in a manner that was consistent with the structures specified in their model, indicating that items could be ordered from easiest to most difficult as levels (a) to (d) were measured, respectively. A latent-structure analysis was also conducted to evaluate students' performance level by item, relative to the predicted model structure. Again, Okamoto and Case's results suggested that the items measured distinct conceptual structures, as outlined in the cognitive model. Hence, the mental counting line cognitive model is useful in supporting specific inferences about students' knowledge and skills with whole numbers. The benefit of using the test in conjunction with the model is that it allows instructors to systematically measure key components in students' mental counting, so that specific strengths and weaknesses can be identified. By modeling these knowledge and skills, instructors not only observe a profile of student performance that can inform their teaching, but they can also begin to understand, from a cognitive development perspective, how students think about and solve problems involving whole numbers in early elementary school (e.g., Griffin, 2002, 2004; Griffin & Case, 1997).

DEFINING CHARACTERISTICS OF COGNITIVE MODELS USED IN EDUCATIONAL ASSESSMENT

In 2001, the National Research Council (NRC) claimed:

> Every assessment, regardless of its purpose, rests on three pillars: a model of how students represent knowledge and develop competence in the subject domain [i.e., a cognitive model of learning], tasks or situations that allow one to observe students' performance, and an interpretation method for drawing inferences from the performance evidence thus obtained. (p. 2)

Despite their foundational role in assessment, learning scientific cognitive models have received limited use in test design and development, in part because the models are difficult to specify and then map onto current assessment practices. To promote a better understanding and to further their use, the NRC identified five key features of cognitive models. First, they claim that a cognitive model of learning should be based on empirical studies of skill acquisition in the domain of interest. These studies yield rich descriptions about the domain and the types of knowledge and skills examinees require to solve problems in the domain. Test developers can profit from these descriptions by developing tasks that elicit relevant cognitive skills.

Second, the NRC (2001) claims that a cognitive model of learning should differentiate the performance of novices and experts. Domain mastery may serve as a target for assessment and instruction because experts not only have extensive knowledge, but they also articulate skills that allow them to organize, manipulate, and represent information in a manner that promotes effective reasoning, thinking, and problem solving. The transition from novice to expert performance may also suggest developmental paths or learning progressions that allow us to understand how cognitive skills change over time. Assessments can be designed to measure and monitor the development of these cognitive skills as students become more competent in a domain.

Third, the NRC claims that a cognitive model of learning should be dynamic and robust enough to capture different ways that students learn and come to understand concepts in a domain, given that many learning styles can be paired with many instructional approaches to promote thinking, learning, and instruction. Presumably, a comprehensive cognitive model will provide a broader perspective of how students think and learn domain-specific ideas leading to varied assessment methods and strategies.

Fourth, they claim that a cognitive model of learning should be specified in such a way that the concepts in the model align most closely with the test-score inferences the model is intended to support. Because cognitive models can be defined broadly and they can include may different aspects of thinking and learning, decisions must be made about which aspect of the models to use when designing a test. One way to make this decision is to ensure that the model is used to support the purpose of the test and its intended score inferences.

Fifth, they claim that a cognitive model of learning should support flexibility of test development and use, particularly in score reporting. Fine-grain models, where cognitive skills are specified in a detailed manner, should be developed to support aggregation to coarse-grain models, where the cognitive skills are specified in a more general manner. This feature allows the test developer to use the assessment for different purposes and in more varied testing situations.

Leighton and Gierl (2007a) responded to these features by noting that although the NRC's description of a cognitive model is broad and inclusive, few assessments are designed or developed from a cognitive model of learning that would satisfy the NRC's description. In fact, large-scale educational assessments designed from cognitive models of test specifications – which reflect the majority of tests in use today – fail to meet any of the NRC's features, except, perhaps, for the fifth (if we consider sub-scores as an approach for refining grain size in score reporting). This contradictory situation – the claim that all assessments are based on a cognitive model with the fact that few operational assessments satisfy the NRC's five-feature description of a cognitive model – suggests that a less restrictive description of a cognitive model must be used to understand how the modeling process can guide the design and development of large-scale educational assessments. Next, we offer a less restrictive and more inclusive *characterization* of a cognitive model that may allow us to begin to link the learning sciences with assessment practices.

LEIGHTON AND GIERL'S CHARACTERIZATION OF A COGNITIVE MODEL FOR EDUCATIONAL ASSESSMENT

The NRC offered five *specific features* of a cognitive model of learning that could inform assessment design. We offer three *general characteristics* of a cognitive model for educational assessment that may allow us to link the learning sciences to test design and development. Our three characteristics include grain size, measurability, and instructional relevance.[3]

GRAIN SIZE

The first characteristic of a cognitive model necessary to link learning with assessment is the specification of grain size, where grain size refers to both the depth and breadth of knowledge and skills measured. To promote specific cognitive inferences, for instance, models must contain knowledge and skills that are specified at a fine grain size to magnify the processes underlying test performance broadly (i.e., several content areas) or narrowly (i.e., one concept in one content area). Cognitive models containing many knowledge and skills can only be operationalized with exams containing many test items. Grain size must be also be specified consistently within the assessment so the knowledge and skills can be ordered, if desired. The ordering of knowledge and skills within a domain can reflect developmental and/ or learning progressions. Ordered knowledge and skills are also necessary when the purpose of the assessment is to make diagnostic inferences so the examinees' problem-solving strengths and weaknesses can be identified. The identification and evaluation of specifically ordered knowledge and skills may also be helpful during instruction because students are developing more complex knowledge and skills using basic and often easier concepts and ideas as their foundation.

---

[3] In Chapters 3, 4, and 5, we do not include empirical verification as a fourth feature of cognitive models. It is assumed that all learning scientific cognitive models are based on empirical evidence. That is, they have evidentiary support rooted in the learning sciences. To be useful in assessment, cognitive models should help designers and developers identify the knowledge and skills that will be the targets for assessment. Ideally, these models are based on empirical studies of learning in a specific domain using examinees from the target population, where basic cognitive principles that are relevant and applicable to test design and development are articulated and used to create the model.

However, the grain size issue will always elicit important tradeoffs in testing. A cognitive analysis at a fine-grain size, for example, will limit construct representation and content coverage because the depth of representation or coverage will typically be achieved at the expense of breadth of representation or coverage, unless the test contains an unusually large number of items.

With a cognitive model of test specifications, the grain size is often coarse because content coverage is broad. The content-by-skill interaction, as outlined in the cells of the test specifications, is typically used perfunctorily to develop test items, leading to general and often uninformative test-score inferences. With a cognitive model of task performance, the grain size is expected to be less coarse, and therefore content coverage will be more limited. Test-score inferences are also expected to be more targeted because the components of the cognitive model of task performance are articulated at a finer grain size. The *Number Knowledge Test*, for example, measures examinees' informal knowledge of whole numbers, including some operations and representations related to whole number concepts. On a typical grade-three mathematics achievement test, informal knowledge of whole numbers, as measured by the *Number Knowledge Test*, would account for one or two items, at most, in a forty- or fifty-item test measuring many math concepts in many content areas.

MEASURABILITY

The second characteristic of a cognitive model necessary to link learning with assessment is measurability of the knowledge and skills in the model. The knowledge and skills included in the model must be described in a way that would allow a developer to create a test item to measure that knowledge or skill. The items must also be permissible for a typical educational-assessment administration (i.e., paper-based test or, in some cases, a computer-based test). Every educational test is developed with the belief and expectation that different types of items can be created to elicit the knowledge and skills outlined in the test specifications. Item development is guided by "best practices," standards for test design and development, and conventional wisdom to ensure high-quality testing tasks – as determined by substantive and statistical requirements (e.g., Downing & Haladyna, 2006; Schmeiser & Welch, 2006; *Standards for Educational and Psychological Testing*, 1999). Currently, however, practices, standards, and conventions are not available for developing items designed to link the knowledge and skills in cognitive models with test-based inferences about examinees. Test-development procedures and, by implication, quality control standards, required for creating fine-grained, cognitively based tasks have not been established (Gierl, Alves, Roberts, & Gotzmann, 2009).

With a cognitive model of test specifications, content experts use the content-by-skill interaction in each cell of the two-way matrix to craft items that are expected to measure domain-specific knowledge and skills. The judgments used by each content expert to initially create the items, and then the consensus reached between experts during the item review, allows developers to create items believed to measure the knowledge and skills outlined in the specifications. Unfortunately, little or no evidence exists to support the link assumed to exist between the items developed and the knowledge and skills elicited during testing. With a cognitive model of task performance, judgment is also required to develop tasks for measuring the knowledge and skills outlined in the model. Okamoto and Case (1996) developed items to measure the knowledge and skills identified in the mental counting line cognitive model for the *Number Knowledge Test*. Their items were adapted from previous studies on children's numerical understanding, and were also developed specifically for their test by extracting key concepts from their cognitive model. Empirical evidence was also collected for their items using examinee response data to ensure the items measured the knowledge and skills specified in the model. For example, Okamoto and Case reported that items produced proportion-correct scores that were ordered from least to most difficult in a manner that was predicted by structures specified in their model. They also found, using results from a latent-structure analysis, that their items measured distinct conceptual structures as outlined in their cognitive model.

INSTRUCTIONAL RELEVANCE

The third characteristic of a cognitive model necessary to link learning with assessment is that the knowledge and skills must be instructionally relevant and meaningful to a broad group of educational stakeholders, including students, parents, and teachers. Knowledge and skills must also be reported to stakeholders as scores, and information must be presented on how these scores are intended to guide remediation and instruction. Hence, the score reporting and performance feedback must be communicated clearly. Huff and Goodman (2007) surveyed a representative sample of educational stakeholders in the United States and found they overwhelmingly wanted more instructionally relevant information from large-scale educational assessments. Because assessment is situated in a much larger integrated educational context that includes cognition, learning, and instruction, many researchers and practitioners now believe that by providing more specific information on students' knowledge and skills, teachers will benefit by acquiring a better understanding on how students think about and solve problems on tests, which in turn may help structure and direct instruction. Or, as we described earlier, remedial decisions could be based on how students actually think about and solve problems. Assessments provide one source of evidence for making students' thinking overt, so their knowledge and skills can be identified and evaluated. Feedback can then focus on retaining cognitive strengths while overcoming weaknesses.

With a cognitive model of test specifications, instructional relevance is acquired by using the content knowledge and skills specified in the curriculum to design the assessment; that is, the curricular and assessment objectives are aligned with the test specifications. For our grade-three mathematics test specification example (see Figure 2.1), content experts first reviewed the mathematics program of study to identify the assumptions, outcomes, and indicators in the content areas of Number, Patterns and Relations, Shape and Space, and Statistics and Probability. Second, content experts used their knowledge, beliefs, and experiences to translate these concepts into the test specifications. The end result is a set of knowledge and skills in the four content areas that serves to design the assessment and to guide test development and score interpretation. In other words, the test is intended to measure key outcomes in the curriculum and thus provide information about students that is instructionally relevant to educational stakeholders, based on the judgments and interpretations of content experts.

With a cognitive model of task performance, items are created to measure specific components in the cognitive model. The tasks may or may not have instructional relevance, depending on the purpose of the model. Case and Okamoto (1996) initially developed the *Number Knowledge Test* as a research tool to evaluate their theory about the development of the central conceptual structures required for understanding whole-number concepts. Eventually, however, the test evolved into a diagnostic tool for identifying conceptual weaknesses in elementary school students' thinking about whole numbers, which could then be used to guide instruction in mathematics. In particular, their model and test have been used to create intervention programs for disadvantaged students that allow teachers to not only identify areas of strength and weakness, but also to create individualized remedial strategies to overcome weaknesses (Griffin, 2002, 2004; Griffin & Case, 1997; Griffin, Case, & Siegler, 1994).

A summary of our three cognitive model characteristics along with guiding questions for assessment design is shown in Table 2.2. In the next three chapters, we provide a targeted review of influential diagrammatic cognitive models in reading (text) comprehension, scientific, and mathematical reasoning. We also evaluate these models

TABLE 2.2. *Using Leighton and Gierl's three general characteristics of a cognitive model to guide assessment design*

Cognitive model characteristic	Guiding questions
1. Grain Size	• How many cognitive components (e.g., knowledge and skills) does the model contain? • How specific are these knowledge and skills and, by implication, how many items would be required to measure them? • Do the knowledge and skills need to be ordered?
2. Measurability	• Once the knowledge and skills have been identified, can tasks be developed (i.e., item types) to measure these components in a typical educational test administration situation (e.g., paper- or computer-based test)? • Would the tasks meet the requirements of "best practice" established in the educational measurement literature? Do new standards of practice for item development need to be created?
3. Instructional Relevance	• If the knowledge and skills can be identified and measured, will test scores derived from these knowledge and skills provide information that can guide learning and instruction? • Can these knowledge and skills be reported to stakeholders as scores in a way that will promote remediation and guide instruction?

from a test-design perspective using the characteristics of grain size, measurability, and instructional relevance.

REFERENCES

Alberta Education (2007). *The Alberta K–9 mathematics program of studies with achievement indicators.* Edmonton, AB: Alberta Education.

Alberta Education (2008). *Alberta provincial achievement testing, subject bulletin 2008–2009: Grade 3 mathematics.* Edmonton, AB: Alberta Education.

American Educational Research Association, American Psychological Association, & National Council on Measurement in Education (1999). *Standards for educational and psychological testing.* Washington DC: Author.

Bloom, B., Englehart, M. Furst, E., Hill, W., & Krathwohl, D. (1956). *Taxonomy of educational objectives: The classification of educational goals. Handbook I: Cognitive domain.* New York: Longmans, Green.

Brown, J.S. & Burton, R.R. (1978). Diagnostic models for procedural bugs in basic mathematics skills. *Cognitive Science, 2,* 155–192.

Busemeyer, J.R. & Diederich, A. (2010). *Cognitive modeling.* Thousand Oaks, CA: Sage.

Case, R. (1992). *The mind's staircase: Exploring the conceptual underpinnings of children's thought and knowledge.* Hillsdale, NJ: Erlbaum.

    (1996). Reconceptualizing the nature of children's conceptual structures and their development in middle childhood. *Monographs of the Society for Research in Child Development, 61* (1–26), Serial 246.

Case, R. & Griffin, S., (1990). Child cognitive development: The role of central conceptual structures in the development of scientific and social thought. In E. A. Hauert (Ed.), *Developmental psychology: Cognitive, perceptuo-motor, and neurological perspectives* (pp. 193–230). North-Holland: Elsevier.

Chi, M.T.H. (1997). Quantifying qualitative analyses of verbal data: A practical guide. *The Journal of the Learning Sciences, 6,* 271–315.

Dawson, M.R.W. (1998). *Understanding cognitive science.* Blackwell.

    (2004). *Minds and machines: Connectionism and psychological modeling.* Malden, MA: Blackwell.

Downing, S.M. & Haladyna, T.M. (2006). *Handbook of test development.* Mahwah, NJ: Erlbaum.

Ericsson, K.A. & Simon, H.A. (1993). *Protocol analysis: Verbal reports as data.* Cambridge, MA: The MIT Press.

Gierl, M.J. (1997). Comparing the cognitive representations of test developers and students on a mathematics achievement test using Bloom's taxonomy. *Journal of Educational Research, 91,* 26–32.

Gierl, M.J., Alves, C., Roberts, M., & Gotzmann, A. (2009, April). Using judgments from content specialists to develop cognitive models for diagnostic assessments. In J. Gorin (Chair), *How to build a cognitive model for educational assessments.* Symposium conducted at the meeting of the National Council on Measurement in Education, San Diego, CA.

Huff, K. & Goodman, D. (2007). The demand for cognitive diagnostic assessment. In J. P. Leighton & M. J. Gierl (Eds.), *Cognitive diagnostic assessment for education: Theory and applications* (pp. 19–60). New York: NY: Cambridge University Press.

Griffin, S. (2002). The development of math competence in the preschool and early school years: Cognitive foundations and instructional strategies.

In J. Royer (Ed.), *Mathematical cognition* (pp. 1–32). Greenwich, CT: Information Age Publishing.

(2004). Building number sense with number worlds: A mathematics program for young children. *Early Childhood Research Quarterly, 19,* 173–180.

Griffin, S. & Case, R. (1997). Re-thinking the primary school math curriculum: An approach based on cognitive science. *Issues in Education, 3,* 1–49.

Griffin, S., Case, R., & Sandieson, R. (1992). Synchrony and asynchrony in the acquisition of children's everyday mathematical knowledge. In R. Case (Ed.), *The mind's staircase: Exploring the conceptual underpinnings of children's thought and knowledge* (pp. 75–97). Hillsdale, NJ: Erlbaum.

Griffin, S., Case, R., & Siegler, R. (1994). Rightstart: Providing the central conceptual prerequisites for first formal learning of arithmetic to students at-risk for school failure. In K. McGilly (Ed.), *Classroom lessons: Integrating cognitive theory and classroom practice* (pp.24–49). Cambridge, MA: Bradford Books MIT Press.

Leighton, J.P. (2004). Avoiding misconceptions, misuse, and missed opportunities: The collection of verbal reports in educational achievement testing. *Educational Measurement: Issues and Practice, 4,* 1–10.

Leighton, J.P. & Gierl, M.J. (2007a). Defining and evaluating models of cognition used in educational measurement to make inferences about examinees' thinking processes. *Educational Measurement: Issues and Practice, 26,* 3–16.

(2007b). Verbal reports as data for cognitive diagnostic assessment. In J. P. Leighton & M. J. Gierl (Eds.), *Cognitive diagnostic assessment for education: Theory and applications.* (pp. 146–172). Cambridge, UK: Cambridge University Press.

Leighton, J.P. & Gokiert, R.J. (2008). Identifying test item misalignment using verbal reports of item misinterpretation and uncertainty. *Educational Assessment, 13,* 215–242.

Lohman, D. & Nichols, P. (1990). Training spatial abilities: Effects of practice on rotation and synthesis tasks. *Learning and Individual Differences, 2,* 67–93.

Marr, D. (1982). *Vision.* San Francisco, CA: W. H. Freeman.

National Research Council (2001). *Knowing what students know: The science and design of educational assessment.* Committee on the Foundations of Assessment. J. Pellegrino, N. Chudowsky, and R. Glaser (Eds.). Board on Testing and Assessment, Center for Education. Washington, DC: National Academy Press.

Newell, A. & Simon, H.A. (1972). *Human problem solving.* NJ: Prentice Hall.

Norris, S.P., Leighton, J.P., & Phillips, L.M. (2004). What is at stake in know-ing the content and capabilities of children's minds? A case for basing high stakes tests on cognitive models. *Theory and Research in Education, 2*, 283–308.

Okamoto, Y. & Case, R. (1996). Exploring the microstructure of children's central conceptual structures in the domain of number. *Monographs of the Society for Research in Child Development, 61* (27–58), Serial 246.

Poggio, A., Clayton, D.B., Glasnapp, D., Poggio, J., Haack, P., & Thomas, J. (April, 2005). *Revisiting the item format question: Can the multiple choice format meet the demand for monitoring higher-order skills?* Paper presented at the annual meeting of the National Council on Measurement in Education, Montreal, Canada.

Schmeiser, C.B. & Welch, C.J. (2006). Test development. In R. L. Brennan (Ed.), *Educational measurement* (4th edition, pp. 307–353). Westport, CT: Praeger.

Snow, R.E. & Lohman, D.F. (1989). Implications of cognitive psychology for educational measurement. In R. L. Linn (Ed.), *Educational measurement* (3rd ed., 263–331). New York: American Council on Education, Macmillan.

Taylor, K.L. & Dionne, J-P. (2000). Accessing problem-solving strategy knowledge: The complementary use of concurrent verbal protocols and retrospective debriefing. *Journal of Educational Psychology, 92*, 413–425.

Wellman, H.M. & Lagattuta, K.H. (2004). Theory of mind for learning and teaching: The nature and role of explanation. *Cognitive Development, 19*, 479–497.

3

Cognitive Models of Task Performance
for Reading Comprehension

Reading comprehension is a central skill students must learn to become successful learners in other content domains. For example, adequate reading skills are required to acquire scientific and mathematical literacy skills. In the present volume, then, we begin by describing cognitive models of task performance in reading comprehension, because reading skills function as a gatekeeper for the acquisition of most other academic skills.

Although students typically prefer reading over mathematics (OECD, 2004), many students continue to struggle with their reading performance. According to 2003 PISA results (Lemke et al., 2004), students in the United States scored 495 on the reading component, which is not measurably different from the OECD average of 494 (PISA results are scaled to have a mean of approximately 500 with a standard deviation of 100). This is good news for American students. However, it should be noted that among the thirty-eight countries participating in the assessment, eleven countries scored higher in reading than the United States.

More recently, the U.S. National Center for Education Statistics (2009) reported that although students' reading scores on the National Assessment of Educational Progress (NAEP) have increased since 1992, they remain unchanged from 2007 to 2009. In particular, 67 percent of students in grade four read at a basic level, and only 33 percent were classified as either proficient or advanced. At the basic level, grade-four students should "locate relevant information, make simple inferences, and use their understanding of the text to identify details that support a given interpretation or conclusion. Students should [also] be able to interpret the meaning of a word as it is used in the text" (NCES, 2009, p. 18). At the basic level, the integration of ideas in the written text, a skill one would expect to be a critical aspect of reading comprehension, is not considered a basic requirement for grade-four reading. Instead, the integration of ideas is a skill expected of grade-four students at the proficient level. In particular, "Fourth-grade students performing at the Proficient level should be able to integrate and interpret texts and apply their understanding of the text to draw conclusions and make evaluations" (p. 18). Given that only 33 percent of students were classified at the proficient level, it is possible to conclude that most U.S. students at grade four lack a critical aspect of reading comprehension – integration of ideas from written text. For grade-eight students, most were classified at the basic level, but only 32 percent were at or above the proficient level. At the basic level, grade-eight students "should be able to locate information; identify statements of main idea, theme, or author's purpose; and make simple inferences from texts. They should be able to interpret the meaning of a word as it is used in the text. Students performing at this level should also be able to state judgments and give some support about content and presentation of content" (p. 36). The finding that only 32 percent of grade-eight students are proficient readers is problematic because students at this age are only five years away from potentially entering the workforce or embarking on post-secondary education. In other words, only five years away from potentially entering the work-force, only a minority of grade-eight students can perform the functions of a proficient reader, namely, "provide relevant information and summarize main ideas and themes ... make and support inferences about a text, connect parts of a text, and analyze text features ... fully substantiate judgments about content and presentation of content" (p. 36). We highlight these results from this large-scale achievement test for students in grades four and eight to contextualize the challenge ahead for educators. Large-scale assessment results provide a snapshot of how students are performing at any given time, and the findings across studies suggest that there is much work to be done to improve students' reading comprehension skills.

Snowling and Hulme (2005, p. 207) assert that "to fully understand reading comprehension would be to understand most of the fundamental problems in cognition. The challenge is daunting." As a starting point, it is important to note that it is beyond the scope of this chapter to identify and review all theories and models of reading comprehension that may be relevant to large-scale educational assessment. The science of reading is vast with numerous authored books, edited books, journal articles, and even entire scholarly publications devoted to the study of every aspect of reading – word recognition processes, decoding, phonological awareness, learning to read and spell, reading comprehension, reading in different languages, disorders of reading and spelling, the biological bases of reading, and the teaching of reading. In this chapter, we present a targeted review of major models of text or reading comprehension[1] for the purpose of large-scale educational-assessment design.

According to Verhoeven and Perfetti (2008, p. 293), "it is generally agreed upon that the understanding of written text calls upon both bottom-up word recognition processes and top-down comprehension processes." Bottom-up processes include decoding printed words into meaningful propositions. Top-down processes include integrating the propositions with background knowledge. Cognitive models of text comprehension that capitalize on the interaction of bottom-up and top-down processes are currently considered the best frameworks for understanding individual differences in reading comprehension (see e.g., Bower & Morrow, 1990; Cain & Oakhill, 1999; Fox & Alexander, 2009; Graesser, Singer, & Trabasso, 1994; Just & Carpenter,

---

[1] Text comprehension and reading comprehension are terms used interchangeably in the present chapter.

1980; Jenkins, Fuchs, van den Broek, Espin & Deno, 2003; Kintsch & Kintsch, 2005; Leslie & Caldwell, 2009; Oakhill, Cain, & Bryant, 2003; Perfetti, 1999; Perfetti, Landi, & Oakhill, 2005; Verhoeven & Perfetti, 2008). Verhoeven and Perfetti (2008) identify three major models of text comprehension that have garnered substantial empirical support and capitalize on the interaction between bottom-up and top-down processes. These models are the *construction integration model* (e.g., Kintsch, 1988; Kintsch & Rawson, 2005; see also Just & Carpenter, 1987), the *resonance model* (e.g., Gerrig & McKoon, 1998; Myers, O'Brien, Albrecht, & Mason, 1994; Myers & O'Brien, 1998), and the *landscape model* (e.g., Gaddy, van den Broek, & Sung, 2001; Linderholm, Virtue, Tzeng, & van den Broek, 2004; van den Broek, Rapp, & Kendou, 2005; van den Broek, Risden, Fletcher, & Thurlow, 1996).

Not everyone will agree that the focus should be on these three models. For example, Graesser (2007) indicates that text comprehension models can be categorized into three classes depending on the emphasis placed on either bottom-up or top-down processing. According to Graesser (2007), the three classes of models on which to focus are: (a) *bottom-up models* such as Kintsch's (1998) construction-integration model and Myers's et al. (1994) resonance model; (b) *strategy-driven models*, including Graesser's et al. (1994) constructionist model and Zwaan and Radvansky's (1998) event-indexing model; and (c) *embodied cognition models* such as Glenberg and Robertson's (1999) indexical hypothesis[2] (see also Zwaan, Stanfield, & Yaxley, 2002). Graesser (2007) also points to what he calls *hybrid models* such as van den Broek's et al. (1996; van den Broek et al., 2005) landscape model, which attempts to balance more evenly the contributions of both bottom-up and top-down processes. Another motivation for partitioning text-comprehension models into these three classes is,

---

[2] Although Glenberg and Robertson's (1999) indexical hypothesis is not yet fully articulated as a model (see Glenberg, Jaworski, Rischal, & Levin, 2007), Graesser (2007; see also Whitten & Graesser, 2003) treats it as a model because of its potential to evolve into a complete framework for text comprehension.

according to Graesser (2007), to distinguish theoretical perspectives on the role of reading comprehension strategies. A reading comprehension strategy is "a cognitive behavioral action that is enacted under particular contextual conditions, with the goal of improving some aspect of comprehension" (Graesser, 2007, p. 6). For example, in bottom-up models, Graesser (2007) explains that reading comprehension strategies are considered equivalent to any other type of knowledge structure that can be activated from long-term memory. As such, reading comprehension strategies are not viewed as having a unique role in comprehension relative to other knowledge structures. In contrast, in strategy-driven models, reading comprehension strategies are given special status because they are viewed as actively directing the comprehension process.

FOCUS OF THE CHAPTER

This chapter will review reading comprehension models based on the recommendations of Verhoeven and Perfetti (2008) and Graesser (2007). Our review therefore focuses on Kintsch's *construction-integration model* (referred to as the *CI* model from this point forward) and Graesser's *constructionist model*. These two cognitive models are reviewed because they have diagrammatic representations, they reflect theoretically distinguishable frameworks that have received substantial empirical support, and they have influenced the development of subsequent models in the field of reading comprehension. For example, the *resonance model* (e.g., Myers & O'Brien, 1998) is similar to the CI model and, therefore, a description of the CI model provides a window into related reading comprehension frameworks such as the resonance model for large-scale educational-assessment design. Likewise, Graesser's constructionist model includes assumptions and top-down processes that are shared by other frameworks such as the *landscape model* (van den Broek, Young, Tzeng, & Linderholm, 1998; van den Broeck et al., 2005). Consequently, we believe the CI model and the constructionist model provide theoretically substantive frameworks from which to illustrate distinct perspectives on the knowledge and skills involved in reading comprehension.[3]

The chapter is organized into three main sections. First, the CI model (Kintsch, 1988; Kintsch & Rawson, 2005; see also Just & Carpenter, 1987) is presented and then considered using the criteria of granularity, measurability, and instructional relevance outlined in Chapter 2 (see Francis, Fletcher, Catts, & Tomblin, 2005, for alternate dimensions or criteria to evaluate reading models). Second, the constructionist model (Graesser, 2007; Graesser et al., 1994) is presented and considered using the same criteria. Third, concluding remarks are offered about both models regarding their feasibility for use in the design and development of large-scale educational assessments.

Although the CI and the constructionist models are presented in this chapter, the CI model is described and discussed in more detail. This is done because the CI model is considered to be the "most comprehensive model of reading comprehension ... [and] support for the constructionist model is not as extensive as for the CI model" (Graesser, 2007, p. 11, 14; Whitten & Graesser, 2003; see also Singer & Kintsch, 2001). Furthermore, in our presentation of the CI and constructionist models, we do not provide an exhaustive review of all their components. It is impossible to do so in the space allotted given the proliferation of research associated with these two models. For example, one of the first scholarly papers describing the precursors of the CI model (i.e., Kintsch & van Dijk, 1978) had a citation count of 2,550 according to Google Scholar at the time this chapter was written. Likewise, one of the first papers describing the constructionist model (i.e., Graesser et al., 1994) had a citation count of 865. Instead of providing an exhaustive review of their components, we outline their basic features to create a

---

[3] We do not review embodied cognition models because they have not yet accumulated the theoretical details and empirical support required to permit an even-handed comparison with the other models described in this chapter.

platform of common knowledge from which to begin considering the possibilities of each model for assessment design. For a complete presentation of the CI and constructionist models, the reader is referred to Kintsch (1998) and Graesser et al. (1994), respectively.

KINTSCH'S CONSTRUCTION-INTEGRATION (CI) MODEL

Model Description

Background

Analyzing comprehension as a psychological process is rooted in the work of Kintsch and van Dijk (1978; van Dijk & Kintsch, 1983; see also Butcher & Kintsch, 2003). In 1978 Kintsch and van Dijk proposed a cognitive process model of reading comprehension. This process model, also called a "functional architecture" or programming language for reading comprehension (see Chapter 2, footnote 1), described the underlying algorithms for the implementation of reading. In this model, the reader was said to generate two representations, a *microstructure* and *macrostructure* of written text. Shown in Figure 3.1 is a simple example of the microstructure for the following sample of text, "Running in Cold Weather": "The runners can jog in the snow because they wear multiple clothes. Wearing multiple clothes is called dressing in layers because each level protects extremities like hands, feet, and head to let the body conserve heat." As illustrated in Figure 3.1, the microstructure represents the syntactic and semantic relations among specific propositions in the text. Bottom-up, word-decoding processes generate the microstructure (Holmes, 2009). Moreover, constraints from both long-term memory (LTM) and working memory (WM) influence the type and strength of links among propositions (Butcher & Kintsch, 2003). Figure 3.2 is an example of the macrostructure that may accompany the full text associated with "Running in Cold Weather." The macrostructure is also generated by bottom-up processes and represents the hierarchical relations among various parts

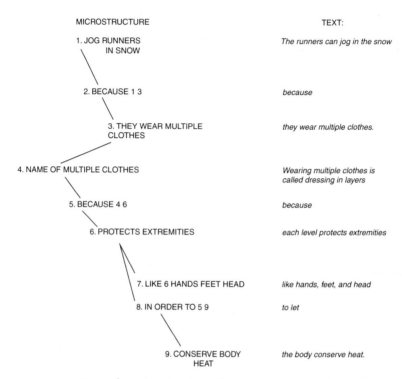

FIGURE 3.1. Example microstructure for two sentences from the text "Running in Cold Weather": *The runners can jog in the snow because they wear multiple clothes. Wearing multiple clothes is called dressing in layers because each level protects extremities like hands, feet, and head to let the body conserve heat.*

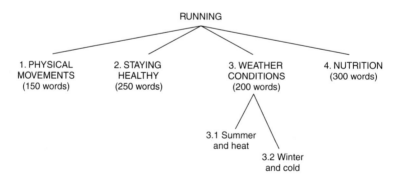

FIGURE 3.2. Example macrostructure based on the text "Running in Cold Weather."

of the written text at a more general or global level of detail (Kintsch & van Dijk, 1978). Top-down processes, particularly knowledge from LTM, also guide the creation of the macrostructure by helping to select the most relevant, meaningful propositions to include in the macrostructure, thereby creating an overall theme or gist of the written material (see Butcher & Kintsch, 2003). Both the microstructure and macrostructure are combined to form an integrated propositionally based representation of textual information.

Although Kintsch and van Dijk's (1978) original model received substantial empirical support for predicting the performance of participants' comprehension and memory for text in psychological experiments (e.g., Graesser, Mills, & Zwaan, 1997), it was challenging to use this model to account for other experimental findings, particularly those from studies of lexical decision making and eye movements during reading (for a review, see Rayner, Pollatsek, & Starr, 2003). These latter studies showed that, contrary to the predictions of Kintsch and van Dijk's 1978 model, top-down processes did not strongly guide the reading process by priming context-appropriate meanings or filtering out inappropriate word senses for ambiguous text. Rather, bottom-up processes appeared to have an immediate, direct role by activating multiple word meanings and only later allowing for top-down processes (e.g., prior knowledge) to suppress inappropriate meanings in particular contexts. Thus, by 1988, Kintsch (1993) recognized that "the next step beyond ... was a 1988 paper, where the previously neglected problem of knowledge use was approached in a new way: A hybrid model combining the virtues of production systems and connectionist constraint satisfaction mechanisms ... to model the role of knowledge in comprehension" (p. 1).

Framework

As shown in Figure 3.3, Kintsch and van Dijk's 1978 model was revamped to produce the CI model, where text or reading comprehension was defined as a "loosely structured, bottom-up process that

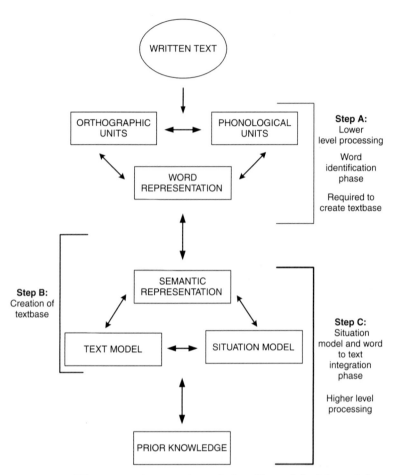

FIGURE 3.3. Diagrammatic overview of the CI model. Adapted from Verhoeven, L. & Perfetti, C. (2008). Advances in text comprehension: Model, process, and development. *Applied Cognitive Psychology*, 22, 293–301. Step A reflects the most basic processing needed to decode and identify words. Step A is needed to generate the textbase, which is shown in Step B. Finally, Step C reflects the higher-level processing consisting of the situation model and the integrative mechanisms to amalgamate prior knowledge with a coherent textual representation – the final semantic representation.

is highly sensitive to context and ... flexibly adjusts to shifts in the environment" (Kintsch, 1998, p. 94; Kintsch, 1988, 2005). In this newly revamped model, bottom-up, lower-order processes continued to have a significant role. However, the influence of top-down processes was reconfigured. In Kintsch's view, readers were normally unaware of the chaotic but primary activity of bottom-up processes, which triggered an initially disordered and nonsensical basic mental representation of text (i.e., involving the microstructure and macrostructure). A process of integration, which often relied on top-down processes, was only applied secondarily to this initially messy representation. This integration process yielded an increasingly structured and coherent semantic account of the written material.

In the CI model, two essential representations are systematically combined to form a coherent semantic account of the written text. Both the microstructure and macrostructure comprise the first essential representation, called the *textbase*. The textbase reflects primarily the work of bottom-up, word-decoding processes that operationalize the propositional structure of text (see Kintsch & Kintsch, 2005). In addition to the textbase, another essential representation, called a *situation model*, is formed. The situation model reflects the work of top-down processes, including background knowledge from LTM, which clean up, order, and integrate the textbase to promote an accurate, coherent, and meaningful semantic account of written text (Kintsch, 1988, 1998). For example, skilled readers often fixate on most words in a sentence, with fixations being longer at the end of sentences (Just & Carpenter, 1992; Reichle, Pollatsek, Fisher, & Rayner, 1998). End-of-sentence fixations indicate that integrative, situation-model processes are working to clean up and yield coherent semantic representations of the written text. Updates to the situation model occur throughout the reading cycle to form the most accurate and coherent semantic account of the text.

Shown in Figure 3.3 is a diagrammatic summary of the basic components of the CI model (see Verhoeven & Perfetti, 2008). Text or reading comprehension begins with bottom-up, lower-order processes translating the written text into a symbolic, linguistic, or word representation. The symbols we call words are meaningfully identified using retrieval or, more basically, a phonological code, along with information about orthography and syntactic relations among propositional units.[4] This basic linguistic representation is then fed "up the cognitive chain" to inform the textbase. The textbase, as mentioned previously, represents the local and global propositional structure of the written text, including hierarchical relations among propositional units. The textbase interacts with the situation model, which reflects prior or background knowledge and integrates the textbase with what a reader already knows to be true about the world. The situation model and textbase are continually updated with incoming textual information and culminate to form a final integrated and coherent semantic representation of the written text. Interestingly, a diagram of the combined components of the CI model, shown in Figure 3.3, was not found in Kintsch's writings but, rather, in Verhoeven and Perfetti (2008). Although Kintsch offers illustrations of the CI model, most notably in his 1998 book on text comprehension, most of these illustrations are pictorials of specific propositional networks. In fact, a combined diagram of the CI model's key components was challenging to find in Kintsch's writings. We therefore offer an adaptation of Verhoeven and Perfetti's diagrammatic summary of the text or reading comprehension process as a useful outline of the CI model's key features and relationships.

The situation model described by Kintsch (1998) is closely related to Johnson-Laird's (1983) notion of a *mental model*. A mental model

---

[4] Mastery or automation of decoding skills is related to fluent reading (see Samuels, 1994; Stanovich, 2000). The development of automatic word identification frees valuable cognitive resources for other text comprehension skills such as generating inferences and, thus, meaning from written text, which makes possible the acquisition of new information and knowledge (NRP, 2000; Samuels & Flor, 1997; Verhoeven & Perfetti, 2008).

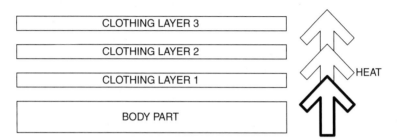

FIGURE 3.4. Possible situation model for the text "Running in Cold Weather."

is a semantic representation of a situation, event, or state of affairs. This semantic representation is minimalist insofar as it preserves only the basic relations among key components or "tokens" in the situation or event being considered. The mental model, once generated, can be used by the individual to draw inferences about explicit or implicit relationships among the tokens. A situation model is similar to a mental model to the extent that it reflects a semantic representation of the basic relations and key components encountered in written text. Figure 3.4 shows a possible situation model for the sample text "Running in Cold Weather." A reader's situation model is not constrained by the textbase and often includes elements that are personally relevant to the reader, such as spatial perceptions of written descriptions, imagery, and emotions elicited by the text (Kintsch & Kintsch, 2005). As the individual processes written text, the representations associated with the textbase and the situation model are continuously and simultaneously combined into a final semantic representation or *network*.[5] This confluence of representations is

---

[5] The term *network* is used by Kintsch (1998) to convey the final representation of the written text. This term is compatible with the connectionist architecture that

necessary for a full account of the written material. Kintsch (1998) claims that the textbase alone would "yield an impoverished and often even incoherent network" (p. 103).

It is important to reiterate that the CI model was proposed at the algorithmic level of analysis (see Chapter 2, footnote 1). Descriptions of the model's components are articulated at an exceedingly precise level, allowing the components (information-processing steps) to be instantiated in the form of a computer program. For example, the following four categories of components are stipulated for the creation of a textbase representation and a situation model:

1. Rules for construction of propositions (large set of rules that decode text);
2. Rules for interconnecting the propositions in a network (three levels of links are possible – propositions may be directly related, indirectly related, or one may be subordinate to another);
3. Rules for the activation of knowledge (knowledge is assumed to be associative and to be activated in working memory); and
4. Rules for constructing inferences (examples include rules for transitive inference and generalization).

The first two rules create the textbase. The third and fourth rules activate the situation model and stabilize the final semantic representation or network of propositions subject to constraints not only in the textbase, but also in the situation model. Further, in the notation of Kintsch (1998), three important processes related to the network of propositions include: (1) *node activation,* $a_i(t)$, where nodes are any proposition, inference, or elaboration in a propositional network created to facilitate the representation of the text; (2) *strength of link,* w_{ij},

is used to model some aspects of the processing requirements of the CI model at the algorithmic level (see Chapter 2 of this volume).

between nodes *i* and *j*; and (3) *memory strengths*, m_{ij}, the final product of node activation and strength between nodes. These processes are formalized as follows:

(1) Node activation is formalized as a vector $\mathbf{A}(t) = (a_1(t), a_2(t), \ldots a_n(t)) = \{a_i(t)\}$ where each node in the network has an activation value, a, at a given time t. Moreover, activation is spread from all the neighboring nodes to one node, so that the activation of a node at time $t + 1$ is given by

$$a_{ij}(t+1) = \frac{\sum_{i=1}^{n} a_i(t) w_{ij}}{\max a_j(t+1)};$$

(2) The pattern of links among all nodes is given by the connectivity matrix $\mathbf{W} = \{w_{ij}\}$, where w_{ij} is the strength of the connection between nodes *i* and *j*; and

(3) The connectivity matrix $\mathbf{W}$ and the final activation vector $\mathbf{A}$ are combined to produce the final matrix of memory strengths for each node in the network, $m_{ij} = \sum_{c=1}^{k} w_{ij} * a_i * a_j$, where w_{ij} is an element of $\mathbf{W}$, and the final activation of a node is represented by a_i, and c and *k* reflect the network iterations over *k* cycles (starting with cycle 1) required to converge to a final, stable semantic representation that has met the bottom-up and top-down constraints associated with the textbase and situation model, respectively.

Text comprehension in the CI model is the resulting outcome of a series of evaluations made by the reader about the nature of incoming information, thereby placing strong demands on the coordination of WM and LTM (Kintsch & Kintsch, 2005). Verhoeven and Perfetti (2008, p. 296) suggest that "the basic premise is that text comprehension involves the mental simulation of the referential situation, and that these mental simulations are constrained by the linguistic and pictorial information in the text, the processing capacity of the human brain and the nature of human interaction with the world (Zwaan & Radvansky, 1998)."

Model Evaluation: Granularity, Measurability, and Instructional Relevance

The CI model is a key model for understanding text or reading comprehension (Graesser, 2007; Kinstch, 2005; see Verhoeven & Perfetti, 2008). Test developers wanting to capitalize on the scientific basis of this cognitive model for designing student assessments of reading comprehension should consider at least three criteria. First, the model needs to be considered in terms of its granularity; that is, the model must be specified at a level of detail that clearly and usefully distinguishes the knowledge and skills involved in reading comprehension. The model must also be specified at a level of detail that permits its components to be ordered and then mapped onto test specifications. Second, the model needs to be considered in terms of its measurability. Each knowledge or skill component must be described in way that allows a test developer or researcher to design a test item to measure that component. Items developed from the CI model must also meet conventional psychometric standards of performance (e.g., item difficulty and discrimination). Third, the model needs to be instructionally relevant; that is, the knowledge and skills included in the model should be sufficiently meaningful to permit test scores to be formed. These scores, in turn, must be understandable to stakeholders such as teachers so as to help them guide instruction and learning (see Chapter 2, Table 2.2).

Granularity
The CI model involves components that are specific and others that are general. For example, node activation, strength between nodes, and memory strengths formalize basic processes underlying reading

comprehension at an exceedingly fine grain size associated with the algorithmic level of analysis. Although these highly specific and basic processes allow for the information-processing steps of the CI model to be instantiated, the specificity of these processes also make them impractical for large-scale educational assessment. That is, test developers are unlikely to design test items measuring *node activation* because this is too basic a process, which is often outside of human awareness and self-regulation and too elementary to match educators' broad instructional objectives. Consider the following learning outcomes included in the 2009, grade-four National Assessment of Educational Progress (NAEP) in reading (National Center for Education Statistics [NCES], 2009, p. 19):

- Recognize technique author uses to develop character.
- Recognize the meaning of a word that describes a character's actions.
- Provide text-based comparison of change in main character's feelings.
- Provide text-based comparison of two characters' feelings.
- Infer and provide relationship between main subject and historical movement.
- Use information from an article to provide and support an opinion.

These learning outcomes suggest broad levels of thinking, reflecting a coarser level of granularity than node activation or strength between nodes.

The CI model also includes components described at a coarse grain size, namely, the textbase representation and the situation model (see Figure 3.3). In particular, the situation model is defined at a grain size that includes many of the knowledge and skills test developers and teachers are interested in assessing and teaching. For example, many of the learning outcomes just described from the 2009 grade-four NAEP would fall within the scope of the situation model. The situation model comprises higher-level background knowledge and inferences, including readers' goals and expectations, that function to clarify or clean up the textbase representation. Most test-based inferences of reading comprehension (i.e., reading literacy, critical reading) would be designed to inform stakeholders about how adept examinees are at generating and using a situation model of written text.

Measurability

We are aware of no published accounts of large-scale reading assessments developed directly from the CI model (see Campbell, 2005; Francis et al., 2005, for discussion of psychometric issues in large-scale assessment of reading). However, there are some empirical analyses of reading comprehension test items based on select aspects of the CI model (e.g., Gorin, 2005; Gorin & Embretson, 2006; Embretson & Wetzel, 1987; Sheehan & Ginther, 2000). For instance, Embretson and Wetzel (1987) developed a general model based on Kintsch and van Dijk's (1978) early framework to investigate sources of complexity in multiple-choice paragraph comprehension items. Embretson and Wetzel's model included text representation and decision processes. The decision processes in Embretson and Wetzel's model reflected the application of Kintsch and van Dijk's model to an operational, educational assessment. The decision processes included mechanisms for mapping the multiple-choice response alternatives to relevant text under consideration. Embretson and Wetzel found that the model they developed based on Kinstch's early work provided relatively good prediction of item difficulty. In fact, the decision processes required for selecting correct multiple-choice response alternatives were found to be the most important model component for predicting item difficulty. In another example, Gorin and Embretson (2006) investigated the difficulty of reading comprehension test items on the Graduate Record Exam (GRE™) using a simplified version (i.e., Embretson and Wetzel's [1987] Reading Comprehension Processing Model; Sheehan and Ginther's [2000] model) of the CI model. One of the main findings reported by Gorin and Embretson was that processing difficulty of GRE verbal test items is influenced by the decision processes required of examinees as they map information between textual passages and multiple-choice response alternatives. Interestingly, the source of this processing difficulty pertained more to the format of the test items than to components of the CI model, leading Gorin and Embretson (2006) to warn test developers to be aware "of the potential unintended impact of item design characteristics on construct meaning [reading comprehension]" (p. 408).

The measurability of the CI model is most evident in learning scientific experimental studies of the model (e.g., Britton & Gülgöz, 1991; Ferstl & Kintsch, 1998; Miller & Kintsch, 1980; Kintsch, 1998; Kintsch & Kintsch, 2005). In these studies, single or multiple tasks are designed to evaluate components of the model based on participants' responses. For example, tasks designed to assess the texbase require participants to engage in free recall, cued recall, simple summarization, recognition, and answering explicit probes about the written text. Tasks designed to assess the situation model require participants to generate inferences by integrating the written text with prior knowledge or to arrange textual words or ideas into a concept map. Once the concept map is produced, it can then be used to evaluate the reader's organization of knowledge by comparing their map with how experts in the field organize the textual concepts (Kintsch, 1998). Britton and Gülgöz (1991; see also Gilabert, Martínez & Vidal-Abarca, 2005) provide a typical example of how Kintsch's CI model is evaluated in experimental studies. Britton and Gülgöz used the CI model to improve the comprehensibility of a one-thousand-word instructional passage by inserting relevant inferences in the text where readers would normally be expected to make the inferences. To test whether the one-thousand-word passage had been improved with the added inferences, undergraduate students were randomly assigned to read either the original text or the improved text with added inferences. Students demonstrated better recall of the improved text compared with the original text. By illustrating how textual comprehensibility could be improved with the CI model, Britton and Gülgöz provided evidence for the efficacy of the CI model. However, Britton and Gülgöz's study did not show how the instructional text might distinguish the comprehension levels of individual students.

Ferstl and Kintsch (1998) describe a more direct method than the one illustrated by Britton and Gülgöz for assessing individual differences in reading comprehension. Ferstl and Kinstch's method involved asking participants to read two types of stories about a familiar concept (e.g., after-school detention). One story was presented using a conventional structure (e.g., detention takes place after school at 3 P.M., and students sit quietly at their desks), whereas the other story was presented using a distorted or unconventional structure (e.g., detention takes place in the morning at 8 A.M. and involves dancing). After reading the stories, participants were asked to apply what they had learned about the stories to perform a sorting of key words or, alternatively, a cued association task related to the stories they had read. Ferstl and Kintsch anticipated that if participants had learned the underlying structure of the unconventional story, their sorting should differ compared to the sorting produced with the conventional story. Ferstl and Kintsch (1998) found that, as expected, participants sorted key words and responded to cued associations differently as a function of the conventionality of the story they read. These results led Ferstl and Kintsch to conclude that having participants read stories and sort key words (or respond to cued associations) was an adequate measure of participants' situation models and their ability to learn the underlying structure of a story.

Although measures of the CI model have been designed for learning scientific experimental studies, comparable measures for large-scale educational tests have not been developed. The absence of such efforts is perhaps unsurprising given the exceedingly fine-grained account of reading comprehension specified in the CI model. However, other coarser aspects of the CI model may be amenable for test design.

Kintsch and Kintsch (2005) have taken note of the absence of educational tests based on the CI model with their claim that current reading comprehension tests (e.g., SAT™ critical reading subtest) "do not reflect our understanding of comprehension processes" (p. 86). They argue that comprehension as a unitary skill should not be measured. Instead, different knowledge and skills should be measured, such as mining the meaning from text, generating the situation model, and integrating prior knowledge and goals with words and propositional structures gleaned from the text. In particular, Kintsch and Kintsch (2005) warn that most educational tests, which involve short texts or passages with few questions targeted to each passage, do not promote deep comprehension (i.e., generation of a situation model) in examinees. However, they do highlight the work of Hannon and Daneman (2001), who investigated the adequacy of a reading comprehension test for distinguishing the lower-level skill of reproducing text using simple knowledge from the higher-level skill of reproducing text using inference generation and integration. Hannon and Daneman (2001) found that four factors predicted differences among skilled versus unskilled readers: recall of new information, making inferences from the text, access to prior knowledge, and integration of prior knowledge with text. From these results, Kintsch and Kintsch (2005) concluded that "test items directed at different levels or aspects of comprehension yields a more complex view of comprehension ability and its assessment" (p. 88).

According to Kintsch and Kintsch (2005), essay formats are appropriate measures of text comprehension because they require examinees to read longer texts, contemplate deeper issues, and express their responses in an open-ended format that allow them to elaborate on their inferences. However, it is well-known that essay grading by expert judges has proven onerous, expensive, and unreliable (Bejar, Williamson, & Mislevy, 2006). A theoretically motivated solution to the challenge of cost-effective and objective essay grading is provided by Kintsch and Kintsch (2005) in their description of Latent Semantic

Analysis (LSA). LSA is a machine learning method that generates a geometric representation of meaning from words and texts resembling those produced by human beings. LSA models the relationships of words to other words using a mathematical technique known as *singular value decomposition for optimal dimension reduction*. This technique removes unwanted variability in data, thereby producing a representation of text meaning. Using a calculation that is similar to a correlation coefficient, LSA identifies the semantic relatedness among all words to generate meaning from the text without the need for word definitions. For instance, LSA exploits the fact that some words tend to co-occur together in good writing such as *she* and *her* (similarity measure of .98), whereas other word pairs such as *blackbird* and *black* (similarity measure of .04) do not. *Blackbird* and *black* do not tend to co-occur in good writing because when a compound word is used, it is typically uncommon to mention the words making up the compound in isolation. In this way, LSA imitates human word selection decisions and category judgments (Landauer, Laham, & Foltz, 2003). The LSA system has been used to grade essays and, so far, has yielded results that are as reliable as those produced by expert human graders (see Landauer, Laham, & Foltz, 2000, as cited in Kintsch & Kinstch, 2005). LSA is also the text-analysis method used by Pearson Knowledge Analysis Technologies for developing the *Intelligent Essay Assessor* system, which is used for commercial automated essay scoring. A review of the *Intelligent Essay Assessor* can be found in Dikli (2006).

Instructional Relevance

Although the textbase and the situation model both contribute to forming a coherent, semantic representation of the written text (Kintsch, 1998, p. 107), the situation model is arguably the most sought-after component to teach and to assess. The situation model directs the generation of inferences and the integration of meanings from the textbase representation. Teaching students how to generate a situation model involves teaching them how to actively "make sense" of what they read as they are reading (Kinstch & Kinstch, 2005). This type of instruction entails teaching students to reread, paraphrase, and summarize in their own words; reorganize written content into hierarchical schemes; show relations among ideas; seek connections between new and existing information; self-explain; form analogies, hypothesize, draw conclusions, and make predictions; formulate questions; and evaluate the text for internal cohesion. This type of instruction also entails teaching students to monitor their ongoing comprehension, identify inconsistencies, and attempt to resolve points where comprehension breaks down (see Kintsch, 2005; Kinstch & Kinstch, 2005; also Pressley, Woloshyn, & Associates, 1995, for a review). Kintsch (1998, p. 295) states that although the formation of a situation model is an integral part of learning from textual material, teaching and assessing components of the situation model are not straightforward. Kintsch (1998, p. 295) warns against superficial instructional initiatives that narrowly focus on the creation of situation models, as deep textual comprehension and learning more generally rely heavily on memory not only for words, propositions, sentences, but also for agents, motives, actions, and events.

GRAESSER'S CONSTRUCTIONIST MODEL

Model Description

Background

The constructionist model, shown diagrammatically in Figure 3.5, is based on the premise that a psychological theory of reading comprehension should account for how and why motivated readers can develop highly integrated and thematic knowledge-based inferences in response to certain types of texts such as narratives (Graesser et al., 1994; Graesser, 2007; see also Goldman, 1985). According to Graesser and his colleagues (1994), successful readers generate *multiple representations* of written material and generate *multiple inferences* about the content of

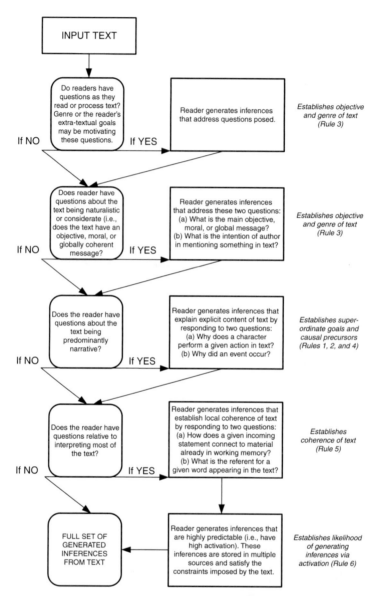

FIGURE 3.5. Diagrammatic overview of the constructionist model. Adapted from Graesser, A.C. & Kreuz, R.J. (1993). A theory of inference generation during text comprehension. *Discourse Processes, 16*, 145–160. Italicized notes to the right of this figure indicate the correspondence between the model components and the six production rules described in the chapter.

their representations. Although there is little debate as to how readers generate simple or shallow inferences about syntactic or propositional aspects of written material (Graesser et al., 1994; McKoon & Ratcliff, 1992), there is considerable debate on how deep, knowledge-based inferences are generated (e.g., Fox & Alexander, 2009).

Graesser et al. (1994) propose that the key element that distinguishes successful from not-so-successful readers is the *referential situation model*. A referential-situation model is a "mental representation of the people, setting, actions, and events that are mentioned in explicit clauses [in text] or that are filled in inferentially by world knowledge" (Graesser et al., 1994, p. 371). Although the notion of a situation model was originally developed by Kintsch (1998), Graesser (2007) extended this notion by proposing that the goals a reader possesses in relation to written text are critical for creating the most relevant referential-situation model for comprehension. According to Graesser et al. (1994, p. 373), "deeper meaning is [specifically] achieved by computing a *referential* specification for each noun ... *causes and motives* that explain why events and actions occurred ... [and] the *global message*, or *point*, of the text. .." A relevant referential-situation model promotes the generation of additional text-based and knowledge-based inferences that are essential for the reader to process written text in a meaningful way. Thus, successful readers use their referential-situation model to generate deep, knowledge-based inferences about written text, and actively use these inferences to form mental maps or evocative representations of incoming information. The goals readers impose on written text are therefore important drivers of the meaning they generate and the success they experience during the reading process.

A question that the constructionist model aims to answer is: Of all possible inferences that readers could potentially construct of narrative text, why are only some generated and not others? According to Graesser (2007), this question can be answered by recognizing that a reader's goals, and his or her referential-situation model, constrain the types of inferences generated. These constraints function to achieve maximum targeted efficiency and relevancy in the process of comprehension. Consider the following sentences (see a similar illustration in Graesser et al., 1994):

> *The bank teller saw the clown hold out a bag. She opened her safe, but she knew the manager was on the case.*

As an individual reads these sentences, multiple representations and inferences could be generated. For instance, a basic representation of the text would involve the propositional structure of the sentences, including their syntax, predicates, and arguments. However, in the construction of deeper, knowledge-based representations, what guides the reader to form some inferences and not others? Typically, a knowledge-based representation of the text would be based on inferences about the *relations* among agents and objects; that is, the referential specification for each noun. For example, it is inferred that the manager is not literally on top of a piece of furniture, or "the case." Rather, in this contextual situation, it is inferred that being "on the case" means that the manager is busy making arrangements to secure bank holdings in response to the robbery. Moreover, a knowledge-based representation would be based on inferences about the *causes and motives* underlying the occurrence of actions and events among agents and objects. Readers would be expected to infer that the bank teller opened the safe because he or she recognized that the clown was not a real clown but, instead, a robber dressed in a clown costume. Finally, a knowledge-based representation would be based on inferences that surmise the point or gist of the text, such as "bad events come in many forms." These are typical inferences associated with knowledge-based representations.

The reader could, in principle, elaborate on the physical movements the bank teller used to open the safe. However, most readers avoid drawing irrelevant inferences or excessive elaborations in relation to their knowledge-based representations unless they have reason to include them (Graesser et al., 1994). For example, if a reader happened to be a manufacturer of security safes and was trying to figure out how the bank teller bypassed the security mechanism, the reader may then elaborate on the physical movements used to open the safe in order to fulfill his or her curiosity of how the mechanism was disabled. However, in the absence of such specific goals, the inference or elaboration would not be expected. According to Graesser et al., readers avoid drawing an endless set of inferences or elaborations by using their goals to channel and constrain the mechanisms by which inferences are generated. Only inferences that meet specific reader goals are considered permissible (see Rips, 1994, for the logical processes that could underwrite this ability).

Framework

According to the constructionist model, the driving principle underlying a reader's capability to generate deep, knowledge-based inferences is the *search after meaning* (see Bartlett, 1932; Graesser et al., 1994). This principle includes three assumptions that are unique to the constructionist model:

1. The *reader-goal assumption*: This assumption postulates that readers have objectives when they read, and often these objectives involve attaining deep levels of meaning; that is, they aim to generate mental representations that map out the meaningful aspects of the material being processed. These meaningful aspects involve attending to semantics and developing a referential situation model.

2. The *coherence assumption*[6]: This assumption postulates that readers try to generate mental representations of the written

---

[6] In the landscape model (van den Broek, Risden, & Husebye-Hartmann, 1995; see also Kendou & van den Broek, 2007), a reader's effort to establish coherence in text comprehension is a source of individual differences. There are two standards for coherence: referential and causal. Referential coherence involves establishing word-to-referent coherence, such as knowing that a pronoun (e.g., he) refers to a

text that are locally and globally coherent. Local coherence involves making logical sense of adjacent clauses and short sequences of clauses. Global coherence involves making sense of larger, inter-related sequences of written text.

3. The *explanation assumption*: This assumption proposes that readers seek to explain actions, events/occurrences, and psychological states in written text; that is, they seek to form naïve or folk theories of the physical and non-physical causality for actions, events, and states. The readers' aim to explain occurrences in text ties in with the assumption to establish local and global coherence among distinct parts of the text, and with the assumption of goal-directedness. Thus, goal-directed readers want to understand what they read at a deep level, and this entails establishing coherence locally and globally via explanations as to why things are happening in the situations described in the written text (see also Trabasso & van den Broek, 1985).

These three assumptions outline the incentives for making knowledge-based inferences; that is, they are designed to explain how a reader selects information from LTM to integrate, make sense, and understand written text as it is being processed in WM. This coordination of top-down and bottom-up processing is similar to what Kintsch (1998; Kintsch & Kintsch, 2005) proposes in the CI model as necessary for text comprehension. However, what is unique about the constructionist model is that the catalyst for coordinating top-down and bottom-up processing is the readers' goals. In Graesser's constructionist model, then, goals drive the kind of information activated from LTM, which can include specific beliefs, knowledge, and individual

---

particular noun (e.g., driver). Causal coherence involves establishing a cause or antecedent condition for an event described in the text, which is believed by the reader to provide a causal explanation for the event. Referential and causal standards are associated with the reader's goal-driven behavior.

emotional experiences. Alternatively, information activated from LTM can be general, including schemata, scripts, frames, stereotypes, or information from other written material a reader has encountered and used to make sense of the world (Graesser et al., 1994).

The constructionist model also includes the following six components and/or assumptions that are shared by other models of text comprehension, some of which were described in the introduction to this chapter (e.g., Fox & Alexander, 2009; Kintsch, 1998; Kintsch & Kintsch, 2005; van den Broek et al., 2005; Myers & O'Brien, 1994):

1. Information sources for text comprehension include the written text, background knowledge structures, and the pragmatic context of the text.

2. Three levels of representation are created. A surface code representation is based on the wording and syntax of the text, a textbase level of representation is created based on explicit text propositions and localized inferences needed to establish text cohesion, and the situation model representation is created based on background knowledge structures and reader goals.

3. Three memory stores are used. Short-term memory (STM) is used to hold the most recent text clause, WM is used to hold the last two sentences in addition to information that is rehearsed, and LTM is used to activate background knowledge structures, and goals.

4. Discourse has a focus. A reader can alternate his or her focus among all three levels of representation (i.e., surface code, textbase, and/or situation model; see Figure 3.3).

5. Text comprehension is subject to convergence and constraint satisfaction. An inference that is generated increases in strength to the extent that it is activated by several sources of information (i.e., written text, background knowledge, and pragmatic context of text) and satisfies the constraints of those sources of information.

6. Repetition and automaticity influence text comprehension. Repetition or practice can increase the speed with which knowledge structures are accessed in LTM. Moreover, to the degree that written text activates highly familiar knowledge structures, these structures are accessed holistically and require minimal WM resources.

According to Graesser et al. (1994), the algorithms (i.e., underlying processes) responsible for implementing these six components are "built on the computational platform of Just and Carpenter's READER model (1992)" (p. 380). The READER model uses algorithms, in the form of production rules, to detect conditions in the reader's WM, which lead to executable actions. These production rules provide the functional architecture needed to explain the phenomenon of reading comprehension with the precision of a programming language. A production rule has a formalized structure with the following form (see Newell & Simon, 1972):

IF condition, THEN action.

The production rule is interpreted as follows: *If* the contents of WM match the *condition* of the production rule (i.e., meets or exceeds some specified activation value), *then* the rule is triggered and a cognitive action is executed. When a rule is triggered and the subsequent cognitive action is executed, the contents of WM are updated to reflect the application of the rule. Unlike other production systems that execute rules sequentially, production rules in the READER model execute simultaneously or in parallel meaning that multiple underlying processes can be executed at once, thus, approximating real-life neural processing. READER production rules reside in LTM.

According to the constructionist model, a series of production rules scan the contents of WM during a reading cycle to check whether specific processes need to be executed to generate desired inferences. Graesser et al. (1994) outline six production rules that allow the motivated reader to establish goals, local and global coherence, and explanations of written text. The six rules are as follows (see also table 2 in Graesser et al., 1994, p. 381):

1. ***IF*** explicit statement in text involves a character's intentional action (A) or goal (G), ***THEN*** explain why the character performed A or has G;
2. ***IF*** explicit statement in text involves an intentional action (A), a goal (G), or an event (E), ***THEN*** explain why the character has performed A, why the character has G, or why E occurred;
3. ***IF*** explicit statement (S) in the text occurs, ***THEN*** explain why the writer mentions S;
4. ***IF*** explicit statement in text is an intentional action (A) or an event (E), ***THEN*** track emotional reaction of characters;
5. ***IF*** WM includes a given configuration (C) of goals, actions, events, emotions, and/or states that meet some threshold of activation, ***THEN*** create global structures; and
6. ***IF*** an implicit statement or structure in WM meets some threshold of activation, ***THEN*** construct inferences that receive high activation in WM.

Production rule 1 executes inferences that establish super-ordinate goals about events in written text. Production rule 2 executes inferences that determine the causal precursors of actions, goals, and events. Production rule 3 executes inferences that elaborate explicit statements in text, including the genre for a particular type of narrative. These three production rules, along with production rule 6, are needed for the reader to generate what are called *explanation inferences* about written text. Production rule 4 executes inferences that establish the emotion of characters. Production rule 5 executes global structures to help organize the coherence of narrative elements in the text. Graesser et al. (1994) consider all six rules to "implement the reader's active comprehension strategies when reading narrative text" (p. 380). In other words, these are the rules that instantiate readers' goals in the creation of a referential-situation model and in the comprehension of written text. Figure 3.5 illustrates a diagrammatic summary of the constructionist model, along with the six production rules (shown italicized on the right-hand side of the figure).

Model Evaluation: Granularity, Measurability, and Instructional Relevance

Granularity

The details of the constructionist model are similar to the CI model insofar as both models have specific and general components, depending on the part of the model being considered. The production rules of the constructionist model are described at a fine level of granularity. These rules, which facilitate the generation of inferences and help form a mental representation of the written text, are assumed to operate at a subconscious level outside of human awareness. Although these rules are fine grained, they do appear to better approximate the types of educational outcomes included in large-scale assessments of reading. For example, production rule 4 executes inferences that establish the emotion of characters. This production rule would be relevant to one of the learning outcomes associated with the 2009 grade-four NAEP (NCES, 2009, p. 19), namely, to provide a text-based comparison of two characters' feelings. The constructionist model also highlights the importance of the referential-situation model as a critical aspect of text comprehension. The referential-situation model is specified at a coarse grain size.

Measurability

Graesser et al. (1994) claim that when comprehension works, readers "construct a meaningful referential situation model that addresses the readers' goals, that is coherent, and that explains why actions, events, and states are mentioned in the text" (p. 372; see also Graesser, 2007). The creation of a referential-situation model is, therefore, associated with a series of meaningful outcomes that supposedly distinguish successful and not-so-successful readers. Successful readers should be able to draw accurate and pertinent inferences from their referential-situation model in relation to text (Graesser et al., 1994). Successful readers should be able to use their referential-situation model as a guide to posing questions about knowledge gaps, anomalies, and prospective contradictions found in the text. In particular, questions beginning with the interrogative adverb, *why*, prompt readers to consolidate their text comprehension. Questions beginning with other adverbs such as *how, where, when,* and *what happens next* have been found to disrupt comprehension (see Magliano, Trabasso, & Graesser, 1999) and, therefore, may not strengthen comprehension relative to *why* questions. Successful readers should be able to construct answers to their own questions and address knowledge gaps, anomalies, and contradictions encountered in the text by consulting their referential-situation models. Finally, successful readers should be able to paraphrase the written text meaningfully and generate an appropriate summary.

Although we have found no published accounts of operational, large-scale educational test items designed directly from the constructionist model, items that measure the referential-situation model would include features requesting or prompting students to engage in one of the following activities: (a) draw appropriate inferences, (b) ask relevant questions, (c) answer these questions, (d) paraphrase, and/or (e) summarize written text. For instance, a story could be presented to students along with a set of items designed to query text-based information about key points in the story. These types of items could be used to evaluate how well students detect and respond to contradictory, anomalous, or irrelevant statements in the text and, in general, how well they draw appropriate inferences at key points during their reading comprehension (see Kendou & van den Broek, 2007, for experimental variations of such an approach). In other words, items could be designed to probe the coherence of readers' referential-situation models and readers' ability to draw additional appropriate inferences, including detecting anomalous segments of text. Items developed based on the constructionist model could also help to differentiate readers who generate deeper-level, knowledge-based representations from those who simply construct shallow representations of the text.

Magliano, Millis, Ozuru, and McNamara (2007), in an analysis of reading assessment tools such the Gates McGinitie and Nelson-Denny, indicate that most educational tests are not constructed based on theories of reading comprehension, because psychometric properties often take precedence over psychological veracity. They also proposed a taxonomy for classifying and evaluating, ad hoc, the cognitive demands measured by reading test items. The taxonomy is based on the work of many reading researchers (e.g., Kintsch, 1988; Trabasso, van den Broek, & Suh, 1989), including Graesser (e.g., Graesser, McNamara, Louwerse, & Cai, 2004). The taxonomy can be used to evaluate multiple-choice items, in addition to other formats, by matching item features (e.g., stems and answer options) to the types of cognitive demands expected to be measured by those features. For example, a stem beginning with the words "The passage suggests that the teacher would have thought that today's cars are . . ." (Magliano et al., 2007, p. 118) would be categorized as measuring the process of *inference*.

Graesser (2007) claims that most text comprehension models, which involve multiple levels of representation, clash with current psychometric tests. They also clash with the canonical methodology of test design, which typically includes three to five content domains along with multiple items per domain to measure relevant knowledge and skills. Graesser et al. (1994) also caution that tasks designed to assess reading comprehension need to be evaluated for the cognitive demands they make of readers, because these demands have implications for the goals and levels of inferences readers generate about the text. Tasks requiring a nominal amount of reading under timed conditions do not prompt readers to expend the effort required to generate meaningful, deeper-level inferences. Graesser and his associates caution assessment specialists and test developers by claiming that students are unlikely to generate deeper-level inferences for reading comprehension tasks when these tasks can also be solved with shallow inferences.

Instructional Relevance

The constructionist model is instructionally relevant. The notion that readers' goals are critical to text comprehension suggests that readers can be encouraged to value and apply strategies for reading (Graesser, 2007). Teachers could use the components of the constructionist model to help instruct students about ways to generate richer referential-situation models. In particular, teachers could monitor the relations students attend to as they read, the questions students ask (especially why questions), and the anomalies they detect in written text. In addition, one-to-one methods such as think-aloud interviews could be conducted with students as they read, and verbal reports collected to evaluate the quality of inferences generated and questions posed (Pressley & Afflerbach, 1995). Graesser (2007; see table 1.1, p. 16) recommends teaching students a series of strategies to strengthen their strategic approach to reading, including self-explanation, active reading, reciprocal teaching and questioning, concept mapping, peer-assisted learning, and concept-oriented mining of text.

CONCLUSION

Kintsch and Kintsch (2005) indicate that "as long as reading comprehension tests are composed of a theoretically unmotivated collection of test items – the criterion being whether an item discriminates good from poor reader ... a picture [of true reading comprehension] cannot emerge" (Kintsch & Kintsch, 2005, p. 88). In the knowledge-based environments of the twenty-first century, the ability to learn from written text is a defining line between knowledge "haves" and "have-nots" (Stanovich, 2000). Graesser's et al. (1994) constructionist model emphasizes the value of reader goals in the process of text or reading comprehension. Reader goals influence the richness of the representations generated from textual material and the precision of attempts to address gaps in understanding. Successful readers generate coherent explanations of the events and actions that occur in text and paraphrase, summarize, and predict outcomes based on written text. The constructionist model involves six production rules, specified at a fine level of granularity. These production rules are specific and therefore unlikely to be of interest to test developers for large-scale educational assessments. However, the referential-situation model, a coarser component of the constructionist model could form the basis of assessment design. Attempts to measure the referential-situation model could involve designing test items that assess readers' goals, representational coherence, and explanations for textual events. That is, items could be designed to measure the types of deeper-level inferences expected to emerge from rich knowledge-based representations comprising a strong referential-situation model of written text.

Kintsch's CI model also emphasizes the function of a situation model to integrate and clean up an otherwise chaotic propositional representation of text. However, Kintsch (1998) recognizes the difficulty of designing assessments of reading comprehension, even those designed to evaluate aspects of the situation model. He states, "... asking questions to assess knowledge for scientific purposes is limited in its effectiveness because we do not have a detailed theory of question answering. As long as it is not known just what psychological processes and what knowledge are involved in answering a particular question, we simply do not have a reliable way of constructing the right questions for our purposes" (Kintsch, 1998, p. 296). Although the CI model provides a theoretically and empirically rich account of the psychological processes in reading comprehension, the challenge remains on how to measure these processes, especially the operations of the situation model. The development of LSA provides a promising avenue for ensuring the objective and affordable scoring of essay items designed to measure the complexity of knowledge-based inferences and the situation model.

Kintsch's CI model is considered to be the "most comprehensive model of reading comprehension" (Graesser, 2007, p. 11). However, in the CI model, goals do not have a unique role in directing the reading process (see Gerrig & McKoon, 1998, p. 69). Rather, reading is considered to be a fluid, automatic process driven largely by the textual and long-term memory associations made by the reader (Raaijmakers & Shiffrin, 1981). In the CI model, specialized rules that facilitate the generation of inferences such as establishing the coherence of text do not exist. Rather, inferences are generated through associative processes (see previous section on CI framework). There is no question that the interaction of top-down and bottom-up processes is an integral part of both the CI and the constructionist models (Verhoeven & Perfetti, 2008). However, the goal-driven processing illustrated by the constructionist model requires an added liability that the CI model does not assume. Goal-driven processing assumes a level of human intentionality that has traditionally been difficult for cognitive scientists to model algorithmically (see Marr, 1982; Dawson, 1998).

The CI and constructionist models provide major frameworks with which to conceptualize text or reading comprehension (Graesser, 2007; Verhoeven & Perfetti, 2008), but there needs to be considerable planning in their adaptation to test design. There are aspects of the CI and the constructionist models that are specified at exceedingly fine levels of detail, thus making their relevance for test design problematical. For example, the connectivity matrix of the CI model or even the production rules of the constructionist model are specified at a level of granularity that may be too detailed in light of most broad educational objectives (see, for example, learning outcomes for grade-four NAEP outlined in NCES, 2009). It is important to note, however, that of the two models, the production rules of the constructionist model are specified at a level of granularity that better approximates educational objectives. Although experimental tasks have been designed to measure aspects of these models, these tasks are often singular in focus, thereby making them quite different from most items on large-scale educational assessments. Test developers interested in increasing the scientific basis of reading comprehension assessments face the intimidating task of how to select relevant aspects of a cognitive model for assessment design. In addition to the daunting task of selecting the most relevant aspects of the model, assessment specialists must also recognize that a model developed based on one group of students may not necessarily generalize to other groups, such as students with distinct learning styles, language proficiencies, and/or even general ability levels (see Jackson, 2005; see also Chapter 6 of this volume). If it seems perplexing that a model of reading comprehension should not be readily translatable into test design, then we are in danger of overlooking the fact that learning scientific cognitive models and theories aim to account for mental phenomena without necessarily aiming to evaluate those phenomena in applied educational settings (Crocker, 2005; Leighton & Gierl, 2007).

REFERENCES

Bartlett, F.C. (1932). *Remembering: A study in experimental and social psychology.* Cambridge, UK: Cambridge University Press.

Bejar, I.I., Williamson, D.M., & Mislevy, R.J. (2006). Human scoring. In D.M. Williamson, R.J. Mislevy, and I.I. Bejar (Eds.), *Automated scoring of complex tasks in computer-based testing* (pp. 49–81). Mahwah, NJ: Erlbaum.

Bower, G.H. & Morrow, D.G. (1990). Mental models in narrative comprehension. *Science, 247,* 44–48.

Britton, B.K. & Gülgöz, S. (1991). Using Kinstch's computational model to improve instructional text: Effects of repairing inference calls on recall and cognitive structures, *Journal of Educational Psychology, 83,* 329–345.

Butcher, K.R. & Kintsch, W. (2003). Text comprehension and discourse processing. In A.F. Healy and R.W. Proctor (Eds.), *Handbook of psychology: Volume 4 experimental psychology,* (pp. 575–595). Hoboken, N.J.: Wiley.

Cain, K. & Oakhill, J.V. (1999) Inference making and its relation to comprehension failure. *Reading and Writing, 11,* 489–503.

Campbell, J.R. (2005). Single instrument, multiple measures: considering the use of multiple item formats to assess reading comprehension. In S.G. Paris & S.A. Stahl (Eds.), *Children's reading comprehension and assessment* (pp. 347–368). Mahwah, NJ: Erlbaum.

Crocker, M.W. (2005). Rational models of comprehension: Addressing the performance paradox. In A. Culter (Ed.), *Twenty-first century psycholinguistics: Four cornerstones* (pp. 363–380). Hillsdale, NJ: Erlbaum.

Dawson, M.R.W. (1998). *Understanding cognitive science.* Blackwell.

Dikli, S. (2006). An overview of automated scoring of essays. *Journal of Technology, Learning, and Assessment, 5*(1). Retrieved May 21, 2010 from http://www.jtla.org.

Embretson, S.E. & Wetzel, C.D. (1987). Component latent trait models for paragraph comprehension. *Applied Psychological Measurement, 11,* 175–193.

Ferstl, E.C. & Kintsch, W. (1998). Learning from text: Structural knowledge assessment in the study of discourse comprehension. In S.R. Goldman & H. van Oostendorp (Eds.), *The constructions of mental representations during reading,* (pp. 247–277). Mahwah, NJ: Erlbaum.

Francis, D.J., Fletcher, J.M., Catts, H.W., & Tomblin, J.B. (2005). Dimensions affecting the assessment of reading comprehension. In S.G. Paris & S.A. Stahl (Eds.), *Children's reading comprehension and assessment* (pp. 369–394). Mahwah, NJ: Erlbaum.

Fox, E. & Alexander, P.A. (2009). Text comprehension: A retrospective, perspective, and prospective. In S.E. Israel & G.G. Duffy (Eds.), *Handbook of research on reading comprehension* (pp. 227–239). New York City: Routledge.

Gaddy, M.L., van den Broek, P., & Sung, Y-C. (2001). The influence of text cues on the allocation of attention during reading. In T. Sanders, J. Schilperoord, & W. Spooren (Eds.), *Text representation: Linguistic and psycholinguistic aspects,* (pp. 89–124). Amsterdam, Netherlands: John Benjamins Publishing Company.

Gerrig, R. & McKoon, G. (1998). The readiness is all: The functionality of memory-based text processing. *Discourse Processes, 26,* 67–86.

Gilabert, R., Martínez, G., & Vidal-Abarca, E. (2005). Some good texts are always better: text revision to foster inferences of readers with high and low prior background knowledge. *Learning and Instruction, 15,* 45–68.

Glenberg, A.M., Jaworski, B., Rischal, M., & Levin, J. (2007). What brains are for: Action, meaning, and reading comprehension. In D.S. McNamara (Ed.), *Reading comprehension strategies: Theories, interventions, and technologies,* (pp. 221–240). New York: Erlbaum.

Glenberg, A.M. & Robertson, D.A. (1999). Indexical understanding of instructions. *Discourse Processes, 28*, 1–26.

Goldman, S.R. (1985). Inferential reasoning in and about narrative texts. In A.C. Graesser & J.B. Black (Eds.), *The psychology of questions* (pp. 247–276). Hillsdale, NJ: Erlbaum.

Gorin, J. (2005). Manipulating processing difficulty of reading comprehension questions: The feasibility of verbal item generation. *Journal of Educational Measurement, 42*, 351–373.

Gorin, J. & Embretson, S.E. (2006). Item difficulty modeling of paragraph comprehension items. *Applied Psychological Measurement, 30*, 394–411.

Graesser, A.C. & Kreuz, R.J. (1993). A theory of inference generation during text comprehension. *Discourse Processes, 16*, 145–160.

Graesser, A.C., Singer, M., & Trabasso, T. (1994). Constructing inferences during narrative text comprehension. *Psychological Review, 101*, 371–395.

Graesser, A.C., McNamara, D.S., Louwerse, M.M., & Cai, Z. (2004). Coh-Metrix: Analysis of text on cohesion and language. *Behavior Research Methods, Instruments, & Computers, 36*, 193–202.

Graesser, A.C., Millis, K.K., & Zwaan, R.A. (1997). Discourse comprehension. *Annual Review of Psychology, 48*, 163–189.

Graesser, A.C. (2007). An introduction to strategic reading comprehension. In D.S. McNamara (Ed.), *Reading comprehension strategies: Theories, interventions, and technologies,* (pp. 3–26). New York: Erlbaum.

Hannon, B. & Daneman, M. (2001). A new tool for measuring and understanding individual differences in the component processes of reading comprehension. *Journal of Educational Psychology, 93*, 103–128.

Holmes, V.M. (2009). Bottom-up processing and reading comprehension in experienced adult readers. *Journal of Research in Reading, 32*(3), 309–326.

Jackson, N.E. (2005). Are university students' component reading skills related to their text comprehension and academic achievement? *Learning and Individual Differences, 15*, 113–139.

Jenkins, J.R., Fuchs, L.S., van den Broek, P., Espin, C.A., & Deno, S.L. (2003). Accuracy and fluency in list and context reading of skilled and RD groups: Absolute and relative performance levels. *Learning Disabilities Research and Practice, 18*, 222–236.

Johnson-Laird, P. N. (1983). *Mental models. Towards a cognitive science of language, inference, and consciousness.* Cambridge, MA: Harvard University Press.

Just, M.A. & Carpenter, P.A. (1980). A theory of reading: From eye fixations to comprehension. *Psychological Review, 87*, 329–354.

(1987). *The psychology of reading and language comprehension.* Boston, MA: Allyn and Bacon.

(1992). A capacity theory of comprehension: Individual differences in working memory. *Psychological Review, 99*, 122–149.

Kendeou, P. & van den Broek, P. (2007). The effects of prior knowledge and text structure on comprehension processes during reading of scientific texts. *Memory & Cognition, 35(7)*, 1567–1577.

Kintsch, W. (1988). The use of knowledge in discourse processing: A CI model. *Psychological Review, 95*, 163–182.

Kintsch, W. (August 23, 1993). The long and crooked way toward a model of text comprehension. *Current Contents, 34*. Accessed from World Wide Web on September 10, 2009, at http://garfield.library.upenn.edu/classics1993/A1993LR55300001.pdf.

(1998). *Comprehension: A paradigm for cognition*. Cambridge, UK: Cambridge University Press.

(2005). An overview of top-down and bottom-up effects in comprehension: The CI perspective. *Discourse Processes, 39 (2,3)*, 125–128.

Kintsch, W. & van Dijk, T.A. (1978). Towards a model of text comprehension and production. *Psychological Review, 85*, 363–394.

Kintsch, W. & Kintsch, E. (2005). Comprehension. In S.G. Paris & S.A. Stahl (Eds.), *Children's reading comprehension and assessment* (pp. 71–92). Mahwah, NJ: Erlbaum.

Kintsch, W. & Rawson, K.A. (2005). Comprehension. In M.J. Snowling and C. Hulme (Eds.), *The science of reading*, (pp. 209–226). Malden, MA: Blackwell.

Landauer, T.K., Laham, D., & Foltz, P.W. (2000). The Intelligent Essay Assessor. *IEEE Intelligent Systems*, 27–31.

(2003). Automated essay scoring: A cross disciplinary perspective. In M. D. Shermis and J. C. Burstein (Eds.), *Automated essay scoring and annotation of essays with the Intelligent Essay Assessor* (pp. 87–112). Mahwah, NJ: Erlbaum.

Leighton, J.P. & Gierl, M.J. (Eds.). (2007). *Cognitive diagnostic assessment for education. Theories and applications*. Cambridge, MA: Cambridge University Press.

Lemke, M., Sen, A., Pahlke, E., Partelow, L., Miller, D., Williams, T., Kastberg, D., & Jocelyn, L. (2004). *International Outcomes of Learning in Mathematics Literacy and Problem Solving: PISA 2003 Results From the U.S. Perspective*. (NCES 2005–003). Washington, DC: U.S. Department of Education, National Center for Education Statistics.

Leslie, L. & Caldwell, J.S. (2009). Formal and informal measures of reading comprehension. In S. Israel and G. Duffy (Eds.), *Handbook of research on reading comprehension* (pp. 403–427). Mahwah, NJ: Erlbaum.

Linderholm, T., Virtue, S., Tzeng, Y., & van den Broek, P. (2004). Fluctuations in the availability of information during reading: Capturing cognitive processes using the landscape model. *Discourse Processes, 37*(2), 165–186.

Magliano, J.P., Trabasso, T., & Graesser, A.C. (1999). Strategic processing during comprehension. *Journal of Educational Psychology, 91*, 615–629.

Magliano, J.P., Millis, K., Ozuru, Y., & McNamara, D.S. (2007). A multidimensional framework to evaluate reading assessment tools. In D.S. McNamara (Ed.), *Reading comprehension strategies: Theories, interventions, and technologies* (pp. 107–136). New York City: Erlbaum.

Marr, D. (1982). *Vision*. San Francisco: W.H. Freeman.

McKoon, G. & Ratcliff, R. (1992). Inferences during reading. *Psychological Review, 99*, 440–466.

Miller, J.R. & Kintsch, W. (1980). Readability and recall of short prose passages: A theoretical analysis. *Journal of Experimental Psychology: Human Learning and Memory, 6*, 335–354.

Myers, J.L., O' Brien, E.J. Albrecht, J.E., & Mason, R.A. (1994). Maintaining global coherence during reading. *Journal of Experimental Psychology: Learning, memory, and Cognition, 20*(4), 876–886.

Myers, J. & O'Brien, E. (1998). Accessing the discourse representation during reading. *Discourse Processes, 26*(2), 131–157.

National Center for Education Statistics (2009).*The Nation's Report Card: Reading 2009* (NCES 2010–458). Institute of Education Sciences, U.S. Department of Education, Washington, D.C.

National Reading Panel (NRP). (2000). *Teaching children to read: An evidence-based assessment of the scientific research literature on reading and its implications for reading instruction*. Washington, DC: The National Institute of Child Health and Human Development.

Newell, A. & Simon, H.A. (1972). *Human problem solving*. New Jersey: Prentice-Hall.

Oakhill, J.V., Cain, K.E., & Bryant, P.E. (2003). The dissociation of word reading and text comprehension: Evidence from component skills. *Language and Cognitive Processes, 18*, 443–468.

Organization for Economic Cooperation and Development. (2004). *Learning for tomorrow's world: First results from PISA 2003*. Paris, France: Author.

Perfetti, C.A. (1999). Comprehending written language: A blueprint of the reader. In C.M. Brown, & P. Hagoort (Eds.), *The neurocognition of language processing* (pp. 167–208). London: Oxford University Press.

Perfetti, C.A., Landi, N., & Oakhill, J. (2005). The acquisition of reading comprehension skill. In M.J. Snowling and C. Hulme (Eds.), *The science of reading*, (pp. 227–247). Malden, MA: Blackwell.

Pressley, M. & Afflerbach, P. (1995). *Verbal protocols of reading: The nature of constructively responsive reading.* Hillsdale, NJ: Erlbaum.

Pressley, M., Woloshyn, V., & Associates. (1995). *Cognitive strategy instruction that really improves children's academic performance* (2nd ed.). Cambridge, MA: Brookline Books.

Raaijmakers, J.G. & Shiffrin, R.M. (1981). Search of associative memory. *Psychological Review, 88,* 93–134.

Rayner, K., Pollatsek, A., & Starr, M. (2003). Reading. In A.F. Healy and R.W. Proctor (Eds.), *Handbook of psychology: Volume 4 experimental psychology,* (pp. 549–574). Hoboken, N.J.: Wiley.

Reichle, E.D., Pollatsek, A., Fisher, D.L., & Rayner, K. (1998). Toward a model of eye-movement control in reading. *Psychological Review, 105,* 125–157.

Rips, L.J. (1994). *The psychology of proof.* Cambridge, MA: MIT Press.

Samuels, S.J. (1994). Word recognition. In R. B. Ruddell, M. R. Ruddell, & H. Singer (Eds.), *Theoretical models and processes of reading* (pp. 359–380). Newark, DE: International Reading Association.

Samuels, S.J. & Flor, R. (1997). The importance of automaticity for developing expertise in reading. *Reading and Writing Quarterly, 13,* 107–122.

Sheehan, K.M. & Ginther, A. (2000, April). *What do passage-based multiple-choice verbal reasoning items really measure? An analysis of the cognitive skills underlying performance on the current TOEFL reading section.* Paper presented at the annual meeting of the National Council of Measurement in Education (NCME), New Orleans, LA.

Singer, M. & Kintsch, W. (2001). Text retrieval: A theoretical explanation. *Discourse Processes, 31,* 27–59.

Snowling, M.J. & Hulme, C. (2005). Editorial part III. In M.J. Snowling and C. Hulme (Eds.), *The science of reading,* (pp. 207–208). Malden, MA: Blackwell.

Stanovich, K.E. (2000). *Progress in understanding reading: Scientific foundations and new frontiers.* New York: Guilford.

Trabasso, T. & van den Broek, P.W. (1985). Causal thinking and the representation of narrative events. *Journal of Memory and Language, 24,* 612–630.

Trabasso, T., van den Broek, P., & Suh, S. (1989). Logical necessity and transitivity of causal relations in the representation of stories. *Discourse Processes, 12,* 1–25.

van Dijk, T.A. & Kintsch, W. (1983). *Strategies of discourse comprehension.* New York: Academic Press.

van den Broek, P., Risden, K., & Husebye-Hartmann, E. (1995). The role of readers' standards for coherence in the generation of inferences during reading. In R.F. Lorch Jr. & E.J. O'Brien (Eds.), *Sources of coherence in text comprehension* (pp. 353–373). Hillsdale, NJ: Erlbaum.

van den Broek, P., Risden, K., Fletcher, C.R., & Thurlow, R. (1996). A "landscape" view of reading: Fluctuating patterns of activation and the construction of a stable memory representation. In B.K. Britton & A.C. Graesser (Eds.), *Models of text understanding* (pp. 165–187). Mahwah, N.J.: Erlbaum.

van den Broek, P., Young, M., Tzeng, Y., & Linderholm, T. (1998). The Landscape model of reading: Inferences and the online construction of memory representation. In H. van Oostendorp & S.R. Goldman (Eds.), *The construction of mental representations during reading* (pp. 71–98). Mahwah, N.J.: Erlbaum.

van den Broek, P., Rapp, D.N., & Kendeou, P. (2005). Integrating memory-based and constructionist approaches in accounts of reading comprehension. *Discourse Processes, 39,* 299–316.

Verhoeven, L. & Perfetti, C. (2008). Advances in text comprehension: Model, process, and development. *Applied Cognitive Psychology, 22,* 293–301.

Whitten, S. & Graesser, A.C. (2003). Comprehension of text in problem solving. In J.E. Davidson and R.J. Sternberg (Eds.), *The psychology of problem solving* (pp. 207–229). New York: Cambridge University Press.

Zwaan, R.A. & Radvansky, G.A. (1998). Situation models in language comprehension and memory. *Psychological Bulletin, 123,* 162–185.

Zwaan, R.A., Stanfield, R.A., & Yaxley, R.H. (2002). Do language comprehenders routinely represent the shapes of objects? *Psychological Science, 13,* 160–171.

4

Cognitive Models of Task Performance
for Scientific Reasoning and Discovery

Science and scientific progress are products of skilled methods of thinking about and acting on the world. The innovation, systematicness, and logic comprising scientific reasoning and discovery are therefore natural goals for governments interested in cultivating a literate, technologically savvy, and economically productive citizenry in the twenty-first century (Hanushek, 2005). As noted in Chapter 1, recent international assessments indicate variability in how well students of different nations have mastered scientific knowledge and skills. For example, U.S. examinees scored below average on two out of three content area sub-scales in the 2006 Programme for International Student Assessment (PISA), namely, explaining phenomena scientifically and using scientific evidence (see Baldi et al., 2007; see also Organization Economic Cooperation Development [OECD], 2006). This finding is not new. In 1982–1983, the National Commission on Excellence in Education, composed of a select group of university presidents, professors, and K–12 teachers, compiled a grim report on the state of science and mathematics' education in the United States: *A Nation at Risk*. Moreover, the National Research Council's (2007) *Taking Science to School* indicates that at the time *A Nation at Risk* (1983) was disseminated, U.S. President Ronald Reagan had already cautioned the National Academies of Sciences and Engineering of an impending decline in science and mathematics achievement, and of the erosion this decline could eventually cause the American people in their standards of living.

U.S. efforts at addressing the decline in science education are illustrative of how elusive the solution to educational problems can be, even when the amount of human capital invested in analyzing, documenting, and solving the issue is tremendous. During the 1990s, two documents, *Benchmarks for Science Literacy* (American Association for the Advancement of Science, 1993) and *The National Science Education Standards* (National Research Council, 1996), served to guide U.S. state education officials in their efforts to improve science education standards, curricular frameworks, and assessments (National Research Council, 2007). Although reform-based programs met with various successes during this decade, especially for helping students from economically disadvantaged backgrounds and school systems that kept pace with initiatives (see Boyd, Banilower, Pasley, & Weiss, 2003; Kim et al., 2001; see also National Research Council [NRC], 2007), glitches in planning and delivery arose from political, technological, and preparatory sources. These glitches limited the influence of these programs to produce desired changes (NRC, 2007). Aside from these setbacks, it also became clear that focusing attention on reforming *science education* standards without also focusing on *science learning* was insufficient in the face of a systemic educational crisis with complex structural and pedagogical roots. In particular, reform efforts did not appear to embrace or incorporate decades-long, empirically based educational and psychological knowledge on the cognitive and learning processes by which individuals conceptualize, learn, and demonstrate scientific understanding (Newcombe et al., 2009; NRC, 2007). The omission of educational and psychological research from science education policies and initiatives is also of concern in other countries such as Canada (see Leighton, Gokiert, & Cui, 2007).

According to several National Research Council publications, there is a vast amount of scientific knowledge and skills expected to be taught in the classroom and assessed on large-scale assessments (e.g., NRC, 1996, 2007). With the increasing prevalence of international and national assessment programs such as PISA (OECD, 2009), TIMSS

(Third International Mathematics and Science Study; see Gonzales et al., 2008), NAEP (National Assessment of Educational Progress; see Grigg et al., 2006), legislation such as the U.S. based No Child Left Behind Act (NCLB) of 2002, and Race to the Top Fund, attention to the need for accountability in science education has gained momentum. With the NCLB Act specifically, yearly science tests are administered in U.S. schools to all students, and these students must show regular improvement of science achievement scores encompassing many knowledge and skills. *The National Science Education Standards* (NRC, 1996) stipulate eight broad categories or learning goals for science instruction: Students are expected to learn about unifying concepts and processes in science, science as inquiry, physical science, life science, earth and space science, science and technology, science in personal and social perspectives, and the history and nature of science. Within each of these general categories, specific knowledge and skills are targeted. In science as inquiry, for instance, students are expected to acquire abilities necessary to form hypotheses, conduct experiments, and evaluate evidence. Moreover, the National Research Council's (2007) Committee on Science Learning indicates that students need to learn about knowledge of the natural world, how scientific knowledge is constructed, how to generate and evaluate scientific evidence and explanations, and how to participate in scientific practice and discourse. Although these objectives outline instructional goals for the knowledge and skills students are expected to acquire in science, a notable absence in both *The National Science Education Standards* and *Taking Science to School* is specification of the methods by which these objectives should be taught to and measured in students. The absence of these methods, including cognitive models for instruction and assessment, may be intended to promote flexibility in the procedures teachers use to prepare students for large-scale assessments. Alternatively, the absence of direction may also be leading to confusion about how to reach pedagogical goals and how to interpret test scores in the realm of science achievement.

Incorporating empirically based cognitive models of scientific reasoning and discovery for the design and development of large-scale educational assessments may be especially relevant at this point in time. Not only may cognitive models provide a stronger scientific basis for K–12 educational testing than current behavioral models provide, but they may also prove to be instrumental in guiding the instruction of a highly complex content domain (Newcombe et al., 2009). A number of esteemed researchers of scientific reasoning and discovery, including cognitive scientist David Klahr of Carnegie Mellon University (see Newcombe et al., 2009), indicate that teaching science is especially challenging compared to other disciplines. What makes science challenging is that two aspects must be taught simultaneously – content-based knowledge (e.g., life sciences, physical sciences) and process-based skills (e.g., hypothesis formation, hypothesis testing, evidence evaluation). Both content and skill are fundamental to scientific reasoning and discovery. The importance of both scientific content and skill is unlike other disciplines such as mathematics, for example, where content knowledge and process-based skills are often indistinguishable (Newcombe et al., 2009).

The study of scientific knowledge and skills has attracted attention from cognitive, developmental, and educational psychologists interested in capturing the essential aspects of what it means to think innovatively, systematically, and logically (e.g., Dunbar & Fugelsang, 2005; Gorman, Tweney, Gooding, & Kincannon, 2005; Klahr, 2000; Koerber, Sodian, Thoermer, & Nett, 2005; Kuhn, 2002; Kuhn & Franklin, 2006; Koslowski & Masnick, 2002; Tschirgi, 1980; Zimmerman & Glaser, 2001). In a recent review of the literature, Zimmerman (2007) defined scientific thinking "as the application of the methods or principles of scientific inquiry to reasoning or problem-solving situations, and [involving] the skills implicated in generating, testing and revising theories, and in the case of fully developed skills, to [reflecting] on the process of knowledge acquisition and change ..." (Zimmerman, 2007, p. 173; see also Zimmerman, 2000). This description is similar to others such as Dunbar and Fugelsang's (2005, p.705) definition: "Scientific thinking refers to the mental processes used when reasoning about the content of science (e.g., force in physics), engaged in typical scientific activities (e.g., designing experiments), or specific types of reasoning that are frequently used in science (e.g., deducing that there is a planet beyond Pluto)."

Interestingly, much of the learning scientific research conducted on scientific knowledge and skills has focused on the acquisition of process skills rather than content knowledge. In each of the definitions just presented, the focus is on skills such as Zimmerman's (2007) "methods or principles of scientific inquiry" or "skills implicated in generating, testing and revising theories." Likewise, Dunbar and Fugelsang (2005) adopt a similar focus by emphasizing "mental processes used when reasoning about the content of science." Not surprisingly, this definitional focus extends into the empirical research literature. The following process skills have been subjects of empirical investigations: experimental-design skills (e.g., Klahr, 2000) and evidence-evaluation skills (e.g., Kuhn, 2002), including evaluating covariation-type data (e.g., Masnick & Morris, 2002), coordinating theory with covariation-type data (Koerber et al., 2005), distinguishing covariation and causation (e.g., Koslowski & Masnick, 2002), generating causal inferences and increasing epistemological understanding (e.g., Kuhn & Franklin, 2006), distinguishing causal inferences versus scientific thinking (e.g., Kuhn & Dean, 2004), and evaluating anomalous and non-anomalous evidence (Chinn & Malhotra, 2002). Additional process skills that have been investigated include integrative approaches to scientific reasoning that focus on partially guided and self-directed inquiry (e.g., Khlar, Trionna, & Williams, 2007), searching in a hypothesis space (Dunbar & Klahr, 1989), bridging the search for hypotheses with experimentation (Klahr, Fay, & Dunbar, 1993; Kuhn & Dean, 2005), searching in an experiment space (e.g., Tschirgi, 1980), managing data (e.g., Dunbar & Klahr, 1989; Garcia-Mila & Andersen, 2007), evaluating evidence using partial self-directed inquiry (e.g., Masnick & Klahr,

2003; Schauble, 1996), processing knowledge change (e.g., Kanari & Millar, 2004), possessing personal dispositions as theorist versus experimenter in inquiry (e.g., Dunbar & Klahr, 1989; Klahr, 2000), and perceiving goals of inquiry (e.g., Tschirgi, 1980; Kuhn, 2001).

When the acquisition of science knowledge has been investigated in content areas such as physics, biology, psychology, and/or cosmology (e.g., Agan & Sneider, 2004; Chi, 2005; Choe, Keil, & Bloom, 2005; Flores, Tovar, & Gallegos, 2003; Lehrer & Schauble, 1998; Leighton & Bisanz, 2003; Siegler, 1998; Shtulman, 2006; Vosniadou & Brewer, 1992), it is done primarily in the service of uncovering process skills in scientific reasoning and discovery. For example, Shtulman (2006) showed that both children and adults who have misconceptions about evolution and natural selection are prone to draw erroneous conclusions about evolutionary events such as variation, inheritance, and extinction. Likewise, Leighton and Bisanz (2003) studied how elementary school children's and university students' knowledge of the ozone layer influenced their reasoning about the origins of the ozone hole. In a landmark study, Vosniadou and Brewer (1992; see also Stathopoulou & Vosniadou, 2007) investigated how elementary school children's knowledge of the shape of the earth (e.g., flat versus spherical) influenced their reasoning about physical events. Vosniadou and Brewer (1992, p. 542) asked the children to respond to questions such as the following: "If you were to walk for many days in a straight line, where would you end up? Would you ever reach the end or edge of the earth?" and "Does the earth have an end or an edge?" Depending on whether children thought the Earth was a flat disc, a sphere, or some other shape (see Vosniadou and Brewer, 1992, for the five mental models), they provided distinct answers about what would happen to a person walking in a straight line. Children who thought the Earth was a flat disc said a person would fall off the Earth because they had reached the end, whereas children who thought the Earth was a sphere said the person would never reach the end but would just go around in circles.

It is beyond the scope of this chapter to provide a comprehensive review of all psychological and educational research on scientific reasoning and discovery. Notwithstanding the profusion of research, diagrammatic representations of cognitive models that interconnect or link the relevant knowledge and skills identified in these particular lines of research have been surprisingly limited. Cognitive diagrammatic models that link the knowledge and skills inherent to generating hypotheses, designing experiments, and evaluating evidence and drawing conclusions are relatively uncommon. However, in her review of the literature, Zimmerman (2007) notes that the Scientific Discovery as Dual Search (SDDS) model proposed by Klahr and Dunbar (1988; see also Dunbar & Fugelsang, 2005; Klahr, 2000) serves as a useful framework for organizing a variety of the empirical findings in the literature. The SDDS model is able to illustrate "the complexity and the cyclical nature of the process of scientific discovery" (Zimmerman, 2007, p. 174). Another cognitive model that visually captures the relevant knowledge and skills inherent to scientific reasoning and discovery is Kuhn's (2001, 2005) Knowing/Phases of Inquiry model (KPI). This model can be used to account for thinking generally and brings together multiple lines of research on multivariable causal reasoning, the coordination of theory and evidence, and epistemological understanding more specifically (Kuhn, 2001, 2005; Kuhn, Katz, & Dean Jr., 2004). Although Zimmerman (2007) does not identify Kuhn's KPI model as a general framework, the importance of the KPI model is nonetheless apparent. Zimmerman cites numerous research studies conducted by Kuhn and her colleagues that cut across almost all distinct lines of scientific reasoning and discovery research (e.g., research on experimentation skills [e.g., Kuhn & Phelps, 1982; see also Kuhn, Iordanou, Pease, & Wirkala, 2008], research on the evaluation of evidence [e.g., Kuhn, 2002], and integrated approaches to the study of scientific reasoning [Dean & Kuhn, 2007]). Consequently, the KPI model may be seen as an alternative to the SDDS model in outlining the key processes of scientific reasoning and discovery with strong theoretical and empirical support (e.g., Kuhn, 1989, 2001, 2002, 2005; Kuhn et al., 2008).

This chapter will review Klahr and Dunbar's (1988) SDDS model and Kuhn's (2001; Kuhn, 2005; Kuhn & Dean, 2004) KPI model, and will consider their components for the design and development of large-scale educational assessments in terms of the criteria outlined in Chapter 2 – granularity of knowledge and skills, measurability for facilitating the development of test items, and instructional relevance for aligning with educational objectives. The chapter is organized into three main sections. First, the SDDS model (Klahr & Dunbar, 1988; see also Dunbar & Fugelsang, 2005; Klahr, 2000) is presented and then considered using our three criteria. Second, the KPI model (Kuhn, 2001; Kuhn & Dean, 2004) is outlined and considered using the same criteria. Third, concluding remarks are offered about the models in terms of their use in the design and development of large-scale educational assessments.

KLAHR AND DUNBAR'S SCIENTIFIC DISCOVERY
AS DUAL SEARCH (SDDS) MODEL

Cognitive models of complex thinking processes are challenging to produce. However, a good model must simplify even the most complex of processes. In the science domain, Gorman et al. (2005) claim:

> What makes models powerful and predictive is their selectivity. A good model simplifies the modeled world so as to make it amenable to one's preferred methods of analysis or problem solving. However, selectivity can make one's models limited in scope and, at worst, unrealistic. Insofar as this is a problem, it is often stated as a dichotomy between abstraction and realism. (p. 3–4)

As discussed in Chapters 2 and 3, often what makes a model successful in the learning sciences is the selectivity and specificity of the underlying processes identified at the algorithmic level of analysis (Dawson, 1998). Whereas these selective and specific underlying processes may be of value to the cognitive scientist because it makes the model programmable on a computer or empirically testable in the psychological laboratory, such details may be less relevant to test developers and psychometricians who want to use the model for educational-assessment design and development. Educational assessments are often specified at a coarse grain size, reflecting broad achievement standards or objectives (see the National Science Education Standards, NRC, 1996, 2007). Given sufficient discrepancy between broad assessment goals on the one hand, and the specificity of an algorithmic or cognitive (processing) model on the other hand, the broad goals will prevail and the cognitive model will likely be cast aside. As Gorman et al. (2005; see also Gleick, 1987) stated, "a good model must simplify" and yet not be too selective in the process of simplification. This is one challenge with using any cognitive model to guide the design and development of educational test items. Similar to the models of text or reading comprehension described in Chapter 3, Klahr and Dunbar's SDDS model is of interest because it has garnered significant empirical support, reflects relevant coarse and fine levels of grain size, and has a diagrammatic representation.

Model Description

Background
Klahr and Dunbar's (1988) SDDS model attempts to illustrate the basic and most relevant knowledge and skills inherent to scientific reasoning and discovery. The main components of the model are based on Simon's (1977; see also Newell & Simon, 1972; and Simon & Lea, 1974) pioneering and highly influential research on problem solving as a *search through a problem space* (Dunbar & Fugelsang, 2005; Klahr,

2000; Klahr & Simon, 1999). According to Simon (1977), the problem space is a metaphorical workspace that includes all components required to solve a problem. This space includes the following: (a) an initial knowledge state in which the problem solver has a question, no solution, and desires a solution; (b) a set of operators or strategies that can be applied by the problem solver to the problem, given the satisfaction of specific constraints; and (c) a goal or ideal solution to the problem. The problem-solving process consists of charting out a path through this metaphorical space by mentally searching for knowledge states that permit the application of operators that in turn advance or transform a current knowledge state into the goal state or solution (Newell & Simon, 1972). Knowledge states and operators vary depending on the problem under consideration.

Klahr and Dunbar (1988) propose that scientific thinking can also be conceptualized as a search through a problem space; specifically, a search through two equally important spaces – a *hypothesis* space and an *experiment* space. As will be described in the next section, the knowledge states, operators, and goals for the hypothesis and experiment spaces share similarities. In particular, the outcome of the hypothesis space will often constrain the search through the experiment space. As with Simon's (1977) approach, a scientific problem in the SDDS model is believed to consist of an initial knowledge state, a goal knowledge state, and a set of operators or strategies that incrementally advance the process of thinking. That is, the set of operators incrementally transform the initial knowledge state into a more advanced knowledge state with the aim of reaching the solution to the problem. Operators or strategies also have constraints for how they can be applied to knowledge states.

Framework

In the SDDS model, the problem solver must search through two problem spaces – the hypothesis space and the experiment space. In the hypothesis space, the problem is one of finding the best, most parsimonious hypothesis (goal state) to help account for a body of data reflecting a phenomenon of interest (initial knowledge state). How the problem solver navigates through the hypothesis space and selects a hypothesis depends greatly on his or her expertise or familiarity with the domain (Klahr, 2000). Once a hypothesis is generated, it serves as the initial knowledge state in the experiment space where it is tested or evaluated for its adequacy in explaining the body of data. In the experiment space, the problem is one of finding an experiment that is an informative test (goal state) of the hypothesis under consideration (initial state). A primary concern and a major constraint for the problem solver is designing an experiment that will produce interpretable information about the appropriateness of the hypothesis. The search in the two spaces is reconciled by a process of evidence evaluation, which considers the outcome of the designed experiment (evidence) in light of the hypothesis (theory) under consideration for explaining the data of interest.

The SDDS model, including the hypothesis and experiment spaces along with the process of evidence evaluation, is shown diagrammatically in Figure 4.1. It is a complex hierarchical model with three parts. The first part, shown in the left of Figure 4.1, is the hypothesis space and includes five layers of processing. The second part, shown in the middle of Figure 4.1, is the experimental space and includes two layers of processing. The third part, shown in the right of Figure 4.1, includes the process of evidence evaluation and includes a single layer of processing. We review the most relevant aspects of the model in light of the objectives of the chapter and refer the reader to Klahr and Dunbar (1988) and Klahr (2000) for a complete description and review of the SDDS model. The left-hand side of Figure 4.1 illustrates the most elaborate part of the SDDS model, the hypothesis space. In searching the hypothesis space, the problem solver must first generate a *frame* and then assign slot values to the frame (Minsky, 1974). Similar to a script or schema, a frame is a type of representation that organizes knowledge with the assignment of values to *slots* (Minsky, 1974). For example,

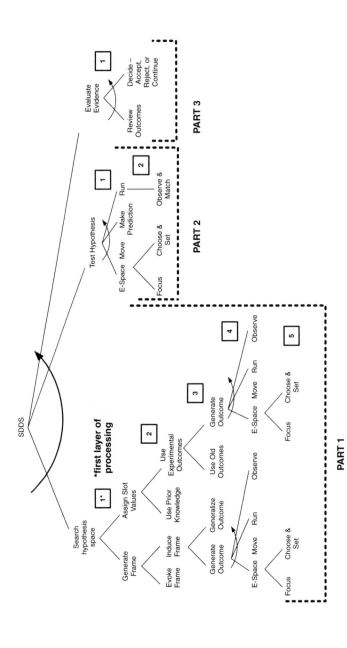

FIGURE 4.1. Diagrammatic overview of the Scientific Discovery as Dual Search (SDDS) Model. Modified and adapted from Klahr and Dunbar (1988). Dual search space during scientific reasoning. *Cognitive Science, 12,* 1–48. Part 1 of the model shows the hypothesis space, part 2 of the model shows the experiment space, and part 3 of the model shows the evidence-evaluation phase of scientific reasoning. Arrows indicate the direction or order in which processes (knowledge and skills) are executed.

Note: The asterisk denotes that this is the first layer of processing as shown by the number 1 in a box. Deeper layers of processing are shown below by the boxed numbers 2, 3, 4, and 5.

the script for dining out at a restaurant may be viewed as a frame with various slots or options in which to include specific information about what to expect from the experience, such as the type of restaurant, the reasons for celebration, the cost of the meal, and the dress code. A frame can be generated either by *evoking* it from long-term memory (LTM) or by *inducing* it from available data. Evoking a frame typically requires less effort than inducing it because the process of evoking simply requires accessing background knowledge. Inducing a frame is more effortful, because it requires conducting a search in experiment space (e-space) to investigate the most appropriate frame in which to cast the hypothesis. Toward this end, a pilot study is initiated and parameterized (see fourth and fifth layers of processing in Figure 4.1) in e-space. Once the pilot study has been formalized in e-space, the study is run and the results are noted (see fourth processing layer). When the results are collected, a decision is made about whether the results are useful or generalize to the original body of data to which the hypothesis is being applied, and whether the frame is the adequate structure for the hypothesis under study. Once a frame is adopted, slot values must be assigned. Slot values may be evoked from LTM or can be selected from the results of the pilot study used to decide on the frame. Alternatively, a lengthier route can be followed in which another pilot study is designed in e-space, this time to inform the slots to include in the frame.

The goal of the search in hypothesis space is to generate a testable hypothesis. The middle of Figure 4.1 shows the processes associated with testing hypotheses in e-space. Once a hypothesis is ready to be tested, e-space is used to identify or focus a study that will yield the most useful information for evaluating the hypothesis (see second processing layer). Choices are also made about the parameters of the study. Once the study is initiated, predictions about the results are made, the study is conducted (run), and the results are recorded. The goal of the search in e-space is to generate experimental evidence to evaluate the hypothesis under consideration. After this is done, the final part of the process is executed, as shown in the right-hand side of Figure 4.1. This part of the SDDS model involves evaluating the evidence obtained in the e-space. In this last major part of the model, the evidence is reviewed and a decision is made about whether the hypothesis should be accepted or rejected. In deciding whether to accept or reject the hypothesis, plausibility, functionality, and parsimony[1] are considered. If the evidence is deemed indeterminate, then another experiment is run in e-space to generate new evidence.

A key component of the SDDS model, which is not explicitly shown in Figure 4.1, involves the methods used to search within and between the hypothesis and experiment spaces. These are the methods that allow progress to be made from initial knowledge states to goal states; for example, to move from conducting a pilot study, to generating a hypothesis, to testing the hypothesis and, finally, to evaluating the evidence. According to Klahr and Dunbar (1988; see also Klahr, 2000; Klahr & Simon, 1999, 2001), two types of methods are used to search hypothesis and experiment spaces. *Strong methods* involve domain-specific knowledge and skills, such as knowledge of the theory of relativity for a search in physics, knowledge of the components of DNA for a search in biology, skill with an electron microscope for a search of viruses in biology, or skill with infrared spectrometry for a search in chemistry. Successful scientists have acquired a large repertoire of shared knowledge and skills, including concepts, theories, models, rules of thumb, techniques, methods, practices, and approaches that are specific to the domain of their professional expertise (see Ericsson, Charness, Feltovich, & Hoffman, 2006, for a comprehensive review of the development of expertise). Strong methods give scientists a privileged path in their search of hypothesis and experimental spaces, because these methods capitalize on prior knowledge and therefore constrain the search significantly, smoothing and expediting

---

[1] Khlar (2000, p. 36) states that the full functioning of these processes is still unknown.

reasoning and discovery. In fact, strong methods often illuminate the path to a solution so quickly that there is surprisingly little search (see Klahr, 2000). This stands to reason, according to Klahr and Simon (1999), because prior knowledge often permits the use of algorithms to solve problems and eliminates trial and error. For instance, finding the maximum of a function is done relatively effortlessly if the problem solver has knowledge and skill of the calculus. In this case, all he or she needs to do is recognize the problem as one that can be solved by taking the derivative and setting it equal to zero. In the absence of this knowledge, the problem solver must begin often through trial and error to find the solution.

Although strong methods are effective at expediting the search for a solution, strong methods may not be as effective when problems are novel or ill-defined. In these cases, the domain-specific algorithms used in the past may fail to provide a solution. When strong methods fail, weak methods are employed. *Weak methods* are domain-general methods that do not capitalize on domain-specific prior knowledge; rather, they are all-purpose tools for solving problems in almost any domain. Although weak methods do not privilege a specific search path toward a solution, they are nonetheless useful methods for both experts and novices alike. Weak methods can be employed when a problem is unlike any other problem encountered in the past and, hence, requires some type of solution, even a creative one. Newell and Simon (1972) and Simon (1977) identified a series of weak methods available to problem solvers, five of which are elaborated in the context of the SDDS model (see Klahr & Simon, 1999). These methods constrain and direct the search of problem spaces in the SDDS model. We describe these methods in some detail because they reflect the types of higher-order thinking skills required by problem solvers who are successful at solving ill-defined problem-solving tasks, many of which require unconventional solutions and challenge algorithmic patterns of thought (see Kuhn, 2005; Perkins, 1995; Resnick, 1987; Stanovich, 2009).

The five methods can be ordered according to the general demands made of LTM and include: generate and test, hill climbing, means-ends analysis, planning, and analogy. The *generate and test* method makes the fewest demands of LTM because it involves simple trial and error. An operator or some action-forcing event is applied to an initial knowledge state to determine whether the result will produce the desired goal state. There are no intermediate knowledge states to evaluate when this method is used. If the desired goal state is not achieved with the initial application of an operator, then another operator is applied to see if it works at solving the problem. An example of this method can be seen when a computer novice systematically presses a series of key combinations (e.g., operators such as Ctrl+Alt+Delete or Fn+Home) to resurrect power to a computer monitor image. If the first key combination fails, then another combination is attempted until something works to revive the image. It is important to reiterate that the generate and test method is used when a problem appears novel to a problem solver and, therefore, specific background knowledge cannot be accessed for a solution. A computer expert would probably not use the generate and test method because a more efficient algorithm involving the proper set of key combinations would be accessed from LTM. Thus, an expert is always expected to use strong methods to solve a problem, unless the problem is sufficiently unusual that even the expert must turn to weak methods for solutions.

The next method, *hill climbing*, involves applying at least two operators to an initial knowledge state to see which of the results yields an intermediate state that is closest to the desired goal state. The intermediate knowledge state that looks most promising in its proximity to the goal state is then submitted to another operator and the result is again evaluated. Hill climbing, unlike generate and test, uses information from intermediate steps in the search path to a solution to determine the next most efficient step to execute.

Means-ends analysis involves a comparison between adjacent knowledge states, including intermediate knowledge states and the goal state. Any differences between states are noted, and an operator is selectively chosen to reduce the most important differences between the two states being considered. If the operator cannot be applied because there is a mismatch in the fit between a knowledge state and the operator, then a sub-goal is introduced to make the knowledge state fit the application of the operator. This method is repeated until the intermediate knowledge state coincides with the goal state.

In comparison to previous weak methods, the fourth method, *planning*, constrains the search for a solution significantly. A typical example of planning involves creating an outline before writing an essay. This method requires generating a basic sketch of the strategy used to meet the requirements of the task, devoid of excessive or complicating details that may distract from the essential components of the task. After the outline is laid out, it is checked against the task objectives to ensure that it satisfies all its requirements. The outline is also used to identify the relevant operators (e.g., relevant research literature to be consulted) that will be needed to make solving the problem fruitful. If the outline is successfully mapped onto the constraints of the task, then it is implemented to solve the problem – writing the essay.

Finally, the weak method that makes the greatest demands on LTM is *analogy*. Analogy exploits a problem solver's background knowledge in multiple domains. The use of analogy involves considering the solution to an already-solved problem (base problem) in one domain to facilitate the solution of a new, unfamiliar problem (target problem) in another domain. Although analogy requires prior knowledge, it is still not a failsafe approach to problem solving. Analogy requires a careful mapping of the features of a base problem to a target problem to determine how the familiarity of one can constrain the novelty of the other and, therefore, facilitate a solution. In particular, the mapping of the base and target problems involves evaluating the features of both problems to determine the extent of surface versus structural similarities, and whether structural similarities are sufficiently relevant to warrant the use of the method.

Although the SDDS model is considered to be an overarching framework for identifying many relevant processes of scientific thinking (Zimmerman, 2007), the details of some of its key underlying processes (e.g., how a hypothesis is evaluated for whether it adequately accounts for data) have not been explicitly articulated (Klahr & Dunbar, 1988, p. 37). In particular, Klahr and Dunbar (1988) state:

> As yet, SDDS is not a running computer model, rather it is a specification of the control structure for a yet to be built program. The actual building of the model will involve a much more extensive and precise specification of the processes involved. (p. 38)

Given that Klahr and Dunbar specified the SDDS model at an algorithmic level of analysis, some computer platforms have already been identified as possible candidates for implementing the underlying processes of the model. These candidates include the BACON series of programs (Langley, Simon, Bradshaw, & Zytkow, 1987), KEKADA (Kulkarni & Simon, 1988), and CDP (Grasshoff & May, 1995). In particular, BACON and KEKADA have been shown to yield successful searches with a relatively small number of methods (Klahr & Simon, 1999), and KEKADA and CDP have been found to use search algorithms that replicate the paths of well-known scientific discoveries (e.g., the reaction path for the in vivo synthesis of urea by Nobel Prize winning medical researcher Dr. Hans Krebs). Next, Khlar and Dunbar's (1988) SDDS model is considered according to the three criteria outlined in Chapter 2 – granularity, measurability, and instructional relevance.

Model Evaluation: Granularity, Measurability, and Instructional Relevance

Granularity
The granularity of the SDDS model is both fine and coarse depending on the aspects of the model being considered (similar to the text or

reading comprehension models considered in Chapter 3). For example, the hypothesis and experiment spaces, in addition to the evidence-evaluation component of the model, are coarse in grain size due to their broad definition and generality. In contrast, the specific processes of the SDDS model, included in some of the initial layers of the hypothesis space shown in Figure 4.1, are finer in their grain size. For example, *generate frame* and *assign slot values* in the hypothesis space (see Figure 4.1) are highly specific processes that may be expected to occur outside a learner's awareness, and may fail to map onto the broad educational objectives large-scale educational assessments typically measure.

Measurability

As with the CI and constructionist models in Chapter 3, the measurability of a cognitive model can be considered from multiple perspectives. On the one hand, the measurability of the SDDS model is observed in the experimental tasks that are designed to test the predictions derived from the model (see Zimmerman, 2007, for a review of tasks). For example, Klahr and Dunbar (1988) designed a task to observe the interplay between the hypothesis and experiment spaces of the SDDS model. Adult participants were introduced in one training session to a computer-programmable robot with multiple basic functions that were under participant control. After the training session, the robot was presented to participants again, and their task was to extend their understanding of the robot by discovering how one of its new computer functions operated. This task required participants to generate a hypothesis of what the robot would do when the new function was in operation (i.e., the behavioral objective of the new function), and then to design an experiment (i.e., write a program) to test the hypothesis. Testing the hypothesis required participants to compare the robot's actual behavior against the hypothesized behavioral outcome of the function. When participants' hypotheses failed to correctly predict the robot's actions, they were allowed to generate a new hypothesis and test their hypothesis again. This type of task allowed Klahr and Dunbar to assess how well participants (a) generated and adapted hypotheses, (b) designed experiments, (c) evaluated evidence, and (d) regulated or coordinated their searches (see also de Jong & van Joolingen, 1998; also Reid, Zhang, & Chen, 2003). The task ended when participants believed they had discovered the objective of the robot's new function.

Van Joolingen and de Jong (1997) provide another example of how experimental tasks are used to test the SDDS model. Van Joolingen and de Jong evaluated the overall search process in the hypothesis space of the SDDS model by presenting tasks to participants that required them to describe aspects of the hypotheses they were considering and generating. The hypotheses were evaluated for correctness, precision, scope, and range. Further, the specific methods used to search for hypotheses were evaluated by asking participants to describe the methods and status of their searches at certain "choice points" in the task. These kinds of experimental tasks (Klahr & Dunbar, 1988; see also van Joolingen & de Jong, 1997; Reid et al., 2003; see also Zimmerman, 2007, for a review of tasks) are designed to evaluate components of the SDDS model – if the participant is observed to pass through or demonstrate certain attributes in the process of hypothesis generation, hypothesis refinement, and experimentation, then evidence in support of the model is noted.

On the other hand, aside from experimental tasks, we have found no published accounts of large-scale test items developed directly from the SDDS model. We speculate that the use of the SDDS model for guiding the design and development of large-scale educational tests will depend on the particular knowledge and skills being considered. Knowledge and skills identified at a coarse grain size, such as methods for searching through the hypothesis and experiment spaces, might be more amenable to measurement with educational test items than knowledge and skills described at a fine grain size. For example, items could be designed to measure strong or weak problem-solving methods as students select testable and informative hypotheses within particular domains. Conversely, knowledge and skills identified at a fine grain size in the SDDS model might be of less interest to test developers. For example, the generation of a frame and selection of slot values may not only be viewed as uninformative and irrelevant to broad educational objectives, but the measurement of these knowledge and skills may also be considered unfeasible using common test-design principles. As we consider the measurability of the SDDS model in light of large-scale educational testing practices, we recognize that a gap exists between the experimental tasks that have been used to evaluate components of the model and the kinds of items normally designed and needed for large-scale educational assessments.

Despite these measurability challenges, Klahr and Dunbar (see also, van Joolingen & de Jong, 1997; Reid et al., 2003) were able to design experimental tasks to evaluate parts of the SDDS model, which is testament to the fact that the model can be evaluated for research purposes. That is, the model is articulated at a sufficiently precise level that its components can be translated into tasks for experimental evaluation. However, the tasks used to evaluate the SDDS model (see Zimmerman, 2007, for a review of tasks) are not comparable to the kinds of test items that would normally comprise a large-scale educational assessment. To this end, many testing specialists would probably take a more critical perspective on how the measurability of the SDDS model was appraised, because the design of a single experimental task does not meet the expectations of a large-scale educational assessment in terms of the most basic psychometric standards for at least two reasons. First, one would need more than a single task (e.g., at least forty to sixty tasks or items for a typical large-scale assessment) to evaluate constructs involving hypothesis formation and experimental testing. Second, most large-scale educational assessments cover a broad range of science topics in order to support broad content-based inferences about what a student has learned. The skills of hypothesis formation, testing, and evidence evaluation would be a set among many other sets of topics across multiple content areas included in the test. In short, large-scale educational items based strictly on the SDDS model have yet to be developed or become operational, hence the measurability of the SDDS model for large-scale assessment remains an open question.

Instructional Relevance

The SDDS model has instructional relevance as it reflects a general framework of knowledge and skills in scientific reasoning and discovery. However, the relative weight between content knowledge and skills included in the model may be considered by some critics as unbalanced. According to *The National Science Education Standards* (NRC, 1996), the expectation is that students will achieve science understanding in eight categories, including unifying concepts and processes in science, science as inquiry, physical science, life science, earth and space science, science and technology, science in personal and social perspectives, and the history and nature of science. With respect to these eight categories, the SDDS model pertains to scientific inquiry explicitly, because the model focuses on hypothesis formation, experimentation skills, and the evaluation of evidence. However, the remaining seven categories are not addressed directly by the SDDS model, because they involve specific forms of content knowledge (e.g., physical science) that are not included in the SDDS model shown in Figure 4.1. In this respect, it may be surprising that content knowledge does not have a more prominent role in the SDDS model given the role of content knowledge in the induction of frames, selection of slot values, and the application of strong (and weak) methods of scientific search. However, before determining that the relatively scanty specification of content knowledge in the model is a drawback for informing instruction and designing and developing large-scale educational testing, consider the alternative. If content knowledge were to be specified in the model, then what specific content areas would need to be specified? Would one include the content of all eight categories listed by the

National Science Education Standards? Upon reflection, it is possible that including content knowledge in a cognitive model such as the SDDS may be more restrictive than not. As soon as content is specified in a model, the ability of the model to serve as a conceptual framework for guiding the design and development of assessments across multiple content areas within a domain is weakened. This occurs because, unsurprisingly, specifying content knowledge would tie the model too closely to a single educational topic or objective. The SDDS model outlines the types of knowledge and skills that students should master in a variety of content areas within the science domain, such as physical science, life science, and earth and space science. Just as Bloom's taxonomy does not include a listing of the specific content knowledge to measure in a given domain, neither does the SDDS model (see Chapter 6 for further discussion of this issue).

KUHN'S MODEL OF KNOWING/PHASES OF SCIENTIFIC INQUIRY

In recent reviews of scientific reasoning and discovery (Zimmerman, 2000, 2007), Kuhn's research is extensively cited in two key categories: experimentation skills (e.g., Kuhn & Phelps, 1982; Kuhn, Black, Keselman, & Kaplan, 2000; see also Kuhn, Garcia-Mila, Zohar, & Andersen, 1995; Kuhn, Schauble, & Garcia-Mila, 1992) and evidence evaluation skills (e.g., Kuhn, 1989, 2001, 2002, 2005; see also Kuhn, Amsel & O'Loughlin, 1988; Kuhn & Dean, 2004). Although Kuhn has not proposed an explicit cognitive model of scientific reasoning and discovery, she has articulated two related models, one of *knowing* (Kuhn, 2001) and one *of scientific inquiry* (Kuhn, 2005). Her model of scientific inquiry is born out of the model of knowing. Therefore, we consider both models as one, the Knowledge/Phases of Inquiry (KPI) model, which captures key knowledge and skills related to scientific reasoning and discovery. Kuhn's (2001, 2005) KPI model is shown diagrammatically in Figure 4.2a.

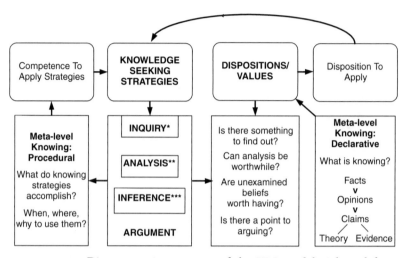

FIGURE 4.2a. Diagrammatic overview of the KPI model. Adapted from Kuhn, D. (2001). How do people know? *Psychological Science, 12,* 1–8.

Note: *Specific model of inquiry shown in Figure 4.2b; **Specific model of analysis shown in Figure 4.2c; and ***Specific model of inquiry shown in Figure 4.2d.

Model Description

Background

Kuhn's (2001, 2005) KPI model is not specified at an algorithmic level of analysis, but rather is presented as a general framework that outlines key knowledge and skill components. As shown in Figure 4.2a, Kuhn identifies four strategies for seeking knowledge: inquiry, analysis, inference, and argument. These four strategies are imbedded within a broader set of components, namely, a meta-cognitive understanding of the procedural and declarative aspects of knowledge seeking and the value of engaging in certain methods of thought. Meta-level *procedural* understanding influences the competence with which a learner applies the strategies of inquiry, analysis, inference, and argumentation to gain knowledge. Learners who have acquired this procedural understanding are likely to apply these strategies successfully and reinforce for themselves the relevance of using strategies to gain knowledge. Alternatively, learners who lack the procedural understanding of what these strategies accomplish, including when, where, and why to apply these strategies, may not apply them correctly and may consequently fail to profit from their use.

Meta-level *declarative* understanding is also related to the use of knowledge-seeking strategies. Meta-level declarative understanding involves knowing what it means to have adequate information on a topic, the differences between facts, opinions, and theories, and how evidence is coordinated to inform theories. Kuhn (2005) explains that learners who have sound knowledge structures are able to distinguish facts, which are typically uncontested statements (e.g., women live longer than men, on average), from opinions (e.g., women live longer than men *because* they are better able to deal with stress). Furthermore, these learners understand that opinions may serve as theories or hypotheses to be empirically tested, and if evidence is collected in their support, only then do opinions become claims. Meta-level declarative understanding also informs values for thinking that in turn either increase or decrease the propensity to use knowledge-seeking strategies. These values about knowledge are manifest through the answers learners provide to questions such as "Is there something to find out?" "Can analysis be worthwhile?" "Are unexamined beliefs worth having?" and "Is there reason for informed debate and argumentation?" In the absence of meta-level declarative understanding, according to Kuhn, facts, opinions, and claims are assumed to be the same, with a similar epistemological worth, and there is little incentive to think critically and scientifically.

The meta-level understanding and values found in Kuhn's KPI model are not found in Klahr and Dunbar's SDDS model. It is reasonable to ask whether these types of conative attributes should be included in a model of scientific reasoning. In his review of the psychological literature on rational thinking, Stanovich (2009; see also

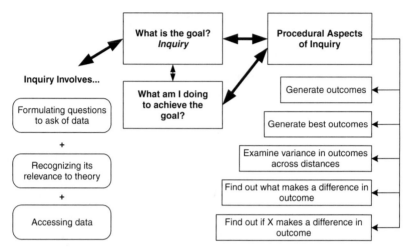

FIGURE 4.2b. Diagrammatic overview of *Inquiry* in KPI model. Adapted from Kuhn, D. (2005). *Education for thinking* (p. 85). Cambridge, MA: Cambridge University Press.

Perkins, 1995) claims that dispositions toward knowledge and/or epistemological values should be included in cognitive models. Stanovich explains that dispositions toward knowledge explain the motivation for why some individuals choose to engage and apply higher forms of thinking skills. He indicates that systematic, logical, and coherent thinking – the very core of scientific reasoning – is greatly facilitated by valuing not only knowledge, but also the methods and strategies that produce justifiable and defensible claims.

Framework

Three of the knowledge-seeking strategies in Figure 4.2a reflect core skills in scientific reasoning and discovery. These strategies are elaborated in Figures 4.2b–4.2d. The first strategy, *inquiry*, shown in Figure 4.2b, involves gathering data and making observations in order to generate a theory about a phenomenon (i.e., hypothesis formation). For instance, if students want to develop a hypothesis about

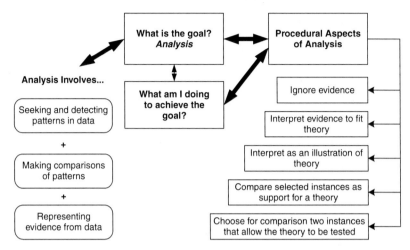

FIGURE 4.2c. Diagrammatic overview of *Analysis* in KPI model. Adapted from Kuhn, D. (2005). *Education for thinking* (p. 87). Cambridge, MA: Cambridge University Press.

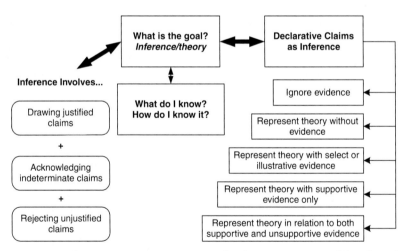

FIGURE 4.2d. Diagrammatic overview of *Inference* in KPI model. Adapted from Kuhn, D. (2005). *Education for thinking* (p. 89). Cambridge, MA: Cambridge University Press.

the risk of earthquakes; then they seek data about variables related to earthquakes such as soil type, water quality, radon gas levels, speed of S waves, and snake activity (see Kuhn, 2005). Shown at the top of Figure 4.2b are the primary queries guiding the inquiry: "What is the goal of the inquiry?" "What are the methods used to achieve this goal?" On the left-hand side of Figure 4.2b are the task objectives associated with the inquiry phase. These task objectives involve having access to data, formulating questions to probe the data, and recognizing the relevance of research questions to a potential theory. On the right-hand side of Figure 4.2b are the procedural strategies that are used to undertake the inquiry. Ordered from least effective to most effective, the strategies include generating outcomes, generating best outcomes, examining variance of outcomes across instances, finding out what makes a difference in an outcome, and finding out if variable X makes a difference in an outcome. The least effective strategy, generation of outcomes, reflects a simple "let's see what happens" approach where variables are manipulated haphazardly. Alternatively, the more sophisticated strategies involve systematically determining the effect of a single variable while holding all other variables constant.

The second strategy, *analysis*, is shown in Figure 4.2c, and it essentially involves theory testing. Shown at the top of Figure 4.2c are the queries guiding the analysis: "What is the goal?" "What are the methods used to achieve this goal?" On the left-hand side of Figure 4.2c are the task objectives to be met in the analysis phase. These objectives include representing evidence, making comparisons, and seeking and detecting patterns in the evidence. On the right-hand side of Figure 4.2c are the procedural strategies used to undertake the analysis. Ordered from least to most effective, these consist of ignoring evidence, inventing evidence to fit the theory, interpreting an instance (i.e., datum, single piece of evidence) as an illustration of the theory, comparing selected instances as providing support for the theory, and choosing for comparison two instances that allow a test of the theory. During this phase, learners are expected to produce a test of the theory or hypothesis generated in the inquiry phase, and then refine the theory or hypothesis based on the results of the test. The least effective analysis strategy is to ignore evidence that challenges an existing theory (i.e., confirmation bias), and the most sophisticated strategy is to systematically evaluate all pieces of evidence in relation to the theory.

The third strategy, *inference*, is shown in Figure 4.2d, and it involves considering the kinds of claims that can be made based on the results of the inquiry and analysis phases. Shown at the top of Figure 4.2d are the queries guiding the inference: "What do I know?" "How do I know this (what is my evidence)?" The left-hand side of Figure 4.2d indicates the task objectives required in the inference phase. These objectives include drawing justified claims, rejecting unjustified claims, and acknowledging when evidence is vague and leads to indeterminate claims. On the right-hand side of Figure 4.2d are the procedural strategies used to generate declarative claims. Ordered from least to most effective, these consist of ignoring evidence, generating claims without evidence, generating claims with illustrative evidence, generating claims by only including supportive evidence, and generating claims by taking into account both supportive and falsifying evidence. During the inference phase, learners are expected to evaluate the evidence collectively and to coordinate the interplay between the theory or hypothesis being evaluated and the evidence found for the theory or hypothesis. Not surprisingly, the least effective inference strategy is to ignore evidence and generate claims in the absence of evidence (i.e., belief or opinion). The most sophisticated strategy is to systematically evaluate all pieces of evidence in relation to the theory or hypothesis, and to generate claims about the status of the theory or hypothesis based on all the evidence collected. Next, Kuhn's (2001, 2005) KPI model is considered according to the three criteria of granularity, measurability, and instructional relevance.

Model Evaluation: Granularity, Measurability,
and Instructional Relevance

Granularity

Unlike the SDDS model considered previously, Kuhn's model is generally specified at a coarse level of granularity. The knowledge and skills needed for scientific inquiry are presented as general strategies. The coarseness is also observed in the inclusion of values. Kuhn's (2001) inclusion of values (see Figure 4.2a) sets the stage for understanding scientific reasoning and discovery more globally, not only in terms of hypothesis formation and testing, but also in terms of the conative dispositions (see Perkins, 1995; Snow, Corno, & Jackson, 1996; Stanovich, 2009) that motivate students to engage in scientific reasoning and discovery. Whereas both the SDDS model and Kuhn's KPI model include key knowledge and skills for hypothesis formation and experimentation (i.e., inquiry, analysis, and inference), the SDDS model focuses on finer processing details such as the generation of frames and the assignment of slot values to frames. In contrast, Kuhn's model consistently focuses on coarser-level processes such as general strategies for seeking knowledge, values, and the meta-cognitive forms of understanding that lead students to examine critically what it means to know and the strategies that lead to substantiated beliefs.

Measurability

As with the SDDS model, experimental tasks have been designed to measure aspects of the KPI model (e.g., Kuhn, 1989, 2001, 2002, 2005; Kuhn & Dean, 2005; Kuhn & Phelps, 1982; Kuhn et al., 2000; see also Kuhn et al., 1995; Kuhn et al., 1992). As an illustration, Kuhn (2005) developed a computer-based, multi-part task on the topic of earthquake risk. Students worked interactively on the computer to answer a series of prompted activity questions as they completed each sub-task. In the first inquiry sub-task, students were shown a computer screen and were prompted with the following instructions (Kuhn, 2005,

p. 81): "Observe cases to find out which features make a difference [for earthquake risk]. Look very carefully at the features of each case you observe and what is the earthquake risk for that case. By studying cases, you'll be able to find out which features matter and which don't in the risk for earthquakes." On the same computer screen, students were shown five object features in vertical ordering related to earthquake risk (i.e., soil type, S-wave rate, water quality, snake activity, and gas level). Students were then prompted to learn more about a particular feature by clicking on the object. Once students selected a particular feature, another screen with additional information and new questions was presented to guide them through the next sub-task (see Kuhn, 2005, pp. 81–84). The earthquake task was designed to measure how students searched for factors influencing earthquake risk, represented evidence, evaluated evidence, and generated inferences. Students were tested once or twice a week over multiple months, and micro-genetic analysis[2] was used to evaluate their performance over time.

Other experimental tasks have also been designed to assess how well participants can evaluate evidence in the presence of conflicting prior beliefs or theories. For example, evidence-based thinking is considered to be superior to theory-based thinking, because it indicates that participants can use empirical data to distinguish between levels of knowledge – that is, they can distinguish what they *think* to be true (i.e., opinion) versus what *is* true based on the data (i.e., a claim that is based on evidence). Kuhn et al. (1988) designed a task in which adults and students in grades six and nine were interviewed about their prior beliefs on the food types (i.e., fruit, cereal, potato, and condiment) most likely to influence whether someone caught a cold. Kuhn and her colleagues found that participants believed fruits and cereals to be the two types of food most likely to influence whether someone

---

[2] Micro-genetic analysis is a type of fine-grained examination of learners' performance, which includes carefully observing learners at closely spaced time intervals to view the development or change of specific psychological processes that could be concealed during a single experimental administration (see Siegler, 2006).

caught a cold. Potato and condiments were thought to be the two types of food least likely to influence whether someone caught a cold. After the interviews, adults and students were presented with the four types of food again and asked to evaluate covariation evidence for whether the evidence indicated that a specific type of food was associated with catching colds. Treatment conditions were arranged so that participants evaluated data *confirming* their pre-existing beliefs about food type and catching colds and data *disconfirming* their pre-existing beliefs. Participants' responses were coded as either evidence-based (sticking to the data even if it meant ignoring pre-existing beliefs) or theory-based (sticking to pre-existing beliefs even if it meant ignoring data). The results revealed that suspending pre-existing beliefs in the evaluation of evidence improved systematically with age. In particular, adults were the most competent in distinguishing and coordinating theory and evidence, followed by grade-nine students, and finally grade-six students. As with the SDDS model, the tasks designed to evaluate component parts of Kuhn's KPI model are experimental, presented within a laboratory context, and usually singular in number. Although such tasks could, in principle, be converted into educational test items for large-scale assessments, we have not found published, operational examples in the research literature.

Instructional Relevance

The KPI model has instructional relevance. The model reflects key cognitive strategies in scientific thought as well as pedagogically relevant conative components (e.g., values). In particular, the thinking values included in the KPI model (e.g., "Is there something to find out?" "Can analysis be worthwhile?") underscore the conative context in which scientific reasoning takes place, and this is likely to resonate with some teachers and parents. Teachers and parents are keenly aware, as are educational psychologists, that success in learning is closely connected to the motivational dispositions that students possess (e.g., Bandura, 2006). Moreover, the knowledge-seeking strategies of inquiry, analysis, and inference complement the science as inquiry category associated with *The National Science Education Standards* (NRC, 1996) mentioned previously. However, some critics may argue that content knowledge does not have a well-defined role in the KPI model. In this sense, the KPI model could be levied the same critique as the SDDS model, because it fails to explicitly include a role for content knowledge, it lacks some instructional relevance. Still, as discussed when evaluating the SDDS model, it is important to consider what might be lost by having content knowledge included explicitly in a model. Although content knowledge is an important component of instruction and large-scale educational tests in science, a single model used to guide assessment design should be able to inform item development across many content areas (e.g., physical sciences, life sciences, earth and space sciences) within the general domain of science (see Chapter 6 for a discussion of this issue). Toward this end, a cognitive model may be more beneficial to assessment specialists by not including specific content knowledge, and, therefore, showing broader applicability within the domain. Alternatively, it may be restrictive to assume that only a single cognitive model should inform the design and development of a domain-specific, large-scale assessment. We consider the limitations of using single cognitive models in assessment design further in Chapter 6.

CONCLUSION AND DISCUSSION

In this chapter, we reviewed Klahr and Dunbar's (1988) SDDS model and Kuhn's (2001, 2005) KPI model. Model components were considered for the design and development of large-scale educational assessment in terms of the three criteria outlined in Chapter 2 (i.e., granularity, measurability, and instructional relevance). These two cognitive models were highlighted because they reflect diagrammatic representations of key knowledge and skills in scientific reasoning and discovery and have garnered substantial empirical support.

The SDDS model provides a broad theoretical framework that can accommodate many of the findings of smaller-scale studies that focus on single aspects of scientific reasoning and discovery (Zimmerman, 2007), namely, research on experimentation skills (including hypothesis formation), evaluation of evidence (including the formation of inferences and conclusions), and integrated approaches consisting of partially guided and self-directed experimentation. Kuhn's KPI model was also highlighted because it encompasses the key processes of inquiry (hypothesis formation), analysis (experimentation), and inference (evaluation of evidence); substantial research work has been conducted on many parts of the model.

When the models were evaluated for their granularity, measurability, and instructional relevance, many similarities were found, with the main differences in granularity. Whereas the SDDS model was found to be specified at both fine and coarse grain sizes, the KPI model was described at a consistently coarse grain size. The SDDS model was coarse insofar as it specified a search through a hypothesis space (using methods at increasingly sophisticated levels) and a search through an experiment space, using similar methods as in the hypothesis space. There was also a phase of evidence evaluation where the results obtained in the experiment space were reviewed. Within the hypothesis space especially, the SDDS model was also described at a fine level of granularity because it included the representational structure of hypotheses (generating frames) and the assignment of slot values to frames.

In terms of measurability, both the SDDS model and the KPI model have been translated into experimental tasks, but these are not the types of tasks typically found on large-scale science assessments. The tasks designed to test the SDDS and KPI models consist of single tasks, with multiple parts often reflecting ill-defined, problem-solving activities associated with searching for ideas, formulating those ideas into testable hypotheses, designing experiments, and evaluating results. Also of interest is the finding that both models favor describing the process of hypothesis formation and experimentation to the relative exclusion of describing how content knowledge in basic domains such as the physical sciences, life sciences, and earth and space sciences inform scientific reasoning and discovery skills. Therefore, test items developed from these models would reflect the skills of scientific inquiry but not necessarily the mastery of content knowledge. Although content knowledge is necessary for the application of strong methods in the SDDS model, the specific processes by which this knowledge informs the selection of methods and search in hypothesis formation and experimentation has yet to be specified (see Klahr & Dunbar, 1988).

The relative absence of content knowledge in the SDDS model and KPI model may be viewed by some as compromising the full instructional relevance of these frameworks for educators. It is evident that scientific inquiry, which the models include, would be of interest to educators. However, the inclusion of content knowledge would also be beneficial, even critical, especially in illustrating when and how content knowledge facilitates the acquisition and successful application of science skills. Newcombe et al. (2009) acknowledge that science education is challenging in part because both content-based knowledge and process-based skills must be taught. It appears that these cognitive models of scientific reasoning and discovery rely heavily on the specification of process skills. The challenge, then, in using and translating these kinds of cognitive models of scientific reasoning and discovery for item design will be in determining how to fill the content knowledge gap for the development of educational test items. Yet this is also a challenge that pertains to all cognitive models described in this volume. The models described in this volume reflect unitary, domain-specific models, reflecting circumscribed sets of knowledge and skills that, in principle, should cut across or be applied to multiple content areas (e.g., physical sciences, biology, chemistry) within a given domain (e.g., science). The CI model, for instance, is not a model of reading comprehension for fiction alone (see Chapter 3, this volume), but rather a model of reading comprehension for many types of textual genres (see Chapter 6, this volume, for further discussion of this issue).

REFERENCES

Agan, L. & Sneider, C. (2004). Learning about the earth's shape and gravity: A guide for teachers and curriculum developers. *Astronomy Education Review*, 2, 90–117. Available at http://aer.noao.edu/cgi-bin/new.pl [accessed Jan. 2010].

American Association for the Advancement of Science. (1993). *Benchmarks for science literacy*. New York: Oxford University Press.

Baldi, S., Jin, Y., Skemer, M., Green, P.J., & Herget, D. (2007). Highlights from PISA 2006: Performance of U.S. 15-year-old students in science and mathematics literacy in an international context (NCES 2008–016). National Center for Education Statistics, Institute of Education Sciences, U.S. Department of Education. Washington, DC.

Bandura, A. (2006). Toward a psychology of human agency. *Perspectives on Psychological Science, 1*, 164–180.

Boyd, S.E., Banilower, E.R., Pasley, J.D., & Weiss, I.R. (2003). *Progress and pitfalls: A cross-site look at local systemic change through teacher enhancement*. Chapel Hill, NC: Horizon Research.

Chi, M.T.H. (2005). Commonsense conceptions of emergent processes: Why some misconceptions are robust. *Journal of the Learning Sciences, 14*, 161–199.

Chinn, C.A. & Malhotra, B.A. (2002). Children's responses to anomalous scientific data: How is conceptual change impeded? *Journal of Educational Psychology, 94*, 327–343.

Choe, K., Keil, F.C., & Bloom, P. (2005). Children's understanding of the Ulysses conflict. *Developmental Science, 8*, 387–392.

Dawson, M.R.W. (1998). *Understanding cognitive science*. Malden, MA: Blackwell.

de Jong, T. & van Joolingen, W.R. (1998). Scientific discovery learning with computer simulations of conceptual domains. *Review of Educational Research, 68*, 179–201.

Dean, D. & Kuhn, D. (2007). Direct instruction vs. discovery: The long view. *Science Education, 91*, 384–397.

Dunbar, K. & Fugelsang, J. (2005). Scientific thinking and reasoning. In K. Holyoak & R.G. Morrison (Eds.), *The Cambridge handbook of thinking and reasoning* (pp. 706–725). New York: Cambridge University Press.

Dunbar, K. & Klahr, D. (1989). Developmental differences in scientific discovery strategies. In D. Klahr & K. Kotovsky (Eds.), *Complex information processing: The impact of Herbert A. Simon* (pp. 109–143). Hillsdale, NJ: Lawrence Erlbaum.

Ericsson, K.A., Charness, N., Feltovich, P.J., & Hoffman, R.R. (Eds.). (2006). *The Cambridge handbook of expertise and expert performance.* Cambridge, UK: Cambridge University Press.

Flores, F., Tovar, M., & Gallegos, L. (2003). Representation of the cell and its processes in high school students: An integrated view. *International Journal of Science Education, 25*, 269–286.

Garcia-Mila, M. & Andersen, C. (2007). Developmental change in note taking during scientific inquiry. *International Journal of Science Education, 29*, 1035–1058.

Gleick, J. (1987). *Chaos: Making a new science.* Harmondsworth, England: Penguin.

Gonzales, P., Williams, T., Jocelyn, L., Roey, S., Kastberg, D., & Brenwald, S. (2008). Highlights from TIMSS 2007:Mathematics and science achievement of U.S. fourth- and eighth-grade students in an international context (NCES 2009–001 Revised). National Center for Education Statistics, Institute of Education Sciences, U.S. Department of Education. Washington, DC.

Gorman, M.E., Tweney R.D., Gooding, D.C., & Kincannon, A.P. (Eds.). (2005). *Scientific and technological thinking.* Mahwah, NJ: Erlbaum.

Grasshoff, G. & May, M. (1995). From historical case studies to systematic methods of discovery. Working notes: AAAI spring symposium on systematic methods of scientific discovery (pp. 46–57). Stanford, CA: AAAI.

Grigg, W., Lauko, M., & Brockway, D. (2006). *The nation's report card: Science 2005* (NCES 2006–466). U.S. Department of Education, National Center for Education Statistics. Washington, DC:U.S. Government Printing Office.

Hanushek, E.A. (2005). The economics of school quality. *German Economic Review, 6*, 269–286.

Kanari, Z. & Millar, R. (2004). Reasoning from data: How students collect and interpret data in science investigations. *Journal of Research in Science Teaching, 41*, 748–769.

Kim, J.J., Crasco, L.M., Smith, R.B., Johnson, G., Karantonis, A., & Leavitt, D.J. (2001). *Academic excellence for all urban students: Their accomplishments in science and mathematics.* Norwood, MA: Systemic Research.

Klahr, D. (2000). Exploring science: The cognition and development of discovery processes. Cambridge: MIT Press.

Klahr, D. & Dunbar, K. (1988). Dual search space during scientific reasoning. *Cognitive Science, 12*, 1–48.

Klahr, D., Fay, A.L., & Dunbar, K. (1993). Heuristics for scientific experimentation: A developmental study. *Cognitive Psychology, 25*, 111–146.

Klahr, D. & Simon, H.A. (1999). Studies of scientific discovery: Complementary approaches and convergent findings. *Psychological Bulletin, 125*, 524–543.

(2001). What have psychologists (and others) discovered about the process of scientific discovery? *Current Directions in Psychological Science, 10*, 75–79.

Klahr, D., Triona, L.M., & Williams, C. (2007). Hands on what? The relative effectiveness of physical vs. virtual materials in an engineering design project by middle school students. *Journal of Research in Science Teaching, 44*, 183–203.

Koerber, S., Sodian, B., Thoermer, C., & Nett, U. (2005). Scientific reasoning in young children: Preschoolers' ability to evaluate covariation evidence. *Swiss Journal of Psychology, 64*, 141–152.

Koslowski, B. & Masnick, A. (2002). The development of causal reasoning. In U. Goswami (Ed.), *Blackwell handbook of childhood cognitive development* (pp. 257–281). Oxford: Blackwell Publishing.

Kuhn, D. (1989). Children and adults as intuitive scientists. *Psychological Review, 96*, 674–689.

(2001). How do people know? *Psychological Science, 12*, 1–8.

(2002). What is scientific thinking and how does it develop? In U. Goswami (Ed.), *Blackwell handbook of childhood cognitive development* (pp. 371–393). Oxford: Blackwell Publishing.

(2005). *Education for thinking.* Cambridge, MA: Harvard University Press.

Kuhn, D., Amsel, E., & O' Loughlin, M. (1988). *The development of scientific thinking skills.* Orlando, FL: Academic Press.

Kuhn, D., Black, J., Keselman, A., & Kaplan, D. (2000). The development of cognitive skills to support inquiry learning. *Cognition and Instruction, 18*, 495–523.

Kuhn, D. & Dean, D. (2004). Connecting scientific reasoning and causal inference. *Journal of Cognition & Development, 5*, 261–288.

(2005). Is developing scientific thinking all about learning to control variables? *Psychological Science, 16*, 866–870.

Kuhn, D. & Franklin, S. (2006). The second decade: What develops (and how). In W. Damon, R.M. Lerner, (Series Eds.), D. Kuhn & R. S. Siegler (Vol. Eds.), *Handbook of child psychology: Vol. 2. Cognition, perception and language* (6th ed.) (pp. 953–993). Hoboken, NJ: John Wiley & Sons.

Kuhn, D., Garcia-Mila, M., Zohar, A., & Andersen, C. (1995). Strategies of knowledge acquisition. *Monographs of the Society for Research in Child Development, 60*, 1–128.

Kuhn, D., Iordanou, K., Pease, M., & Wirkala, C. (2008). Beyond control of variables: What needs to develop to achieve skilled scientific thinking? *Cognitive Development, 23*, 435–451.

Kuhn, D., Katz, J.B., Dean Jr., D. (2004). Developing reason. *Thinking & Reasoning, 10*, 197–219.

Kuhn, D. & Phelps, E. (1982). The development of problem-solving strategies. *Advances in Child Development and Behavior, 17*, 1 – 44.

Kuhn, D., Schauble, L., & Garcia-Mila, M. (1992). Cross-domain development of scientific reasoning. *Cognition & Instruction, 9*, 285–327.

Kulkarni, D. & Simon, H.A. (1988). The process of scientific discovery: The strategy of experimentation. *Cognitive Science, 12*, 139–176.

Langley, P., Simon, H.A., Bradshaw, G.L., & Zytkow, J.M. (1987). *Scientific discovery: Computational explorations of the creative processes.* Cambridge, MA: MIT Press.

Lehrer, R. & Schauble, L. (1998). Reasoning about structure and function: Children's conceptions of gears. *Journal of Research in Science Teaching, 31*, 3–25.

Leighton, J. & Bisanz, G. L. (2003). Children's and adults' knowledge and reasoning about the ozone layer and its depletion. *International Journal of Science Education, 25*, 117–139.

Leighton, J. P., Gokiert, R.J., & Cui, Y. (2007). Using exploratory and confirmatory methods to identify the cognitive dimensions in a large-scale science assessment. *International Journal of Testing, 7*, 1–49.

Masnick, A.M. & Klahr, D. (2003). Error matters: An initial exploration of elementary school children's understanding of experimental error. *Journal of Cognition and Development, 4*, 67–98.

Masnick, A.M. & Morris, B.J. (2002). Reasoning from data: The effect of sample size and variability on children's and adults' conclusions. In *Proceedings of the 24th annual conference of the Cognitive Science Society* (pp. 643–648).

Minsky, M. (June, 1974). A framework for representing knowledge. *MIT-AI Laboratory Memo 306*. Accessed on January 2, 2010, at http://web.media.mit.edu/~minsky/papers/Frames/frames.html.

National Commission on Excellence in Education. (1983). *A nation at risk: The imperative for educational reform.* Washington, DC: U.S. Government Printing Office.

National Research Council. (1996). *National science education standards.* National Committee on Science Education Standards and Assessment. Washington, DC: National Academy Press.

National Research Council. (2007). *Taking science to school: Learning and teaching science in grades K-8.* Arlington, VA: National Science Foundation.

Newcombe, N.S., Ambady, N., Eccles, J., Gomez, L., Klahr, D., Linn, M., Miller, K., & Mix, K. (2009). Psychology's role in mathematics and science education. *American Psychologist, 64,* 538–550.

Newell, A. & Simon, H.A. (1972). *Human problem solving.* Oxford, UK: Prentice-Hall.

No Child Left Behind Act of 2001, Pub Law No. 107–110 (2002, January). Retrieved April 11, 2009 from http://www.ed.gov/policy/elsec/leg/esea02/107–110.pdf

Organization for Economic Cooperation and Development. (2006). *PISA 2006: Science competencies for tomorrow's world: Volume 1: Analysis.* Author.

Organization for Economic Cooperation and Development. (2009). *Education today: The OECD perspective.* Author.

Perkins, D. (1995). *Outsmarting IQ: The emerging science of learnable intelligence.* New York City: The Free Press.

Reid, D.J., Zhang, J., & Chen, Q. (2003). Supporting scientific discovery learning in a simulation environment. *Journal of Computer Assisted Learning, 19,* 9–20.

Resnick, L.B. (1987). *Education and learning to think.* Washington, DC: National Academy Press.

Schauble, L. (1996). The development of scientific reasoning in knowledge-rich contexts. *Developmental Psychology, 32,* 102–119.

Siegler, R. (1998). Emerging minds: The process of change in children's thinking. New York: Oxford University Press.

(2006). Microgenetic studies of learning. In D. Kuhn and R. Siegler (Eds.), *Handbook of child psychology. Vol. 2: Cognition, perception, and language* (6th ed.). Hoboken, NJ: Wiley.

Shtulman, A. (2006). Qualitative differences between naïve and scientific theories of evolution. *Cognitive Psychology, 52,* 170–194.

Simon, H.A. (1977). *Models of discovery.* Dordrecht, Holland: D. Reidel.

Simon, H.A. & Lea, G. (1974). Problem solving and rule induction: A unified view. In L.W. Gregg (Ed.), *Knowledge and cognition* (pp. 105–127). Hillsdale, NJ: Erlbaum.

Snow, R.E., Corno, L., & Jackson, D. (1996). Individual differences in affective and conative functions. In D.C. Berliner & R.C. Calfee (Eds.), *Handbook of educational psychology,* (pp. 243–310). London, England: Prentice Hall.

Stanovich, K.E. (2009). *What intelligence tests miss: The psychology of rational thought.* New Haven, CT: Yale University Press.

Stathopoulou, C. & Vosniadou, S. (2007). Exploring the relationship between physics-related epistemological beliefs and physics understanding. *Contemporary Educational Psychology, 32,* 255–281.

Tschirgi, J.E. (1980). Sensible reasoning: A hypothesis about hypotheses. *Child Development, 51,* 1–10.

van Joolingen, W.R. & de Jong, T. (1997) An extended dual search space model of scientific discovery learning. *Instructional Science, 25,* 307–346.

Vosniadou, S. & Brewer, W. F. (1992). Mental models of the earth: A study of conceptual change in childhood. *Cognitive Psychology, 24,* 535–585.

Zimmerman, C. (2000). The development of scientific reasoning skills. *Developmental Review, 20,* 99–149.

    (2007). The development of scientific thinking skills in elementary and middle school. *Development Review, 27,* 172–223.

Zimmerman, C. & Glaser, R. (2001). Testing positive versus negative claims: A preliminary investigation of the role of cover story in the assessment of experimental design skills (Tech. Rep. No. 554). Los Angeles, CA: UCLA National Center for Research on Evaluation, Standards, and Student Testing (CRESST).

5

Cognitive Models of Task Performance
for Mathematical Reasoning

It is an understatement to say that mathematical knowledge and skill are valuable for the jobs and careers of the twenty-first century. In fact, they are essential for individuals who want to have the widest array of career options available and a high quality of life. Learners who shun mathematics shut themselves off from many lucrative career paths. According to a recently published article in the *Wall Street Journal* (Needleman, January 26, 2009), "Doing the Math to Find Good Jobs," the best occupations in America all required advanced mathematics. According to data compiled by the U.S. Bureau of Labor Statistics and Census, the top five jobs in a list of two hundred included mathematician, actuary, statistician, biologist, and software engineer. These jobs were rated highest because they combined large salaries with desirable working conditions, namely, indoor office environments, unadulterated air, absence of heavy lifting and physical hardship, and conveniences such as controlling one's work schedule. The worst jobs were lumberjack, dairy farmer, taxi driver, seaman, and emergency medical technician. Most of the jobs at the lower end of the list did not require advanced mathematics.

The importance of mathematics for maximizing the likelihood of obtaining a desirable job in the future would make one think that students, desirous of having an edge for a future career, would be clamoring to learn and perform as well as possible in mathematics. Yet this is not the case. Many students, even in post-industrialized countries such as the United States, who once demonstrated unprecedented prowess in the mathematical sciences, are now known to dislike it and to under-perform (National Mathematics Advisory Panel [NMAP], 2008; see also Kloosterman, 2010). Members of a recently convened National Mathematics Advisory Panel (2008, p. xii), many of whom happen to be notable researchers of mathematical cognition and achievement and represent institutions such as Carnegie Mellon, Cornell, Harvard, and Vanderbilt, frame the problem in strikingly succinct terms:

> Particularly disturbing is the consistency of findings that American students achieve in mathematics at a mediocre level by comparison to peers worldwide. On our own "National Report Card" – the National Assessment of Educational Progress (NAEP) – there are positive trends of scores at Grades 4 and 8, which have just reached historic highs. This is a sign of significant progress. Yet other results from NAEP are less positive: 32% of our students are at or above the "proficient" level in Grade 8, but only 23% are proficient at Grade 12.

According to the panel, students are getting worse in mathematics as they grow older. At the very time when their knowledge and skills should be opening doors, these doors are actually closing for students as they enter college and university, and must make consequential decisions about their careers.

To better understand how to open doors for students, the learning sciences are consulted for expert guidance. The learning sciences are rich with empirical studies of mathematical reasoning and cognition, including pre-school mathematical understandings and use of symbolic functions (e.g., McCrink & Wynn, 2004; Munn, 1998); developmental perspectives on counting (e.g., Sophian, 2007); relationships between conceptual and procedural knowledge in mathematical learning (e.g., Fu & Anderson, 2008; Rittle-Johnson, Siegler, & Alibali, 2001; Siegler & Svetina, 2006); numerical competence across ethnic boundaries (Towse & Saxton, 1998); effects of anxiety and age on working memory and mental calculation (Ashcraft & Krause, 2007; Ashcraft & Kirk, 2001); computational models of number conservation

(Simon & Klahr, 1995); mental and spatial representations of numbers (Dehaene, Bossini, & Giraux, 1993; Fias & Fischer, 2005); calculation proficiencies in expert calculators (e.g., Hope, 1985; Dorman, 1991); math performance in girls with Turner Syndrome (e.g., Mazzocco & McCloskey, 2005); what animals know about numbers (Brannon, 2005); numerical estimation (e.g., Kalaman & LeFevre, 2007; Siegler & Booth, 2004); individual differences in normal arithmetical development (e.g., Alibali et al., 2007; Jordan, Mulhern, & Wylie, 2009); and individual differences in special populations with learning disabilities (e.g., Geary et al., 2007; Mabbott & Bisanz, 2008).

Although the diversity of research topics found for mathematical reasoning and cognition is impressive and indicates the scholarly health for research in this domain, this diversity is of surprisingly limited use for at least one real-world application (Davis, 2008) – large-scale educational testing. Part of the challenge is that, aside from the most basic of information-processing metaphors, there is no framework, model, or theory that can be used to categorize the variety of research findings in mathematical reasoning (Newell, 1973). In fact, compiling knowledge of all these studies is not particularly useful for the assessment specialist who may wish to generate a well-defined test item to measure a specific aspect of mathematical reasoning, for example, procedural skill in the transformation of functions at the grade-twelve level (Alberta Education, 2009). The reason for this void is that many of the empirical studies of mathematical reasoning, examples of which are cited in the previous paragraph, focus on processes (e.g., mental representations of parity and numerical magnitude in young children) using measures (e.g., responding to a single digit number on screen and stating whether it is odd or even, see Dehaene et al., 1993) at an exceedingly specific and fairly narrow level of detail. For example, research findings on how children mentally represent numbers are sure to contribute to our understanding of mathematical performance. However, these findings pertain to such an early stage of development as to render their use impractical for the design and development of large-scale educational assessments aimed at older students. What test specialists need are research findings from later stages of mathematical cognition – that is, information about the accumulation of basic processes and how they work together as they materialize into reasoning skills for solving math problems typically encountered by secondary-level students on topics such as systems of equations in algebra or transforming functions. Nonetheless, all is not lost. There are cognitive models that do account for mathematical reasoning and performance that could help steer the design and development of large-scale educational testing.

FOCUS OF THE CHAPTER

It is beyond the scope of the present chapter to provide a complete review of the theories, models, and processes of mathematical reasoning. Such a review would easily fill multiple handbooks. However, as with the previous chapters on reading comprehension and scientific reasoning and discovery, there is a need to reconcile research in the learning sciences with large-scale educational-assessment design and development. Assessments that are designed from well-accepted principles of mathematical reasoning may provide valuable, evidence-based information about the knowledge and skills students are lacking and, more importantly, how to address identified deficiencies through instruction. The focus of this chapter, then, is to present a targeted review of diagrammatic cognitive models in mathematical reasoning that might be translated and used to design and develop large-scale educational assessments in mathematics. The two models we highlight are Anderson's *Adaptive Control of Thought – Rational* (ACT-R; Anderson, 1990; Ritter, Anderson, Koedinger, & Corbett, 2007), which has provided a starting point for other models of mathematical reasoning (e.g., see Transitive Inference Mapping Model [TRIMM] by Halford et al., 1995) and a model called the *Five Strands* (5-S) by Kilpatrick and colleagues (2001), which consolidates many individual research studies of mathematical problem solving in educational domains (see also Mayer, 2003, 2008).

Our decision to review the ACT-R and 5-S models is driven in part by recommendations made from the National Mathematics Advisory Panel (NMAP) members in their 2008 report, *Foundations for Success*. In this report, panel members indicate the need for empirically based cognitive models to inform educational test design and instruction:

> It is essential to produce methodologically rigorous scientific research in crucial areas of national need, such as the teaching and learning of mathematics ... Specifically, more research is needed that identifies: 1) effective instructional practices, materials, and principles of instructional design, 2) mechanisms of learning, 3) ways to enhance teachers' effectiveness, including teacher education, that are directly tied to objective measures of student achievement, and 4) item and test features that improve the assessment of mathematical knowledge. (NMAP, 2008, p. xxvi)

NMAP members also identify the significance of algebra in mathematical learning and the need to identify the preparatory skills students require to enhance their conceptual understanding, computational fluency, and problem-solving proficiency in algebra. Although the panel presented other recommendations, such as making it a goal for students in kindergarten to grade eight to become proficient with fractions, these recommendations take a supportive role in relation to algebra. For example, proficiency in fractions is recommended insofar as it enhances the learning of algebraic knowledge and skills. Why the singular focus on algebra? Knowledge and skill in algebra are pivotal to mathematics achievement in later years (NMAP, 2008) because a solid grounding in algebra is considered a conceptual and procedural gateway for future mathematics courses. For example, in contrast to students who have completed only basic algebra (i.e., algebra I), students who have completed advanced algebra courses (i.e., algebra II) are more than twice as likely to go on to college- or university-level mathematics courses (NMAP, 2008).

Although there are many cognitive models of mathematical reasoning in the research literature, including models that are focused on younger age groups (e.g., Strategy Choice and Discovery Simulation [SCADS], see Shrager & Siegler, 1998; Central Conceptual Structures, see Case & Okamoto, 2000) and on relevant and highly specific cognitive processes (e.g., structure mapping in conceptual representations, see Gentner, Rattermann, Markman, & Kotovsky, 1995; strategy choice, see Siegler & Booth, 2004), few models place the spotlight on algebra proficiency. Additional cognitive models, such as the TRIMM by Halford et al. (1995), are based on Anderson's (1983) ACT* model, a previous version of the ACT-R. Therefore, in the limited space we have available, we will highlight Anderson's (1990) ACT-R model and the 5-S model (Kilpatrick et al., 2001). Both of these models have extensive empirical backing, are subject to diagrammatic representation, and were designed to inform the instruction and assessment of higher-level mathematical skills, including algebra, in adolescent populations. Thus, these models overlap with the target constructs and ages for many large-scale assessments.

The chapter is organized into four main sections. First, key findings of the PISA 2003 and 2006 test results in mathematics are mentioned to set the context for the need to understand mathematical achievement and improve its assessment, but also to show that underachievement in this domain may not reside simply with a lack of understanding about underlying processes in mathematical reasoning. Second, the ACT-R model (Anderson, 1990; Ritter et al., 2007) is presented and evaluated using the criteria of granularity, instructional relevance, and measurability. Third, the 5-S model (Kilpatrick et al., 2001; Mayer, 2003) is outlined and considered using the same three criteria. Fourth, concluding remarks are offered about the models in terms of their granularity, measurability, and instructional relevance vis-à-vis the feasibility of their use in the design and development of large-scale educational assessments.

KEY MATHEMATICAL FINDINGS FROM PISA 2003
AND 2006 ADMINISTRATIONS

The results of the Programme for International Student Assessment
(PISA) are helpful in discussions of achievement and testing for reasons outlined in Chapter 1, such as its methodological and psychometric rigor, focus on literacy (e.g., see de Lange, 2007), and size of
administration. There are other large-scale educational assessments
that highlight the comparatively poor mathematical performance of
U.S. examinees relative to students in other counties (e.g., TIMSS, see
de Lange, 2007; Provasnik, Gonzales, & Miller, 2009; see also NMAP,
2008). However, we focus on the results from the 2003 administration of PISA because these results reveal valuable information not only
about fifteen-year-olds' mathematical knowledge and skills, but also
about their attitudes toward mathematics.

Unlike the 2000 administration of PISA, which focused on reading literacy, the 2003 administration of PISA focused primarily on
mathematical literacy and attitudes toward mathematics. The results
of the 2003 administration were symptomatic of the malaise many
countries are experiencing with mathematics achievement. Although
approximately one-third of students in OECD countries were classified
in the top three levels of the mathematics scale (out of a total of six levels
and where a higher level indicates stronger performance), these propor-
tions varied dramatically across jurisdictions. For example, more than
50 percent of students in Finland and Korea were classified at level 4 or
higher, but just more than 25 percent of students in the United States,
Italy, and Portugal were classified into level 2. Struggling to reach level
2 indicates moderate to weak proficiency and is associated with a not-
so-happy face on the mathematical literacy scale (OECD, 2004, Figure
2.1, p. 45). Clearly, much more work remains to be done to increase
achievement in mathematics. Unlike the 2003 administration of PISA,
the focus of the 2006 administration was science literacy. Nonetheless,
mathematical literacy was still measured, and the results of the 2006

administration revealed that average performance for many students remained unchanged. To use the United States as an illustrative case, the average score in mathematics literacy for American students was 474 and below the average score of 498 for OECD countries (scores are standardized to have a mean of approximately 500 and a standard deviation of 100). The U.S.-based National Centre for Education Statistics (Baldi et al., 2007) reported that thirty-one jurisdictions (twenty-three OECD and eight non-OECD), on average, performed better than the United States, and sixteen jurisdictions performed worse.

What could account for this lackluster performance? A non-trivial number of students may perform poorly in mathematics because they find it boring. According to the attitudinal measures administered for PISA 2003, approximately 50 percent of students indicated being interested in the topics they were learning in mathematics class, but only 38 percent either agreed or strongly agreed that they engaged in mathematics because they enjoyed it (OECD, 2004). Less than 33 percent of students reported looking forward to their mathematics classes. In an index created to show the relationship between interest and enjoyment of mathematics and performance in mathematics, within-country results indicated that a point decrease (or corresponding increase) in interest and enjoyment of mathematics was related to a twelve-point decrease (or corresponding increase) in mathematics performance (OECD, 2004, p. 116). Moreover, girls had even less enthusiasm for mathematics than boys. Across OECD countries, 25 percent of girls agreed or strongly agreed, on average, with the statement that they enjoyed reading about math compared to 37 percent of boys. Although the strength of many of the relationships reported varied by country, it was generally found that students who indicated interest in mathematics tended to also perform better than students who indicated a lack of interest. Of course, no causal statements can be made about the direction of these effects because the data are correlational, so it is unknown whether students lag in their performance in mathematics because they are not interested in it or vice versa.

A more optimistic way to frame the discussion is to acknowledge that although students may not be disposed toward mathematics, they do seem to understand its value for the future. This is to say, students possess *instrumental motivation* for the subject. Again according to PISA 2003, 75 percent of fifteen-year-olds, on average across OECD countries, agreed or strongly agreed that expending effort in mathematics class is valuable because it will help them with their future jobs. However, the strength of the relationship between seeing the value of mathematics for future endeavors and mathematics performance differed by country, and was typically weaker than the association found between interest, enjoyment, and mathematics performance (OECD, 2004). In other words, knowing that mathematics might be helpful for the future may not provide enough direction or motivation for students to improve their mathematical achievement.

Mathematics certainly seems to have an "image problem" when it comes to its likeability among adolescents. Students enjoy mathematics far less than reading (OECD, 2004). There is a message in these types of results for educators, parents, and policy makers. For educators and parents, the message is that mathematics instruction and assessment may need to change, perhaps dramatically, to win back the students who are prone to dislike mathematics and who suffer from associated anxiety (see Spencer, Steele, & Quinn, 1999). The message for policy makers is that resources may not only need to be devoted to transforming how mathematical knowledge and skills are taught in the classroom, but also to how these knowledge and skills are assessed with large-scale tests. Otherwise, in the absence of an image make over, it may become increasingly difficult to change mathematics achievement for young learners.

It is necessary to note that students' mathematical performance is not simply related to interest, enjoyment, and motivation, but also to many other dimensions, some psychological, some environmental, and some that are probably a combination of the two. For instance, mathematics performance is also related to math anxiety (e.g., Morris,

Davis, & Hutchings, 1981; Spencer, Steele, & Quinn, 1999). A one-point increase on the PISA 2003 index of anxiety in mathematics translates, on average, to a reduction of thirty-five points in mathematics performance across OECD countries (OECD, 2004). Likewise, mathematics performance is related to self-efficacy or confidence in mathematics (e.g., Pajares & Miller, 1994; see also Bandura, 2006 for a general framework of social-cognitive theory). For PISA 2003, self-efficacy was found to be one of the strongest predictors of mathematics performance, accounting for 23 percent of the variance, on average, across OECD countries even when other student characteristics such as mathematics anxiety and interest were controlled.

Environmental factors that may contribute to disinterest in and lack of motivation for mathematics include the quality of instruction (Hill, Sleep, Lewis, & Ball, 2007; Wayne & Youngs, 2003) and the nature of assessments (e.g., Cameron & Pierce, 2002; Deci, Koestner, & Ryan, 1999; Hidi & Harackiewicz, 2000). In comparison to mathematics teachers who have less knowledge and skills, teachers who have greater mathematical proficiency tend to be associated with students who show stronger performance in quantitative disciplines (Hills et al., 2007). Presumably, the positive association between content knowledge in mathematics instruction and student achievement occurs because teachers with more content knowledge are better able to articulate, explain, and generate constructive feedback for students than teachers with less knowledge. In terms of assessment, the assignment of numerical or letter grades to student performance, often perceived by students as a distribution of rewards and punishments, has been found to lower levels of interest and motivation for learning mathematics (Deci et al., 1999). However, additional studies (e.g., Hidi & Harackiewicz, 2000) have found that the effects of rewards on motivation are not as straightforward as originally conceived. For example, Hidi and Harackiewicz (2000) found that rewards were less likely to negatively influence students' task motivation when students already expressed little interest in engaging in a task. In their review of the literature, Cameron and Pierce (2002) explain that rewards do not automatically lower motivation for a task. For example, when a reward (such as a grade for an assignment) is directly tied to successful task performance or problem solving, and not simply for participating or expending effort, it does not negatively influence motivation. It appears, then, that when a reward, such as a grade, is perceived as *informative feedback* about the nature of task performance, it may not adversely affect motivation for engaging in problem solving endeavors.

Based on these findings, then, one may speculate that students' motivation or interest for engaging in mathematical performances should not decrease if the grades assigned to these performances are viewed as informative. Toward this end, designing large-scale educational assessments of mathematical knowledge and skills based on empirically based cognitive models of mathematical reasoning that accurately reflect the learning paths students acquire on their way to expertise may be one way to help stave off disinterest in mathematics and lack of motivation among students. That is, measures of mathematical knowledge and skills based on theoretical frameworks that directly link knowledge, skills, and performance may demonstrate to and persuade students that reliable and valid gauges of their proficiency are feasible and even instructive. In the next section, we introduce an empirically based cognitive model of mathematical reasoning that has received substantial empirical backing in the learning scientific literature.

ANDERSON'S ADAPTIVE CONTROL OF THOUGHT – RATIONAL (ACT-R) MODEL FOR MATHEMATICAL REASONING

Model Description

Psychologists at Carnegie Mellon University, led by J. R. Anderson, have been working on understanding the underlying processes associated with quantitative thinking for more than twenty-five years. However, the

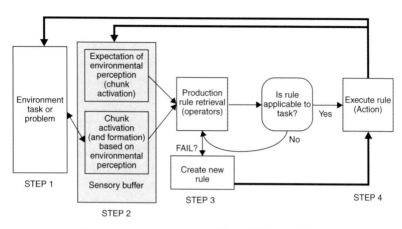

FIGURE 5.1. Diagrammatic overview of the ACT-R model. Step 1 shows the environment and the signal that is perceived when a mathematical problem or task is to be solved. Step 2 shows the activation or formation of chunks (declarative memory) based upon perception of environmental variables (chunks may also be activated based upon the expectation of what is occurring in the environment). Step 3 shows the retrieval of procedural memory (production rules) subject to the matching of antecedent conditions with activated chunks. Step 4 shows the execution of the rule and its feedback to the environmental task or problem that originally gave rise to it.

model, Adaptive Control of Thought – Rational (ACT-R; see Anderson, 1990) was not designed solely to account for mathematical reasoning. ACT-R is a cognitive (processing) model based on accumulated findings in basic, applied, and field-tested research (Ritter et al., 2007). As a cognitive model specified at the algorithmic level of analysis, the mechanisms of ACT-R are described at a sufficiently precise level to facilitate their computer implementation (Ritter et al., 2007, p. 249). The model can also be used to account for cognition in a variety of content domains. Figure 5.1 contains a diagrammatic outline of the model.

Background
ACT-R grew out of human associative memory theory (Anderson & Bower, 1973), an early framework describing the relevant types of knowledge believed to be central to human cognition (Anderson, 1996).

The ACT-R model is also based on Newell's (1972, 1973) *production rule* architecture. With the inclusion of productions, ACT-R provides an account of human cognition with the specificity of a computer programming language. In addition, the inclusion of production rules permits ACT-R to account for a wide array of knowledge and skills. In educational applications, ACT-R is used to account for and predict student learning, thinking, and performance by means of a *cognitive tutor*. The cognitive tutor functions as a working extension of ACT-R to formalize and operationalize the fundamental assumptions and mechanisms of ACT-R within a particular domain such as mathematics (see Anderson, Boyle, Corbett, & Lewis, 1990). Cognitive tutors are designed to embody the domain-specific knowledge and skills necessary to direct instruction, assessment, and feedback for student learning. Cognitive tutors have been used and evaluated in a variety of educational-content domains, including computer programming (Anderson et al., 1990), general mathematics (Anderson, Boyle, Farrell, & Reiser, 1987; Ritter et al., 2007), geometry (e.g., GPT and ANGLE tutors, see Koedinger & Anderson, 1993), and algebra (Koedinger, Anderson, Hadley, & Mark, 1997; Ritter et al., 2007).

Framework

A full description of the ACT-R model is beyond the scope of this chapter, and the reader is referred to Anderson (1990; and Anderson et al., 2004) for complete theoretical and algorithmic details. The key components, summarized in this section, provide the basic information with which to begin considering the model for the design and development of large-scale educational assessments. The ACT-R model is based on three assumptions: First, human cognition is believed to involve two kinds of knowledge: declarative and procedural. Declarative knowledge is knowledge of "facts, images, and sounds" (Ritter et al., 2007, p. 250), and procedural knowledge is knowledge of how to do things. Procedural knowledge is what we often refer to as "skills." Anderson (1990) explains that all tasks involve some combination of both types of knowledge. In the course of acquiring proficiency in a domain, people normally begin with declarative-type knowledge. With sustained practice, however, this declarative-type knowledge morphs into a smooth, effortless form of procedural knowledge that is *automated*. Procedural knowledge is governed by production rules (Newell, 1972, 1973), which specify the conditions under which knowledge should be applied in the form of an action. For example, when the condition of *a ball coming at you* is met, the action of *ducking your head* is executed to avoid the ball. Production rules normally take the form:

IF condition, THEN action.

A second assumption of the ACT-R model is that all tasks can be decomposed into a set of declarative and procedural knowledge components. Successful problem solving is expected to take place when the combination of these knowledge components is activated for fulfilling a task. A third assumption of the ACT-R model is that sustained practice strengthens declarative and procedural knowledge, and lack of practice weakens declarative and procedural knowledge. Knowledge that has been strengthened is expected to be recalled quickly, and knowledge that has not been strengthened is essentially lost unless substantial effort is expended to retrieve it. Declarative and procedural knowledge are used as building blocks to assemble problem-solving strategies. Problem-solving strategies vary in strength among individual students (see also SCADS by Shrager & Siegler, 1998), and any given strategy selected to solve a task is chosen, in part, as a function of its relative strength (Ritter et al., 2007). The goal of mathematics education is to strengthen accurate and adaptive problem-solving strategies and weaken maladaptive strategies for learning.

These three assumptions form the basis of how human cognition and learning are viewed in the ACT-R model. Yet what are the origins of knowledge for ACT-R? Anderson (1996) addresses this question by stating that ACT-R ascribes the origins of knowledge to a sensationalist theory, which means that knowledge is believed to originate from encodings of the environment. For example, our visual system scans the environment and takes in sensory information about objects and their attributes. So far, only knowledge acquired through the visual modality has been considered in the ACT-R model, but there are other modalities that could also be included (Anderson, Matessa, & Douglass, 1995). A second question: How is the knowledge that is encoded from the environment (i.e., the output from our visual system) represented in the mind? The answer to this question touches on key representational assumptions of the ACT-R model. Anderson (1996) explains that all encoded information is initially represented as a *chunk* of declarative knowledge (see Treisman & Sato, 1990). For example, consider the following chunk:

> Fact 2+4
> isa addition-fact
> addend 1   two
> addend 2   four
> sum   six.

Two observations can be made about chunks, generally, based on the chunk for 2 + 4 = 6. First, chunks are akin to schema-like structures with *isa* pointers that indicate the category to which the fact belongs. Second, chunks contain the attributes or features that comprise the fact (e.g., addend 1, addend 2, and sum). Illustrated in Figure 5.2 is a schematic representation of the chunk for the fact 2 + 4 = 6. At the center of the figure, the base-level activation, B_i, for the fact is shown. The strength, S_{ij}, for each attribute is also included, along with the weight, W_j, of each contextual attribute, addend 1 and addend 2. At any given moment, the activation of chunk i in ACT-R is given by the following:

$$A_i = B_i + \Sigma_j W_j S_{ji;}$$

Activation Level = Base Level + Contextual Priming;

Log (posterior odds) = Log(Prior odds) + Log(Likelihood ratio).

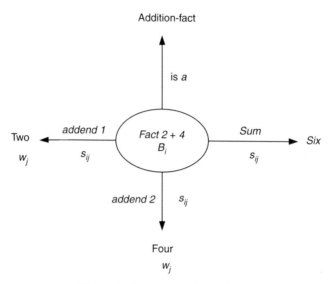

FIGURE 5.2. Network illustration of chunk in ACT-R model.

When mapped onto its Bayesian log form, the activation of chunk *i* is equal to the prior odds that its deployment has been useful in the past (base-level activation) plus the likelihood of its contextual features being primed in a given domain. To the extent that contextual attributes *j* are strongly associated with chunk *i*, the activation of fact 2 + 4 = 6 will be made available to the learner in a given domain.

Unlike declarative knowledge, procedural knowledge (i.e., skill) is not represented as a chunk, but rather as a production rule. As mentioned previously, production rules take the form of *IF condition, THEN action* statements consisting of the antecedent conditions that must be met before actions are executed. Often when the conditions of an initial production rule cannot be met, additional production rules are introduced to create sub-goals that will satisfy the conditions of the initial rules. For example, imagine a student is asked to solve the following set of equations:

$$4x + 8 = 20$$
$$4x = 12.$$

In order to solve these equations, a sub-goal must be introduced, namely, solving for $4x = 12$. However, before the sub-goal is introduced, the student must recognize that the $4x$ in the first equation is the same as the $4x$ in the second, and that $8 + 12 = 20$. Once the student recognizes these relationships, the sub-goal is introduced with the following production rule:

IF the goal is to solve an equation of the form

argument + $n1$ = $n3$ (where argument corresponds to 4x, n1 to 8, and n3 to 20)

and $n1 + n2 = n3$ (where n1 corresponds to 8, n2 to 12, and n3 to 20)

THEN make the goal to solve the equation of the form *argument* = $n2$.

Procedural knowledge, consisting of IF-THEN productions, has a hierarchical structure, where certain conditions must be satisfied before actions can take effect. Declarative knowledge informs production rules by providing the contents of conditions and actions. Knowledge acquisition, and ultimately expertise, within a domain emerges as chunks, and production rules are combined systematically to create complex and multifaceted networks of understanding. However, knowledge acquisition is not simply about accumulating chunks and production rules. According to ACT-R, expertise within a domain is also based on an increasingly accurate reading, based on past performance, of the contextual features in the environment that necessitate specific forms of knowledge (see Anderson, 1996, for full details). Next, the ACT-R model is considered with respect to granularity, measurability, and instructional relevance.

Model Evaluation: Granularity, Measurability, and Instructional Relevance

Granularity

The granularity of the ACT-R model is similar to previous models we have considered, namely, Kintsch's (1998) CI model and Klahr and

Dunbar's (1988) SDDS model. As with the CI and SDDS models, the ACT-R model is specified at both a fine and coarse level of granularity. The fine level of granularity is observed in the specification of chunks, variables associated with the activation of chunks, and production rules needed to program these ACT-R processes. The coarse-level aspects of the ACT-R model are observed in the assumptions made about the structure of cognition, namely, the types of knowledge (i.e., declarative and procedural) underlying learning and problem solving, and the outcomes arising from strong (rehearsed) versus weak (unrehearsed) knowledge. Strong knowledge, in the form of chunks, rules or both, can be recalled and used readily to solve problems and tasks, whereas weak knowledge is retrieved only with considerable effort and, even then, may not correspond to the contextual conditions to which it is needed.

Measurability

As with discussions of previous models, one approach for evaluating the measurability of the ACT-R is to consider how its assumptions have been operationalized in empirical investigations. For example, the ACT-R has been used to account for and predict student learning, thinking, and performance by means of a *cognitive tutor*. The cognitive tutor is an application of ACT-R that operationalizes the declarative and procedural knowledge components within particular domains such as mathematics (see Anderson, Boyle, Corbett, & Lewis, 1990). For instance, consider the PAT (Koedinger & Anderson, 1997) or PUMP Algebra Tutor used to support the PUMP or Pittsburgh Urban Mathematics Project algebra curriculum for grade-nine students. The PUMP curriculum was developed to help teach students algebra skills through relevant real-world problems such as "checking the amount of a paycheck, estimating the cost of a rental car for a trip, and choosing between long-distance telephone service offers from AT&T and MCI" (Koedinger & Anderson, 1997, p. 33). Algebraic problems and tasks were developed and added to the cognitive tutor, PAT, with the help of teachers who entered the problem information into the tutor using authoring functions. These authoring functions allowed the teachers to describe the problems and solutions as well as edit the guesses the tutor made about structural or principled relations in the problems so as to facilitate student problem solving.

The PAT included a specific set of declarative and procedural knowledge components expected to account for algebraic problem solving at a grade-nine level. For example, PAT included inductive routines based not on learned textbook algorithms, but rather on investigations of students' emerging mathematical cognition (see Koedinger & Anderson, 1990, 1991; see also Larkin & Simon, 1987). Inductive routines were formalized as IF-THEN production rules that reflected successful and unsuccessful pathways for algebraic problem solving. Koedinger and Anderson (1990) found that the use of dia-grammatic configurations or geometric images (whole-part schemas, see also Greeno, 1983) aided students as they reasoned to determine when particular algebra procedures were needed. Furthermore, PAT included two methods, *model* and *knowledge tracing*, to inform and monitor student learning explicitly. Model tracing was used to chart students' problem-solving steps on a task as they worked toward a solution, and knowledge tracing kept track of students' overall learn-ing as they responded to all the tasks in the set. Knowledge tracing results were made available to teachers and students with a *skillom-eter window*, which indicated the skills the students had acquired or had yet to learn (see Corbett, Anderson, Carver, & Brancolini, 1994). Students initiated interaction with PAT by taking twenty to thirty min-utes to read through the teacher-developed problems and tasks, and answered questions by considering data tables, spreadsheets, graphs, and symbolic calculators. As students worked through problems, PAT monitored the interactions and provided feedback where needed. When a student committed an error, PAT flagged it without comment and simply highlighted the problematic entry in bold text to draw attention to it. If the error occurred repeatedly (e.g., confusing x and y coordinates in graphing) and PAT recognized it as an instance of a misconception, then PAT introduced a commentary to inform the student of another way to think of the material.

Learning acquired via PAT was evaluated by a series of assessments, including the Iowa Algebra Aptitude Test and a subset of the SAT for grade-nine students. Two additional tests, the Problem Situation Test and the Representations Test, were designed deliberately to reflect the National Council of Teachers of Mathematics (NCTM) learning objectives and the PUMP curriculum. The Problem Situation Test measured students' ability to investigate algebraic problems presented verbally, and the Representations Test measured students' ability to translate algebraic content into graphs and equations.

Surprisingly, neither of these two tests was designed based on the declarative and procedural knowledge components underlying the PAT or the information acquired by PAT (via the model tracing and knowledge tracing) about students' knowledge and misconceptions. As such, the cognitive tutor did not seem to function as a model for assessment as much as a model for instruction – that is, an intelligent tutor guiding the student through a pathway of domain-specific knowledge and skills for problem solving and learning. This outcome suggests that the measurability of the ACT-R might be indirectly observed only by the success rate of cognitive tutors in helping students learn. In other words, the measurability of the ACT-R model might be observed in each interaction that takes place between the cognitive tutor and the student. Every time a student tackles a new problem, the hint or help the tutor extends to the student, with subsequent success, provides evidence for the adequacy of the declarative and procedural routines built into the tutor. In this way, the cognitive tutor *is both teacher and test* to every student it guides – a form of dynamic testing that not only includes presenting problems and tasks to students, but also involves tracking their progress (via model and knowledge tracing) and providing feedback via the skillometer. In the following description by Anderson and Schunn (2000), the aim of the tutor is presented in much the same way as one would describe a good teacher and assessment:

> Our tutors then monitor students' problem-solving and try to diagnose what the students know and do not know, providing help and scaffolding to deal with their weaknesses and dynamic instruction to repair the holes in their knowledge. (p. 19)

In comparison to large-scale testing, however, this is a vastly different form of assessment, because it not only measures student learning (knowledge tracing), but also provides hints when students encounter impasses. It is important to note that although the cognitive tutor operationalizes knowledge and skills outlined in the ACT-R, and although standardized test items (e.g., Iowa Algebra Aptitude Test) have been used to measured student learning with applications of the cognitive tutor, we have found no published accounts of large-scale test items developed *directly* to measure knowledge and skills outlined or derived from the ACT-R.

Instructional Relevance

The ACT-R model along with the cognitive tutor is highly relevant for instructional initiatives. The cognitive tutor mimics the function of teachers by providing individualized instruction to students in specific domains such as algebra. However, the design of cognitive tutors requires extensive work because researchers must first identify and codify relevant declarative and procedural knowledge, including chunks and production rules, and then program these knowledge components and processes into the tutor. Programmed algorithms not only must reflect student thinking, problem solving, and learning at a given age level and domain, but also must include additional functions that help the tutor recognize impasses and the appropriate hints and feedback to provide students in an effort to help them along. It is precisely the identification and codification of domain-specific declarative and procedural knowledge that might be most relevant to using the ACT-R to generate large-scale educational-assessment items.

KILPATRICK, SWAFFORD, AND FINDELL'S FIVE STRANDS (5-S) MODEL

Model Description

Background

In 1998 the Committee on Mathematics Learning was formed by the National Research Council to address concerns about the "shortage of reliable information" (Kilpatrick et al., 2001, p. 3) on how children learn mathematics and the consistently poor performance of American students on international and national assessments. These concerns had originated from the Division of Elementary, Secondary, and Informal Education in the National Science Foundation's Directorate for Education and Human Resources and the U.S. Department of Education's office of Educational Research and Improvement. It was the aim of the National Research Council to have the Committee on Mathematics Learning address these information deficiencies by:

1. Synthesizing the rich and diverse research on pre-kindergarten through eighth-grade mathematics learning.
2. Providing research-based recommendations for teaching, teacher education, and curriculum to improve student learning and identify areas where research was needed.
3. Giving advice and guidance to educators, researchers, publishers, policy makers, and parents.

The committee compiled their findings in a 2001 report, *Adding it Up: Helping Children Learn Mathematics* (Kilpatrick et al., 2001). In the report, students' poor mathematical performance was attributed, in part, to inadequate assessments and poor classroom instruction:

> Although intended to ensure that all students have an opportunity to learn mathematics, some of these [large-scale educational] assessments are not well aligned with the curriculum. Those that were originally designed to rank order students, schools, and districts seldom provide information that can be used to improve instruction. (Kilpatrick et al., 2001, p.4)

In the 2001 report, the 5-S cognitive model was introduced and presented as a framework for synthesizing the research on mathematics learning and as a basis for making recommendations to stakeholders and researchers. One of the recommendations focused on the need to reconsider the design and development of assessments of mathematical proficiency to reflect state-of-the-art research findings. However, as a quick follow-up to this recommendation, Kilpatrick et al. (2001) noted that "much of the research on mathematics teaching and learning has been conducted to address narrower learning goals" (p. 14). We reiterate this observation here because it is also our impression that one of the major challenges for integrating the learning sciences with educational assessment is bridging the gap between the narrow research questions asked by learning scientists and the broad testing objectives required by large-scale educational-assessment programs.

Framework

The 5-S model was developed by the Committee on Mathematics Learning based on their review and synthesis of the research literature on mathematics learning in the educational domain. The 5-S model, shown diagrammatically in Figure 5.3, highlights the following broad components as necessary for the acquisition of mathematical proficiency (see Kilpatrick et al., 2001, p. 6):

1. *Conceptual understanding* of mathematical principles, knowledge, operations, and relations.

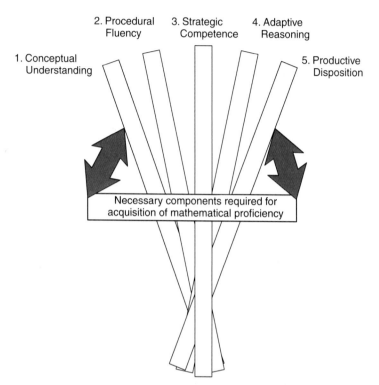

FIGURE 5.3. Diagrammatic overview of the Five Strands (5-S) Model. The first component is conceptual understanding. The second component is procedural fluency. The third component is strategic competence. The fourth component is adaptive reasoning. The fifth component is productive disposition. Adapted from Kilpatrick, J., Swafford, J. & Findell, B. (Ed.). (2001). *Adding It Up: Helping Children Learn Mathematics*. Washington, DC, USA: National Academies Press.

2. *Procedural fluency* in carrying out the skills associated with mathematical knowledge, in particular, showing flexibility, efficiency, and appropriateness in skill deployment.

3. *Strategic competence* as demonstrated by formulating, representing, and solving mathematical problems.

4. *Adaptive reasoning* as shown by the ability to engage in logical thought, reflection, explanation, and justification.

5. *Productive disposition* toward viewing mathematics as useful and as a means for solving problems in the real world, and recognizing the effort and self-efficacy that must be devoted to acquiring competence in mathematics.

The components distilled in the 5-S model appear to be well-established aspects of mathematical reasoning and problem solving. In fact, a similar framework is proposed by Mayer (2003, 2008), who describes proficient mathematical reasoning and problem solving as consisting of a set of four cognitive processes (i.e., [a] problem translation, [b] problem integration, [c] solution, planning, and monitoring, and [d] solution execution) and a set of seven types of knowledge (i.e., factual knowledge, linguistic knowledge, schematic knowledge, strategic knowledge, meta-strategic knowledge, beliefs, and procedural knowledge). The similarities between Kilpatrick's et al. 5-S model and Mayer's framework are striking, including overlap in many of the knowledge and skills identified as central to mathematical reasoning. For example, Kilpatrick's et al. conceptual understanding corresponds to Mayer's factual, linguistic, and schematic knowledge (i.e., facts and concepts).

As shown in Figure 5.3, each component of the 5-S model is presented as interwoven and, hence, inter-dependent with the others. None of the components is individually sufficient for the acquisition of mathematical proficiency; rather, all are necessary to gain mathematical expertise. Kilpatrick et al. cite relevant research to support the inclusion of all five components in the 5-S model. The first component, *conceptual understanding*, is supported by studies indicating that students who have developed well-organized, well-connected knowledge structures exhibit better representations of numerical relations, greater retention of information, more fluent computation, fewer errors, and more effective implementation of strategies in novel situations than students who lack well-structured knowledge (see e.g., Bransford, Brown, & Cocking, 1999; Greeno, Pearson, & Schoenfeld,

1997). Kilpatrick et al. also illustrate that when students acquire basic conceptual knowledge in mathematics, such as the commutative axiom in addition (e.g., 8+7=7+8), they effectively reduce the number of addition facts they need to learn by half.

The second component, *procedural fluency*, is supported by studies indicating that students who possess facility in skill execution are more successful at estimating mathematical solutions, selecting from a variety of strategies, and circumventing basic computational errors than students without this facility. The following example illustrates a common error in subtraction, in which the larger digit is subtracted from the smaller digit even when the smaller digit is the minuend (or top number) in the problem:

4	3
−2	5
2	2.

This error can be avoided when students begin to learn the conceptual knowledge underlying subtraction; namely, that the minuend reflects a set number that needs to be larger than the subtrahend (the number in the bottom), otherwise one cannot take away from a quantity that does not exist. When this problem structure occurs, the next highest number category must be used to "borrow" a set quantity to make the minuend larger (e.g., tens, hundreds, etc.). Conceptual understanding has been shown to foster procedural fluency as students increasingly understand the rationale for the mathematical procedures they implement (see e.g., Alibali, 1999; Brown & Burton, 1978; Hatano, 1988; Hiebert et al., 1997; Kaminski, Sloutsky, & Heckler, 2009; Pesek & Kirshner, 2000; Skwarchuk & Anglin, 2002; Stewart & Thomas, 2010; Wu, 1999).

The third component, *strategic competence*, is what is normally known as *problem-solving* skill. It is born from procedural fluency and marks the ability to correctly represent and apply strategies to generate a solution to a task. Students who exhibit greater strategic competence generate more structurally based representations of problem information, which contain relevant task features, and less surface-based representations. Consider the following sock problem:

> The Bay sells socks for $5/pair.
> This price is $1 **less** than socks at Sears.
> **How much** do 4 pairs of socks cost at Sears?

Students who generate surface-based representations are likely to focus on keywords to make sense of the problem information. In the sock problem, the keyword *less* is mentioned after the amounts of $5 and $1. Given where the word *less* occurs in the problem, many students who are prone to focus on keywords are likely to commit the error of subtracting 1 from 5, yielding 4. The keywords *how much* are also used in the sock problem, again prompting students who focus excessively on keywords to multiply 4 (the number after the words *how much*) by 4 (the number previously computed and associated with the keyword *less*), to generate a solution of $16. Of course, this is not the correct response. However, it is a type of response that often arises from surface-based representations, which tend to include disparate pieces of information and reflect a rigid focus on keywords. A structurally based problem representation focuses less on keywords and, instead, includes a substantive depiction of the problem information, such as a number line to show the relations among numerical entities. A student who generates a structurally based problem representation notices that the price of socks at the Bay is actually smaller in value than the price of socks at Sears, and multiplies the correct price of $6 by 4 to yield $24 for 4 pairs of socks at Sears. Such strategic competence is especially useful when novel problems are encountered, to which no known algorithms can be applied to reach a solution. The ability of students to represent the structural or substantive elements associated with these problem types is essential to the discovery of solutions (e.g., see weak methods of search in SDDS model, this volume, Chapter 4; see also

Gentner, Loewenstein, & Thompson, 2003; Miura & Okamoto, 2003; National Research Council, 2009; Quilici & Mayer, 1996; Siegler & Araya, 2005; Wiest, 2000).

The fourth component, *adaptive reasoning*, requires students to adapt and reason through a variety of problems, even those that are unfamiliar (e.g., Donovan & Bransford, 2005; Hiebert et al., 1997; Schoenfeld, 1992; Wynn, 1995). It involves facility with the use of metaphor, analogy, and the detection of patterns across mathematical exemplars. Adaptive reasoning is exhibited when students understand the rationale for selecting a particular strategy to solve a task and are able to justify their work and their ideas, for example, by recognizing when a proof is useful and when an application of a strategy or principle is appropriate to demonstrate a point (Maher & Martino, 1996). According to Kilpatrick et al., students successfully show reasoning skills in their work when at least three conditions are satisfied: First, students have acquired a sufficiently large conceptual knowledge base along with the procedural fluency to correctly execute selected strategies. Second, the task information is comprehended accurately and offers a motivating experience for students. Third, the environmental context in which problem solving takes place is well known and considered safe by students. Adaptive reasoning therefore requires students to have a solid base in the components already discussed – conceptual understanding, procedural fluency, and strategic competence – in addition to the final strand or component, a productive disposition.

The fifth component, *a productive disposition*, refers to motivation and personal epistemology (e.g., see also KPI model, this volume, Chapter 4); that is, it refers to students recognizing the value of learning mathematics as a tool for problem solving, structuring, and formalizing ideas and concepts. Students who have productive dispositions are able to perceive that mathematics, as any other subject domain, is learned through deliberate practice and effort. Without such a productive disposition, students do not normally exhibit interest in expending the time and effort required to acquire conceptual understanding, fluency in the execution of mathematical strategies, competence in the range and use of particular strategies, and in the chains of reasoning required to substantiate and justify applied procedures. Researchers are increasingly underscoring the importance of learning values across academic domains (e.g., Anderson & Schunn, 2000; Bendixen & Feucht, 2010; Hofer & Pintrich, 1997; Kuhn, 2005; Schommer, 1990; Stanovich, 2009). As with the ACT-R model, in the next section the 5-S model is evaluated in terms of granularity, measurability, and instructional relevance.

Model Evaluation: Granularity, Measurability, and Instructional Relevance

Granularity

The granularity of the 5-S model is coarse. There is no processing model specified at an algorithmic level of analysis underlying each of the five strands or components. Rather, each component reflects general knowledge and skills required for the acquisition and maintenance of mathematical proficiency. However, the knowledge structures and processing skills within each component could be described at a finer level of detail. In the case of strategic competence, for instance, the processes underlying the knowledge and skills associated with formulating problem information, generating numerical, symbolic, verbal, or graphical representations, applying strategies for a plan of execution, and executing the problem-solving plan could be articulated at a finer level of description. The exactitude of these descriptions could be useful in the design of test items that incrementally measure narrow mathematical proficiencies. Such test items are not currently available. Depending on the specificity of the descriptions, however, these descriptions could also prove to be too detailed, and therefore irrelevant, for the broad-bandwidth objectives of large-scale educational assessments.

Measurability

The measurability of the 5-S model is observed in the empirical studies and tasks cited in support of each of the components. Consider strategic competence once again. One type of mathematical task used to assess aspects of strategic competence is the *non-routine problem*. Non-routine problems involve tasks in which the learner cannot directly apply a single algorithm or solution plan, but rather must select from a series of possible strategies or, alternatively, create a unique solution by combining aspects of several algorithms (see weak methods of search in SDDS model, this volume, Chapter 4). The following example is a non-routine problem (Kilpatrick et al., 2001, p. 126):

> *A cycle shop has a total of 36 bicycles and tricycles in stock.*
>
> *Collectively there are 80 wheels.*
>
> *How many bikes and how many tricycles are there?*

According to Kilpatrick et al., there are at least three ways to solve this problem. One way is to reason through the problem information, and to recognize that both bikes and tricycles must have at least 2 wheels. When 36 is multiplied by 2 it yields 72 wheels, which is 8 wheels short of the 80 wheels indicated in the problem. The remaining 8 wheels must belong to the tricycles since they each have 3 wheels. Of the 36 bicycles and tricycles in stock, 28 are bicycles (i.e., $36 - 8 = 28$) and 8 are tricycles. Another strategy is the use of *guess and check* (similar to the *generate-and-test* strategy of Newell & Simon, 1972; see also weak methods of search in SDDS model, Chapter 4, this volume), which involves guessing on a number of bikes (say 18) and a number of tricycles (say 10) and calculating the number of resulting wheels (i.e., $18 \times 2 = 36$ and $18 \times 3 = 30$ for a total of 90 wheels), then readjusting the number of bikes and tricycles entered into the calculation based on this initial result; for instance, increasing the number of bikes to 24, and reducing the number of tricycles to 12. In this case, the resulting number of wheels is 84 (i.e., $24 \times 2 = 48$ and $12 \times 3 = 36$), and the new guess again overshoots the target. Another round of the guess-and-check strategy would take into account this latest result and readjust the next set of values entered into the calculation of bikes and tricycles. Alternatively, a superior strategy involves using an algebraic representation to formulate the problem as follows:

> Let b stand for the number of bikes and t stand for the number of tricycles
> Then $b + t = 36$ and
> $2b + 3t = 80$.

This is now a system of equations that can be solved to yield the answer of 80. Non-routine problems are one way to determine the range of strategic knowledge a student has acquired about problem solving in mathematics. Ideally, students who possess high levels of strategic competence can identify a range of possible approaches, including reasoning through a problem, guess and check, and algebraic approaches.

Many of the tasks used to measure components of the 5-S model involve traditional mathematical stimuli with extended questions designed to evaluate deeper aspects of mathematical proficiency (Niss, 2007). To evaluate adaptive reasoning, for example, a student is asked to justify or *prove* why the answer provided is adequate or follows from the task information. In the example of the non-routine problem mentioned previously, this would entail having students indicate *how they know* that 28 bicycles and 8 tricycles is the correct answer. The aim of this form of open-ended questioning is to evaluate whether a student is simply "plugging-in" numbers or whether a student is aware of the rationale for the formulation and representation chosen to solve the problem. One of the critiques of modern large-scale educational assessments is that they may measure some aspects of conceptual understanding and procedural fluency but often fail to measure higher-level skills such as adaptive reasoning (Bonnet, 2002; Niss, 2007). For example, Niss (2007), in his review of the research of mathematics teaching and learning for the NCTM, indicates:

> Little progress has been made as regards the assessment of essential
> ingredients in mathematical competencies, such as asking questions,
> conjecturing, posing problems, constructing argument, including
> formal proofs, making use of and switching between representa-
> tions, communication, and suchlike. Not only is research lacking,
> assessment instruments are largely lacking as well. (p. 1306)

One challenge to including many open-ended items on large-scale
educational tests is the cost of reliably scoring responses (see measurability of CI model and essay-type items, Chapter 3, this volume). This
problem could be addressed by designing multiple-choice items with
options reflecting rationales, including stronger and weaker justifica-
tions that characterize students' problem-solving approaches (Briggs,
Alonzo, Schwab, & Wilson, 2006).

Instructional Relevance

The instructional relevance of the 5-S model is high. This is not surprising given that the model was developed by the National Research
Council's Committee on Mathematics Learning. The model therefore includes many of the components that researchers and, more
importantly, educators believe are important aspects of mathematical proficiency (e.g., Lester, 2007; see also Clements & Sarama, 2007;
Kieran, 2007; Schoenfeld, 2007, in NCTM's Second Handbook
of Research on Mathematics Teaching and Learning). The model
includes knowledge (conceptual understanding), skill (procedural
fluency), problem solving (strategic competence), higher-order competencies such as reasoning (adaptive), and habits of mind (productive
disposition). These are all components that could be modeled in the
classroom and targeted as outcomes for learning mathematics.

CONCLUSION AND DISCUSSION

This chapter focused on cognitive models of mathematical reasoning.
As with the other academic domains covered in this book, there is

abundant empirical literature on this topic. We did not provide an exhaustive review, but rather a targeted presentation and review of two diagrammatic cognitive models that have garnered extensive empirical support and reflect distinct approaches in the identification of knowledge and skills for mathematical reasoning and performance, including algebraic thinking. Anderson's ACT-R model reflects a cognitive processing model of human cognition that has been applied broadly to mathematical reasoning. As a cognitive processing model, it is specified with sufficient detail to guide the creation of algorithms for implementation on a computer. It is also specified at a coarser level of detail with pointers to two types of knowledge (declarative and procedural) and how these knowledge types are strengthened – via practice. One component the ACT-R model misses but the 5-S model includes is dispositions for mathematical thinking. This is normally a coarse-level component.

As observed in Kuhn's KPI model of scientific reasoning and discovery in the previous chapter, thinking dispositions and values or, alternatively, meta-cognitive strategies have become increasingly important variables in the study of knowledge and skill acquisition. Mathematical reasoning is no exception. Kilpatrick et al. label one of their strands in the 5-S model productive disposition, indicating the supportive nature values and beliefs about mathematical problem solving play in the development of proficiency. As highlighted in our discussion of the 2003 PISA, attitudes are a source of evidence about the thoughts, beliefs, and values students develop in relation to mathematics and the effort they believe is required to acquire mathematical proficiency. These values exert a consequential influence on academic performance. Researchers are also highlighting mathematical affect, beliefs, and metacognition as important variables in how well mathematical content knowledge and skill are learned (e.g., Anderson & Schunn, 2000; Bendixen & Feucht, 2010; Hofer & Pintrich, 1997; Kuhn, 2005; Lesh & Zawojewski, 2007; Lester, Garafalo & Kroll, 1989; Lester & Kehle, 2003; Schoenfeld, 1992; Schommer, 1990; Stanovich, 2009; Wilson & Clark, 2004). Although this component may not serve as a content guide for the design of large-scale educational test items, it is a meaningful component to include in cognitive models of mathematical reasoning, because it may help us to understand the origins of the full range of knowledge and skills associated with mathematical learning that, in turn, may help us develop more comprehensive educational assessments.

REFERENCES

Alberta Education (2009). *Information bulletin: Pure mathematics 30.* Edmonton, Alberta. Author.

Alibali, M.W. (1999). How children change their minds: Strategy change can be gradual or abrupt. *Developmental Psychology, 35,* 127– 145.

Alibali, M., Knuth, E., Hattikudur, S., McNeil, N., & Stephens, A. (2007). A longitudinal examination of middle school students' understandings of the equal sign and performance solving equivalent equations. *Mathematical Thinking and Learning, 9,* 221–247.

Anderson, J.R. (1996). ACT: A simple theory of complex cognition. *American Psychologist, 51,* 355–365.

(1990). *The adaptive character of thought.* Hillsdale, NJ: Erlbaum.

Anderson, J.R., Bothell, D., Byrne, M.D., Douglass, S., Lebière, C., & Qin, Y. (2004). An integrated theory of the mind. *Psychological Review, 111,* 1036–1060.

Anderson, J.R. & Bower, G.H. (1973). *Human associative memory.* Washington, DC: Winston and Sons.

Anderson, J.R., Boyle, C.F., Corbett, A.T., & Lewis, M.W. (1990). Cognitive modeling and intelligent tutoring. *Artificial Intelligence, 42,* 7–49.

Anderson, J.R., Boyle, C.F., Farrell, R., & Reiser, B.J. (1987). Cognitive principles in the design of computer tutors. In P. Morris (Ed.), *Modelling cognition* (pp. 93–133). Chichester, U.K.: Wiley.

Anderson, J.R., Matessa, M. & Douglass, S. (1995). The ACT-R theory of visual attention. In *Proceedings of the Seventeenth Annual Cognitive Science Society,* 61–65.

Anderson, J.R. & Schunn, C.D. (2000). Implications of the ACT-R learning theory: No magic bullets. In R. Glaser (Ed.), *Advances in instructional psychology: Educational design and cognitive science, Vol. 5* (pp. 1–33). Mahwah, NJ: Erlbaum.

Ashcraft, M.H. & Kirk, E.P. (2001). The relationships among working memory, math anxiety, and performance. *Journal of Experimental Psychology: General, 130,* 224–237.

Ashcraft, M.H. & Krause, J.A. (2007). Working memory, math performance, and math anxiety. *Psychonomic Bulletin and Review, 14,* 243–248.

Baldi, S., Jin, Y., Skemer, M., Green, P.J., & Herget, D. (2007). *Highlights from PISA 2006: Performance of U.S. 15-year-old students in science and mathematics literacy in an international context* (NCES 2008–016). National Center for Education Statistics, Institute of Education Sciences, U.S. Department of Education. Washington, DC.

Bendixen, L.D. & Feucht, F.S. (2010). (Eds.). *Personal epistemology in the classroom.* Cambridge, MA: Cambridge University Press.

Bonnet, G. (2002). Reflections in a critical eye: on the pitfalls of international assessment. *Assessment in Education: Principles, Policy, and Practice, 9,* 387–399.

Brannon, E.M. (2005). What animals know abut numbers. In J.I.D. Campbell (Ed.), *Handbook of mathematical cognition* (pp. 85–107). New York: Psychology Press.

Bransford, J.D., Brown, A.L., & Cocking, R.R. (Eds.). (1999). *How people learn: Brain, mind, experience, and school.* Washington, DC: National Academy Press.

Briggs, D.C., Alonzo, A.C., Schwab, C., & Wilson, M. (2006). Diagnostic assessment with ordered multiple-choice items. *Educational Assessment, 11,* 33–63.

Brown, J.S. & Burton, R.R. (1978). Diagnostic models for procedural bugs in basic mathematical skills. *Cognitive Science, 2,* 155–192.

Cameron, J. & Pierce, W.D. (2002). *Rewards and intrinsic motivation: Resolving the controversy.* Westport, CT: Bergin & Garvey.

Clements, D.H. & Sarama, J. (2007). Early childhood mathematics learning. In F.K. Lester Jr. (Ed.), *National Council of Teachers of Mathematics: Second handbook of research on mathematics teaching and learning* (pp. 461–555). Charlotte, NC: Information Age Publishing.

Corbett, A.T., Anderson, J.R., Carver, V.H., & Brancolini, S.A. (1994). Individual differences and predictive validity in student modeling. In A. Ram & K. Eiselt (Ed.), *Proceedings of the Sixteenth Annual Conference of the Cognitive Science Society.* Hillsdale, NJ: Erlbaum.

Davis, S.H. (2007). Bridging the gap between research and practice. Phi Delta Kappan, 88, 568–578.

Deci, E.L., Koestner, R., & Ryan, R.M. (1999). A meta-analytic review of experiments examining the effects of extrinsic rewards on intrinsic motivation. *Psychological Bulletin, 125,* 625–668.

Dehaene, S., Bossini, S., & Giraux, P. (1993). The mental representation of parity and numerical magnitude. *Journal of Experimental Psychology: General, 122,* 371–396.

de Lange, J. (2007). Large-scale assessment of mathematics education. In F.K. Lester Jr. (Ed.), *National Council of Teachers of Mathematics: Second handbook of research on mathematics teaching and learning* (pp. 1111–1142). Charlotte, NC: Information Age Publishing.

Dorman, C. (1991). Exceptional calendar calculation ability after early left hemispherectomy. *Brain & Cognition, 15*, 26–36.

Fias, W. & Fischer, M.H. (2005). Spatial representations of numbers. In J.I.D. Campbell (Ed.), *Handbook of mathematical cognition* (pp. 43–54). New York: Psychology Press.

Fu, W.T. & Anderson, J. (2008). Dual learning processes in interactive skill acquisition. *Journal of Experimental Psychology, Applied, 14*, 179–191.

Geary, D.C., Hoard, M.K., Byrd-Craven, J., Nugent, L., and Numtee, C. (2007). Cognitive mechanisms underlying achievement deficits in children with mathematical learning disability. *Child Development, 78*(4), 1343–1359.

Gentner, D., Loewenstein, J., & Thompson, L. (2003). Learning and transfer: A general role for analogical encoding. *Journal of Educational Psychology, 95*, 393–408.

Gentner, D., Rattermann, M.J., Markman, A., & Kotovsky, L. (1995). Two forces in the development of relational similarity. In T. Simon & G. Halford (Eds.), *Developing cognitive competence: New approaches to process modeling* (pp. 263–313), Hillsdale, N.J.: Erlbaum.

Greeno, J.G., Pearson, P.D., & Schoenfeld, A.H. (1997). Implications for the NAEP of research on learning and cognition. In R. Linn, R. Glaser, & G. Bohrnstedt (Eds.), *Assessment in transition: Monitoring the nation's educational progress* (pp. 151–215). Stanford, CA: National Academy of Education.

Halford, G.S., Smith, S.B., Dickson, J.C., Maybery, M.T., Kelly, M.E., Bain, J.D. & Stewart, J.E.M. (1995). Modeling the development of reasoning strategies: The roles of analogy, knowledge, and capacity. In T. Simon & G. Halford (Eds.), *Developing cognitive competence: New approaches to process modeling* (pp. 77–156). Hillsdale, NJ: Erlbaum.

Hatano, G. (1988). Social and motivational bases for mathematical understanding. *New Directions for Child Development, 41*, 55–70.

Hidi, S. & Harackiewicz, J.M. (2000). Motivating the academically unmotivated: A critical issue for the 21st century. *Review of Educational Research, 70*, 151–179.

Hiebert, J., Carpenter, T.P., Fennema, E., Fuson, K.C., Wearne, D., Murray, H., Olivier, A., & Human, P. (1997). *Making sense: Teaching and learning mathematics with understanding*. Portsmouth, NH: Heinemann.

Hill, H.C., Sleep, L., Lewis, J.M., & Ball, D.B. (2007). Assessing teachers' mathematical knowledge: What knowledge matters and what evidence counts. In F.K. Lester Jr. (Ed.), *National Council of Teachers of Mathematics: Second handbook of research on mathematics teaching and learning* (pp. 111–155). Charlotte, NC: Information Age Publishing.

Hofer, B.K. & Pintrich, P.R. (1997). The development of epistemological theories: Beliefs about knowledge and knowing and their relation to learning. *Review of Educational Research, 67*, 88–140.

Hope, J. (1985). Unravelling the mysteries of expert mental calculation. *Educational Studies in Mathematics, 16*, 355–374.

Jordan, J.A., Mulhern, G., & Wylie, J. (2009). Individual differences in trajectories of arithmetical development in typically achieving 5- to 7-year-olds. *Journal of Experimental Child Psychology, 103*, 455–468.

Kalaman, D.A. & LeFevre, J. (2007). Working memory demands of exact and approximate addition. *European Journal of Cognitive Psychology, 19*, 187–212.

Kaminski, J.A., Sloutsky, V.M., & Heckler, A.F. (2009). Concrete Instantiations of mathematics: A double-edged sword. *Journal for Research in Mathematics Education, 40*, 90–93.

Kieran, C. (2007). Learning and teaching of algebra at the middle school through college levels: Building meaning for symbols and their manipulation. In F.K. Lester Jr. (Ed.), *National Council of Teachers of Mathematics: Second handbook of research on mathematics teaching and learning* (pp. 707–762). Charlotte, NC: Information Age Publishing.

Kilpatrick, J., Swafford, J. & Findell, B. (Ed.). (2001). *Adding It Up: Helping Children Learn Mathematics*. Washington, DC, USA: National Academies Press.

Kintsch, W. (1998). *Comprehension: A paradigm for cognition*. Cambridge, UK: Cambridge University Press.

Klahr, D. & Dunbar, K. (1988). Dual search space during scientific reasoning. *Cognitive Science, 12*, 1–48.

Kloosterman, P. (2010). Mathematics skills of 17-year-olds in the United States: 1978 to 2004. *Journal for Research in Mathematics Education, 41*, 20–51.

Koedinger, K.R. & Anderson, J.R. (1990). Abstract planning and perceptual chunks: Elements of expertise in geometry. *Cognitive Science, 14*, 511–550.

(1991). Interaction of deductive and inductive reasoning strategies in geometry novices. In *Proceedings of the Thirteenth Annual Conference of the Cognitive Science Society*, Hillsdale, NJ: Erlbaum.

(1993). Effective use of intelligent software in high school math classrooms. *In Proceedings of the Sixth World Conference on Artificial Intelligence in Education* (pp. 241–248). Charlottesville, VA: Association for the Advancement of Computing in Education.

Koedinger, K.R., Anderson, J.R., Hadley, W.H., & Mark, M. (1997). Intelligent tutoring goes to school in the big city. *International Journal of Artificial Intelligence in Education, 8*, 30–43.

Kuhn, D. (2005). *Education for thinking.* Cambridge, MA: Harvard University Press.

Larkin, J. & Simon, H. (1987). Why a diagram is (sometimes) worth 10,000 words. *Cognitive Science, 11*, 65–99.

Lesh, R. & Zawojewski, J.S. (2007). Problem solving and modeling. In F.K. Lester Jr. (Ed.), *National Council of Teachers of Mathematics: Second handbook of research on mathematics teaching and learning* (pp. 763–804). Charlotte, NC: Information Age Publishing.

Lester Jr., F.K. (Ed.). (2007). *National Council of Teachers of Mathematics: Second handbook of research on mathematics teaching and learning.* Charlotte, NC: Information Age Publishing.

Lester Jr., F.K. & Kehle, P.E, (2003). From problem solving to modeling: The evolution of thinking about research on complex mathematical activity. In R. A. Lesh & H. M. Doerr (Eds.), *Beyond constructivism: Models and modeling perspectives on mathematics problem solving, learning, and teaching* (pp. 501–518). Mahwah, NJ: Lawrence Erlbaum Associates.

Lester Jr., F., Garofalo, J., & Kroll, D. (1989). Self-confidence, interest, beliefs, and metacognition: Key influences in problem-solving behaviour. In D.B. McLeod & V.M. Adams (Eds.), *Affect and mathematical problem solving: A new perspective* (pp. 75–88). New York: Springer-Verlag.

Mabbott, D.J. & Bisanz, J. (2008). Computational skills, working memory, and conceptual knowledge in older children with mathematics learning disabilities. *Journal of Learning Disabilities, 41*, 15–28.

Maher, C.A. & Martino, A.M. (1996). The development of the idea of mathematical proof: A 5-year case study. *Journal for Research in Mathematics Education, 27*, 194–214.

Mayer, R.E. (2008) *Learning and instruction.* Columbus, OH: Pearson Merrill Prentice Hall.

   (2003). Mathematical problem solving. In J.M. Royer (Ed.), *Mathematical cognition* (pp. 69–92). Greenwich, CT: Information Age Publishing.

Mazzocco, M.M. & McCloskey, M. (2005). Math performance in girls with turner or fragile X syndrome. In J.I.D. Campbell (Ed.), *Handbook of mathematical cognition* (pp. 269–297). New York: Psychology Press.

McCrink, K. & Wynn, K. (2004). Large-number addition and subtraction in infants. *Psychological Science, 15*, 776–781.

Miura, I.T. & Okamoto, Y. (2003). Language supports for mathematics understanding and performance. In A.J. Baroody & A. Dowker (Eds.), *The Development of Arithmetic Concepts and Skills – Constructing Adaptive Expertise: Studies in Mathematical Thinking and Learning* (pp. 229–242). Hillsdale, NJ: Erlbaum.

Munn, P. (1998). Symbolic function in pre-schoolers. In C. Donlan (Ed.), *The development of mathematics skills: Studies in developmental psychology* (pp. 47–71). East Sussex, UK: Psychology Press.

Morris, L.W., Davis, M.A., & Hutchings, C.H. (1981). Cognitive and emotional components of anxiety: Literature review and a revised worry-emotionality scale. *Journal of Educational Psychology, 73*, 541–555.

National Mathematics Advisory Panel. (2008). *Foundations for Success: The Final Report of the National Mathematics Advisory Panel*. U.S. Department of Education: Washington, DC.

National Research Council. (2005). *How Students Learn: History, Mathematics, and Science in the Classroom*. In M.S. Donovan & J.D. Bransford (Eds.), Division of Behavioral and Social Sciences and Education. Washington, DC: The National Academies Press.

National Research Council. (2009). *Mathematics Learning in Early Childhood: Paths Toward Excellence and Equity*. Committee on Early Childhood Mathematics, Christopher T. Cross, Taniesha A. Woods, and Heidi Schweingruber, Editors. Center for Education, Division of Behavioral and Social Sciences and Education. Washington, DC: The National Academies Press.

Needleman, Sarah E. (January 26, 2009). Doing the math to find the good jobs. *Wall Street Journal, p.* D2.

Newell, A. (1973). You can't play 20 questions with nature and win: Projective comments on the papers of this symposium. In W. G. Chase (Ed.), *Visual information processing* (pp. 283–310). New York: Academic Press.

    (1990). *Unified theories of cognition*. Cambridge, MA: Harvard University Press.

Newell, A. & Simon, H.A. (1972). *Human problem solving*. Oxford, UK: Prentice-Hall.

Niss, M. (2007). Reflections on the state and trends in research on mathematics teaching and learning: From here to utopia. In F.K. Lester Jr. (Ed.), *National Council of Teachers of Mathematics: Second handbook of research on mathematics teaching and learning* (pp. 1293–1312). Charlotte, NC: Information Age Publishing.

Organization for Economic Cooperation and Development. (2004). *Learning for tomorrow's world: First results from PISA 2003*. Paris, France: Author.

Pesek, D.D. & Kirshner, D. (2000). Interference of instrumental instruction in subsequent relational learning. *Journal for Research in Mathematics Education, 31,* 524–540.

Provasnik, S., Gonzales, P., & Miller, D. (2009). *U.S. Performance Across International Assessments of Student Achievement: Special Supplement to The Condition of Education 2009* (NCES 2009–083). National Center for Education Statistics, Institute of Education Sciences, U.S. Department of Education. Washington, DC.

Quilici, J.H. & Mayer, R.E. (1996). Role of examples in how students learn to categorize statistics word problems. *Journal of Educational Psychology, 88,* 144–161.

Ritter, S., Anderson, J.R., Koedinger, K.R., & Corbett, A. (2007). Cognitive tutor: Applied research in mathematics education. *Psychonomic Bulletin and Review, 14,* 249–255.

Rittle-Johnson, B., Siegler, R.S., & Alibali, M.W. (2001). Developing conceptual understanding and procedural skill in mathematics: An iterative process. *Journal of Educational Psychology, 93,* 346–362.

Schoenfeld, A.H. (2007). Method. In F.K. Lester Jr. (Ed.), *National Council of Teachers of Mathematics: Second handbook of research on mathematics teaching and learning* (pp. 69–107). Charlotte, NC: Information Age Publishing.

Schoenfeld, A.L. (1992). Learning to think mathematically. Problem solving, metacognition, and sense-making in mathematics. In D.A. Grouws (Ed.), *Handbook of research in mathematics teaching and learning* (pp. 334–370). New York: Macmillan.

Schommer, M. (1990). Effects of beliefs about the nature of knowledge on comprehension. *Journal of Educational Psychology, 82,* 498–504.

Siegler, R.S. & Araya, R. (2005). A computational model of conscious and unconscious strategy discovery. In R. V. Kail (Ed.), *Advances in child development and behavior, Vol.* 33, (pp. 1–42). Oxford, UK: Elsevier.

Siegler, R.S. & Booth, J.L. (2004). Development of numerical estimation in young children. *Child Development, 75,* 428–444.

Siegler, R.S. & Svetina, M. (2006). What leads children to adopt new strategies? A microgenetic/cross sectional study of class inclusion. *Child Development, 77,* 997–1015.

Simon, T.J. & Klahr, D. (1995). A computational theory of children's learning about number conservation. In T.J. Simon & G.S. Halford (Eds.), *Developing cognitive competence: New approaches to process modeling.* Hillsdale, NJ: Erlbaum

Shrager, J. & Siegler, R.S. (1998). SCADS: A model of children's strategy choices and strategy discoveries. *Psychological Science, 9,* 405–410.

Sophian, C. (2007). *The origins of mathematical knowledge in childhood.* Lawrence Erlbaum Associates.

Spencer, S.J., Steele, C.M., & Quinn, D.M. (1999). Stereotype threat and women's math performance. *Journal of Experimental Social Psychology, 35,* 4–28.

Skwarchuk, S.L. & Anglin, J.M. (2002). Children's acquisition of the English cardinal number words: A special case of vocabulary development. *Journal of Educational Psychology, 94,* 107–125.

Stanovich, K.E. (2009). *What intelligence tests miss: The psychology of rational thought.* New Haven, CT: Yale University Press.

Stewart, S. & Thomas, M.O.J. (2010). Student learning of basis, span and linear independence in linear algebra. *International Journal of Mathematics Education, 41,* 173–188.

Towse, J. & Saxton, M. (1998). Mathematics across national boundaries: Cultural and linguistic perspectives on numerical competence. In C. Donlan (Ed.), *The development of mathematics skills: Studies in developmental psychology* (pp. 129–150). East Sussex, UK: Psychology Press.

Wayne, A.J. & Youngs, P. (2003). Teacher characteristics and student achievement gains: A review. *Review of Educational Research, 73,* 89–122.

Wiest, L.R. (2000). Mathematics that whets the appetite: Student-posed projects problems. *Mathematics Teaching in the Middle School, 5,* 286–291.

Wilson, J. & Clark, D. (2004). Towards the modeling of mathematical metacognition. *Mathematics Education Research Journal, 16,* 25–48.

Wu, H. (1999). Basic skills versus conceptual understanding: A bogus dichotomy in mathematics education. *American Educator, 14–19,* 50– 52.

Wynn, K. (1995). Origins of numerical knowledge. *Mathematical Cognition, 1,* 35–60.

6

Putting It All Together: Cognitive Models to Inform the Design and Development of Large-Scale Educational Assessment

In this penultimate chapter, we summarize our impetus for identifying and evaluating diagrammatic cognitive models in reading, science, and mathematics and offer some conclusions about where we go from here. Borrowing the definition from Leighton and Gierl (2007a), a cognitive model was defined as a "simplified description of human problem solving on standardized educational tasks, which helps to characterize the knowledge and skills students at different levels of learning have acquired and to facilitate the explanation and prediction of students' performance" (p. 6). In Chapter 1, we indicated that large-scale educational tests, redesigned and redeveloped from cognitive models in the learning sciences, may offer enhanced information (test-based inferences) about student problem solving and thinking. This enhanced information may help remediate the relatively low test performance of many students, including U.S. students, who are struggling to learn and demonstrate knowledge in core domains. In Chapter 1, we also presented accepted knowledge and principles from the learning sciences about the nature of thinking, learning, and performance to set the stage for what may be required for redesigning and redeveloping large-scale assessments. Illustrative empirical studies in the field of educational measurement were described to demonstrate attempts at redesigning and redeveloping educational assessments based on the learning sciences. Chapters 2, 3, 4, and 5 presented our criteria for evaluating cognitive models and also offered examples of diagrammatic cognitive models in reading, science, and mathematics that have garnered substantial empirical support. In the remainder of this chapter, we describe a secondary impetus for the book, offer lessons learned from the cognitive models of reading, science, and mathematics presented in Chapters 3, 4, and 5, including their granularity, measurability, and instructional relevance, and discuss how these models can begin to inform the design and development of large-scale educational assessments. Finally, we conclude by exploring directions for future research.

ANOTHER IMPETUS: AN EPILOGUE TO LEIGHTON AND GIERL (2007B)

The primary rationale for this book was to present and evaluate types of cognitive models in core academic domains that could be used to enhance the design and development of large-scale educational assessments. However, we would be remiss if we did not also mention another, secondary rationale. We make mention of this additional impetus because, as discussed at the end of this volume, it does not detract from the primary motivation, and it reflects our ongoing interest and responsiveness to the requests of our colleagues and to the needs of the ever-expanding field of educational measurement. In 2007 we edited a book called *Cognitive Diagnostic Assessment for Education: Theory and Applications*. This book included a prominent list of researchers who contributed impressive work on cognitive diagnostic assessment. Cognitive diagnostic assessments, most simply defined, are educational tests designed from learning scientific principles, in addition to well-established psychometric practices, for the purpose of providing stakeholders with psychologically useful information about examinees' problem-solving strengths and weaknesses. The book was also published by Cambridge University Press and was recognized by the American Educational Research Association (AERA), Division D (Measurement and Evaluation section) with the Significant Contribution to Educational Measurement and Research Methodology Prize in 2009.

Although *Cognitive Diagnostic Assessment for Education* presented key accomplishments and initiatives related to the psychometrics of diagnostic assessment, not surprisingly, it could not include all relevant topics. Therefore, the book had some shortcomings. In particular, although the book's title contained the word *cognitive*, the book was essentially about psychometric methods for accommodating learning scientific principles in the design, development, and summary of test performance. What was missing was a chapter on learning scientific principles – the kinds of evidence-based cognitive models from the learning sciences that cataloged component knowledge and skills, which could "plug into" and inform or guide these new psychometric methods. We recognized this limitation at the time and, in chapter 12 of the book, we stated "more general theories of cognition, as they pertain to the knowledge structures and cognitive processes, were not described in our volume ... this is an area of great importance" (Gierl & Leighton, 2007, p. 343). One book reviewer also pointed out this missing piece. In an otherwise enthusiastic review, Everson (2008) wrote:

> One glaring omission, in my view, is the absence of a chapter representing the perspective of cognitive psychology – say, from the point of view of a first-rank scholar with an interest in cognition and learning (e.g., Greeno, Collins, & Resnick, 1996, or Sternberg & Grigorenko, 2003). Scholars of this stripe could comment on what we know today about problem solving, decision making, reasoning, and expertise. Such work would be invaluable in shaping the design and engineering of cognitively rich diagnostic forms of assessment. (p. 6)

We wholeheartedly agreed with Everson in his critique. Yet as the often-quoted adage indicates – the devil is in the details. And the devil of how to condense decades of learning scientific research in a single chapter of a psychometric book on cognitive diagnostic assessment was complicated. Needless to say, at the time we were putting the 2007 book together, we recognized the importance of including the cognitive models that would need to be identified to present a full account of cognitive diagnostic assessment. However, a cursory and, later, a more extensive evaluation of the learning scientific literature revealed to us that a single chapter on the topic of cognitive models would simply not do – the learning sciences are too extensive, and trying to encapsulate this wealth of riches into a single chapter might have allowed us to "check the box," but certainly would not have addressed what we saw as a more fundamental problem with the topic of cognitive models for assessment purposes.

What are the problems with using cognitive models for the design and development of large-scale assessment? In a phrase, *there are no cognitive models readily available*. To elaborate, there are no ready-to-use, off-the-rack cognitive models for assessment design and development. Although learning scientists have developed many cognitive models (some of which have been included in the present volume) to explain a variety of important cognitive and learning processes – reading comprehension, scientific reasoning and discovery, and mathematical reasoning – none of these models specifically reflects the types of processes that are accessed during formal testing or identifies key cognitive components used when students solve problems on achievement tests. In other words, these cognitive models do not specifically pertain to large-scale educational assessments (or even classroom assessments) of reading comprehension, scientific reasoning and discovery, and mathematical reasoning. Thus, the major problem we saw four years ago as we were compiling *Cognitive Diagnostic Assessment for Education* was that we could not find clear-cut, ready-to-use cognitive models to guide educational-assessment design and development. Cognitive models simply did not exist for this particular purpose. This was a problem not only because it meant that we could not neatly compile a chapter on cognitive models in our 2007 book, but more importantly it was a problem because it meant that essential, basic research for the merging of the learning sciences and assessment still needed to be conducted.

As we accumulated research papers and citations, and a growing rationale for the present book, we realized that the idea that educational assessments can be informed by the learning sciences has in part been propagated by two assumptions. The first assumption is that ready-to-use cognitive models do, in fact, exist and can be readily used to guide the design and development of large-scale educational assessments. This assumption is mistaken, because ready-to-use cognitive models for assessment design do not exist. The second assumption is that assessments designed from learning scientific principles will provide better information in terms of test-based inferences about examinees. However, both these assumptions have not been put to the test. In relation to the second assumption, controlled studies have yet to be conducted comparing the informational or inferential value of assessments developed from learning scientific principles against assessments developed from traditional principles (i.e., content-based test blueprints). Moreover, those researchers and practitioners who may have wished to test this second assumption might have been thwarted, because ready to use cognitive models for test design and development do not exist. Thus, the mistakenness of the first assumption could be an impediment to testing the second. So a fundamental problem seems to be one of *identification*. Consequently, the purpose of the present book was to organize in one volume an exploration and targeted review of relevant cognitive models in the domains of reading, science, and mathematics to help inform the possible adaptation and translation of these models into the design, development, and even validation of large-scale educational assessments.

That a book would need to be devoted to identifying relevant cognitive models for assessment purposes is understandable when one considers that the learning scientific literature is extensive. Cognitive models in the learning sciences are developed to account for domain-specific thinking processes, and the challenge in identifying models is to represent them or illustrate them in a way that will promote their consideration and use in educational-assessment design and development. It is important to note that even identifying these models does not fully solve the problem of using cognitive models in assessment design and development. Most, if not all, of the models we have included in this volume cannot be immediately applied to test design and development because they were not created with testing applications in mind. Rather, these models need to be adapted or translated for educational-assessment design and development. As articulated a decade ago in the executive summary of the influential National Research Council's (2001, p. 5) report, *Knowing what Students Know*, is that "[f]urther work is therefore needed on translating what is already known in cognitive science to assessment practice, as well as on developing additional cognitive analyses of domain-specific knowledge and expertise." In order to facilitate thinking and analysis of these diagrammatic models in the learning sciences, in this volume we have reviewed a select number of models for granularity, measurability, and instructional relevance. Granularity refers to the specificity of the knowledge and skill components outlined in the model. Measurability refers to the extent to which educational tasks or items can be developed based on the model. Instructional relevance refers to the importance, usefulness, and desirability of the knowledge and skill components included in the models for informing teaching and instruction.

As we considered how to tackle the sizeable undertaking of presenting a targeted review of cognitive models for the purpose of large-scale educational-assessment design and development, we decided to present cognitive models that met two constraints: The models needed to have substantial empirical support in the learning scientific literature, and they needed to have diagrammatic representations. The first constraint is justified given the limits of space in the present volume and the expediency of presenting evidence-based learning scientific principles for a potentially high-stakes application – large-scale educational assessments. The second constraint evolved from the recognition that Bloom's taxonomy (see Bloom et al., 1956; see also revised Bloom's taxonomy, Anderson et al., 2001) is commonly used in the design and development of educational assessments, and it is represented often as a simple linear hierarchy (see Chapter 1, Figure 1.1). We reasoned that there might be a relationship between the ubiquity of Bloom's taxonomy and its simple diagrammatic representation. A number of psychological investigations have shown that external, diagrammatic (or pictorial) representations facilitate problem solving for classes of tasks (Ainsworth & Loizou, 2003; Greeno, 1983; Koedinger & Anderson, 1990; Larkin & Simon, 1987; Tubau, 2008; Tufte, 1983; Tversky, 2002; see also Mislevy et al., 2010). For example, Larkin and Simon (1987), in their now famous article *Why a Diagram Is (Sometimes) Worth 10,000 Words*, investigated the benefits of diagrammatic representations versus sentential representations (i.e., lists involving primarily propositional structures) in problem solving. What they found in the domains of economics, geometry, and physics is that diagrammatic representations, as opposed to sentential representations, facilitate problem solving for tasks that involve spatial layouts and/or causal structures. The facilitative effect came about, in part, because the diagram effectively eased the processing and searching of information by grouping essential task-related facts into clusters. The diagrammatic illustration of task-related information highlighted the spatial associations and causal connections between components and, therefore, facilitated a series of task-related inferences, including perceptual, implicit, and explicit inferences.

Mislevy et al. (2010) have also written about the significance of external knowledge representations, including both diagrammatic and sentential representations such as "graphs, wiring diagrams, bus schedules, musical notation, mathematical formulas, object models for business systems, and the 7-layer OSI model for computer networks" (p. 3) for assessments. In particular, Mislevy and his colleagues discussed how assessments should be designed and developed in relation to what they call "domain knowledge representations." Domain knowledge representations are the codified and/or symbolic forms in which domain-specific knowledge takes shape in a content domain and to which assessments may be targeted, such as reading, science, and/or mathematics. These representations can guide task analysis (e.g., help identify knowledge and skills for problem solving) and also be adapted or translated into educational test items. The attention Mislevy et al. (2010) bring to the subject of knowledge representations is noteworthy because the methods used to formally configure domain understandings, components, and relationships are undoubtedly a critical part of what is measured and what is not. We concur that special consideration needs to be given to domain knowledge representations, so that test items can be designed to measure important component skills. However, before we can begin to sift through the relevant versus irrelevant aspects of domain knowledge representations in an effort to inform test-item design, we need to tackle the more basic problem of simply identifying and packaging essential knowledge in the learning sciences for assessment specialists. Without this packaging of information, the next step of using a variety of domain knowledge representations in assessment design is unlikely to occur.

To this end, Larkin and Simon's (1987) study is revelatory, not because they state that external representations are useful (we know this to be true because external representations are vital to cognition, with language being one of the most commonly utilized forms of representation). Rather, Larkin and Simon explain that not all external representations are equally useful in the conceptualization of knowledge. What makes an external representation useful in a given domain depends on the nature of the problem under consideration within that domain. For example, in the information processing of a physics problem involving pulleys, weights, and friction, sentential representations (i.e., list structures) are not as useful as diagrammatic representations for summarizing key spatial information with causal links. Applying this idea to the assessment domain, diagrammatic (or pictorial) representations of cognitive models may be especially useful for encapsulating and communicating spatial and/or causal relationships among knowledge and skill components for assessment design. Whether or not diagrammatic representations of cognitive models prove useful in assessment design and development remains to be seen. However, at a minimum in this volume we begin the process of identifying some of these models, including their component knowledge and skills, using a diagrammatic form that highlights their spatial and causal relationships. In the next section, we discuss what we have concluded from the diagrammatic models we have described and evaluated in Chapters 3, 4, and 5.

DIAGRAMMATIC COGNITIVE MODELS IN READING, SCIENCE, AND MATHEMATICS: WHAT HAVE WE LEARNED?

In Chapters 3, 4, and 5, we described and evaluated diagrammatic cognitive models in reading comprehension, scientific reasoning and discovery, and mathematical reasoning. In particular, we focused on Kintsch's (1998) CI model, Graesser's constructionist model (Graesser, Singer, & Trabasso, 1994), Klahr and Dunbar's (1988) SDDS model, Kuhn's (2001, 2005) KPI model, Anderson's ACT-R model, (see Anderson et al., 2004) and Kilpatrick, Swafford, and Findell's (2001) 5-S model. Each model was introduced, its framework was described, and then was evaluated for granularity, measurability, and instructional relevance. Several similarities and differences were noted about the models within the domains of reading, science, and mathematics, and also between the models across academic domains. In the following sections, these similarities and differences are discussed.

Granularity

Granularity refers to the grain size at which the knowledge and skill components in cognitive models are described. Granularity is an important dimension on which to evaluate cognitive models because it has implications for the number and type of educational test items that may need to be designed and developed for large-scale educational assessments. For example, cognitive models that include knowledge and skill components specified at a fine level of granularity would be expected to lead to the development of test items measuring highly specific components. Having items measure highly specific knowledge and skill components could lead to an impractical number of items to be included in a single test. Moreover, if these fine-level knowledge and skill components reflect elementary psychological processes, such as rules for activating the contents of working memory (WM), these components may not match or correspond to the broader objectives of large-scale educational assessments. Alternatively, cognitive models that include knowledge and skill components specified at a coarse level of granularity would lead to a manageable number of test items for development. However, other issues might plague these models, including the possible ambiguity or vagueness associated with operationalizing a broad knowledge and skill description into an explicit item measuring a particular objective. Specified too broadly, the knowledge and skills may also lack instructional relevance.

Most of the cognitive models described and evaluated in this volume contained knowledge and skill components specified at both fine and coarse levels of granularity. In particular, Kintsch's CI model, Graesser's et al. constructionist model, Klahr and Dunbar's SDDS model, and Anderson's et al. (2004) ACT-R model included both fine and coarse levels of granularity in their knowledge and skill components. The two exceptions were Kuhn's KPI model and Kilpatrick's et al. 5-S model. Both of these models were specified solely at a coarse level of grain size. A similarity among the models that included fine-level grain size components was that these components were outlined with a specificity to permit computer programming (see Chapter 1, footnote 1). For instance, the components of Kintsch's CI model described at an exceedingly fine grain size included *node activation*, $a_i(t)$, where nodes were defined as any proposition, inference, or elaboration in a propositional network created to facilitate the representation of the text; *strength of link*, w_{ij}, between nodes i and j; and *memory strengths*, m_{ij}, which were defined as the final product of node activation and strength between nodes (see Chapter 3, this volume). These three components were considered essential to the CI model as they instantiated, on a computer platform, the propositional networks of meaning that gave rise to comprehension of text. In other words, these three components were the building blocks from which the textbase and situation model were generated. The challenge, of course, is that most large-scale educational assessments would not aim to test node activation, strength of link, and memory strengths because these processes are too elementary. Instead, most large-scale educational assessments would aim to measure the interactive product to which these elementary processes give rise – that is, the textbase and the situation model in the domain of reading comprehension. Both of these latter components are coarse in grain size (see Figure 3.3, Chapter 3, this volume).

Other models reviewed in this volume also included knowledge and skill components described at a fine level of granularity, reflecting underlying cognitive processing mechanisms. For example, in reading comprehension, Graesser's et al. (1994) constructionist model postulated a series of six rules to instantiate the types of inferences motivated readers should generate as they read text. At least two of these rules pointed to underlying cognitive processing mechanisms at a fine level of granularity. Consider the fifth rule in the constructionist model: *If WM includes a given configuration of goals, actions, events, emotions, and/or states that meet some threshold of activation, then create global structures.* Further, consider the sixth rule: *If an implicit statement or structure in WM meets some threshold of activation, then construct inferences that receive high activation in WM* (see Chapter 3, this volume). Both of these rules describe mechanisms for generating automatic inferential decisions during reading. These rules are likely to operate outside of the reader's awareness. The other four inference rules in the constructionist model were described at a coarser level of granularity and approximated the types of reading strategies individuals would be expected to consciously employ as they seek to understand the motivational and causal precursors of actions and events depicted in text (see Figure 3.5, Chapter 3, this volume).

Likewise, Klahr and Dunbar's (1988) SDDS model contained underlying cognitive processes described at a fine level of granularity. Specifically, evoking or inducing frames, conducting pilot studies in e-space to evaluate the best frame to use, and assigning slot values to chosen frames (see Figure 4.1, Chapter 4, this volume) reflected basic cognitive processes involved in scientific reasoning. However, these underlying processes are not the type of knowledge and skill components of most interest to test developers who must design large-scale educational assessments. Rather, assessment specialists would be more interested in the coarser-level knowledge and skill components of the SDDS model, such as searching through the hypothesis and experiment spaces (see Figure 4.1, Chapter 4, this volume), and the strong and weak methods that move problem solving forward in the hypothesis and experimental spaces.

The ACT-R model proposed by Anderson and his colleagues (2004) was similar to the SDDS model in its balance of fine- and coarse-level knowledge and skill components. Parts of the ACT-R model, such as chunks and production rules, serve as the underlying mechanisms or building blocks of declarative and procedural knowledge components (see Figure 5.1 and 5.2, Chapter 5, this volume). Chunks and production rules are also specified at a fine level of granularity and, consequently, may be impractical in guiding the design and development of large-scale educational assessments. Instead, assessment specialists are more likely to be aided by the coarser-level components of the ACT-R model, which include task analyses and the broad specification of declarative and procedural knowledge and skills required to successfully solve mathematical tasks.

Although the fine-level knowledge and skill components of models may be inappropriate for the design and development of large-scale educational assessments, it must be noted that these components serve a fundamental role in securing the empirical credibility of the cognitive models presented. That many of these models are specified at an algorithmic level of analysis provides what Newell (1973, see pp. 297–298) termed the *control structure* for cognitive psychological phenomena. The control structure provides the programmable directives (frequently instantiated as a computer program) for how a psychological phenomenon occurs, and often requires identifying the fine-level processes that underwrite broader or coarser-level outcomes. For example, being able to multiply numbers is made possible by a series of underlying processes, including the long-term memory retrieval of number facts, working memory to hold these facts in attention, and the sequential selection of operators that systematically concatenate the numbers to produce a meaningful result. Although the phenomenon of interest may be "multiplying numbers," this observable fact is only able to occur in the mind of a learner because of the many fine-grained processes that allow coarser processes (e.g., addition of numbers) to take place. Without such a control structure or set of programmable directives that specify the sequential order of operations underlying a phenomenon, models fail at their most basic function – to explain an observable fact by narrowing the set of specific processes for materializing the phenomenon. Newell explains that without these programmable directives, models can fall trap to a *deus ex machina* (also known as the *god from the machine*, alternatively see chapter 1 of Ryle, 1949). *Deus ex machina* involves the tendency to stipulate new, abstract components to solve thorny empirical problems without ever having to explicitly show how these components work in practice. The hard work in any empirical science, then, is to explain a phenomenon with sufficient detail to make it come alive with operational specificity. Assessment specialists and test developers may not ever develop educational assessments to measure fine-grained processes, but the use of empirically based cognitive models that involve these processes will fortify any test-based inferences made about students' knowledge and skills.

Measurability

Measurability, as outlined in Chapter 2, refers to the extent to which the knowledge and skill components included in a cognitive model can serve as a basis for designing test items for large-scale educational assessments. This is another important dimension on which to evaluate cognitive models. If a cognitive model does not provide a theoretical or evidence-based framework for the design and development of educational test items, then this shortcoming would discourage use of the model. Ultimately, the successful union between the learning sciences and educational assessment is premised on the informative value of cognitive models for guiding the design of test items for instructional or educational objectives. Toward this end, even if cognitive models must first be adapted or translated before they can be used to inform test-item design, there is an expectation that such an adaptation or translation will be fruitful in guiding the development of test items. Otherwise, there is little incentive to adapt cognitive models and use them for educational assessment purposes.

The cognitive models reviewed in the present volume were comparable in their measurability. First, we were unable to find any published literature indicating that any of the cognitive models included in our review had served as a primary framework for the design and development of large-scale educational test items. This is not surprising because Ferrara and DeMauro (2006), in an extensive review of the literature on achievement testing, indicated that current large-scale educational assessments are not developed from or validated against any evidence-based cognitive model of learning. They state:

> No practical theory or system brings together psychometrics, cognitive psychology, linguistics, and operational test development into a unified approach for designing and developing K-12

achievement assessments and for validating interpretations and uses of achievement test scores. Theory and conception tend to be implicit in or even absent in current practice. (Ferrara & DeMauro, 2006, p. 604)

That Ferrara and deMauro (2006; see also Embretson, 2002 for a similar conclusion) would come to this conclusion is not surprising given that the knowledge and skills measured by most large-scale educational assessments are still based on Bloom's taxonomy (Schmeiser & Welch, 2006; see Chapters 1 and 2, this volume).

It is important to specify the cognitive requirements of the items in the test.... There are many cognitive taxonomies that have been developed, with Bloom's taxonomy (Bloom, Engelhart, Furst, Hill, & Kratwohl, 1956) being one of the best known.... Unfortunately, no current cognitive taxonomy seems to be supported by documented validation evidence. (Schmeiser & Welch, 2006, p. 316)

Bloom's taxonomy, although extensively used, cannot be considered a learning scientific model. Although Bloom's taxonomy is called a cognitive taxonomy because of its content, there is no systematic empirical evidence to justify or explain the ordering of cognitive skills in the taxonomy, why this ordering might reflect distinct levels of expertise within domains, or how this ordering can be used to reliably elicit specific forms of thinking and problem solving in students. Rather, the taxonomy represents a hierarchy of knowledge and skills that provides a guide to designing educational test items aimed at measuring different levels of cognitive complexity.

The cognitive models reviewed in this volume share a second similarity. The main source of evidence for the measurability of these cognitive models came from experimental tasks. Many of these experimental tasks took the form of single laboratory-based tests designed to evaluate component parts of the cognitive models. For example, consider Kinstch's CI model (see Chapter 3, this volume). Experimental tasks designed to assess the textbase typically involve presenting participants with a stimulus such as a reading passage, and then asking participants to engage in free recall, cued recall, simple summarization, recognition, and/or answering explicit probes about the written passage. Alternatively, experimental tasks designed to assess the situation model also involve presenting participants with a reading passage, but this time require participants to generate inferences by integrating the text with prior knowledge or by arranging textual words into concept maps. In Chapter 3, we reviewed Britton and Gülgöz's (1991) test of whether the reader-generated inferences predicted by the CI model were useful for improving the comprehensibility of a one-thousand-word passage. Britton and Gülgöz found that, indeed, participants demonstrated better recall of the one-thousand-word passage when the text had been enhanced in key locations with added inferences than when these inferences had not been added. Likewise, Ferstl and Kintsch (1998) used two types of stories, each with a distinct underlying structure, to evaluate the creation of different situation models. Ferstl and Kintsch found, as expected, that participants created different situation models as a function of the underlying structure of the stories they read. Both of these examples (e.g., Britton & Gülgöz, 1991; Ferstl & Kintsch, 1998) demonstrated the use of single laboratory-based tasks to evaluate coarser-grain components of the CI model. Experimental tasks designed to test fine-grained aspects of the CI model have also been conducted (see Kinstch, 1998, for a review; Kintsch & Kintsch, 2005).

Evidence for the measurability of Graesser's et al. constructionist model, Klahr and Dunbar's SDDS model, Kuhn's KPI model, Anderson's et al. ACT-R model, and Kilpatrick's et al. 5-S model can also be found in the experimental tasks designed to evaluate aspects of these models (see Chapters 3, 4, and 5 for details). This is not surprising because all the cognitive models reviewed in this volume were selected in part because they had garnered substantial empirical evidence in the learning scientific literature. Despite this strong, empirically based substantive foundation, the models in our review have not been adapted or translated into operational test items on large-scale educational assessments. As Ferrara and DeMauro (2006) have indicated, the presence of learning scientific principles in the design and development of large-scale educational assessments is virtually non-existent. Yet why would this be so when there is an apparently strong commitment by assessment specialists to enhance the design and development of educational testing? Mislevy (2006, p. 298) asks a similar question in his review of cognitive psychology and educational assessment: "What is required to bring cognitively grounded assessment to the fore?" He answers:

> Successful examples to emulate, knowledge representations and symbol systems to automatize work, and tools and social processes that embody the principles so users don't need to work them out from scratch. There is much to be done, but we are learning at last to know how to think about it. (Mislevy, 2006, p. 298)

Mislevy's question and answer are useful to consider because they reflect the type of work required to facilitate the adaptation, translation, and use of cognitive models in the design and development of large-scale educational assessments. We think part of this work entails identifying diagrammatic representations of cognitive models and evaluating their knowledge and skill components, so that the relationships among these components are highlighted and contextualized for assessment specialists and test developers. Nonetheless, how cognitive models are specifically adapted or translated for operational test-item design is inevitably dependent on the particular objectives of the assessment under construction.

Instructional Relevance

Instructional relevance was the final dimension on which the cognitive models presented in this volume were evaluated. Instructional relevance refers to the usefulness and practicality of the knowledge and skill components included in cognitive models for enhancing teaching and instruction. This is an important dimension on which to evaluate cognitive models because the learning scientists who have developed these models can be persuasive purveyors of information related to the transformation of student learning and assessment. However, whether or not educators and other stakeholders "buy into" what the learning sciences have to offer will depend on how useful and accessible learning scientific information is made to appear. For example, consider Kuhn's KPI model (see Chapter 4, this volume). Although this model does not include any fine-grained cognitive processes in its description of scientific reasoning and discovery, it does offer multiple coarser-level knowledge and skill components related to the mastery of scientific thinking. The model includes a listing of strategies viewed as essential for masterful scientific thinking, such as inquiry, analysis, and drawing inferences. Moreover, the model includes the category of declarative knowledge – facts, opinions, and claims – which students must learn to recognize in order to distinguish theory from evidence, as well as how theory and evidence are coordinated to produce justifiable arguments to support claims about knowledge. Also of relevance are the conative or dispositional components, including values about the nature of knowledge, which Kuhn suggests are decisive influences on whether learners choose to expend the mental effort needed to learn to reason scientifically (see also Stanovich, 2009). A case could be made that most, if not all, of the knowledge and skill components in the KPI model could be considered highly relevant by teachers and stakeholders to the instruction of students. One reason why these components are relevant is that they are presented as coarse-level components that are easily recognizable as practical forms of knowledge for mastering scientific thinking. Interestingly, whereas the SDDS model also includes coarse-level knowledge and skill components such as the hypothesis and experiment spaces, these are presented alongside fine-grained components, many of which reflect underlying cognitive processes that are less accessible to instruction.

Cognitive models must be viewed as appropriate sources of evidence for the design and development of student large-scale educational assessments. This requirement is reasonable if one of the motives for using cognitive models is to make large-scale educational assessments more informative about student learning. Toward this end, the cognitive tutor in the ACT-R model by Anderson and colleagues (see chapter 5, this volume) is an exemplary illustration of the standard a model should meet in order to be viewed as instructionally relevant. The cognitive tutor is programmed to include declarative and procedural knowledge routines or algorithms that respond to the faulty methods of problem solving students are known to apply when responding to mathematical tasks. When students apply these faulty methods in their planning and execution of solutions to mathematical tasks, the cognitive tutor is able to match the faulty method to one of its routines and offer hints about why a given method is inappropriate and another is appropriate. In the process, the cognitive tutor uses its declarative and procedural knowledge routines to teach students about mathematical thinking and to assess student learning of mathematical strategies and techniques.

What Have We Learned?

As we recap the dimensions of granularity, measurability, and instructional relevance in relation to the cognitive models reviewed and evaluated in this volume, the questions of what we have learned and whether we are any closer to using cognitive models in the design and development of large-scale educational assessments surface. What we have learned is that cognitive models are not yet fully ready for use in the design and development of large-scale educational assessments. They are not ready for use because the knowledge and skill components included in these models do not necessarily correspond to the educational outcomes or knowledge and skills test items are often designed to measure. This is not a trivial conclusion. For example, test items developed for a science assessment often measure content knowledge. Yet neither of the two cognitive models of scientific reasoning and discovery (i.e., SDDS model and KPI model) we reviewed included content knowledge in their knowledge and skill components. Another reason why cognitive models are not ready for use in the design and development of educational assessments is because learning scientists do not develop these models to account for test-item performance, but rather they develop models to explain cognitive and learning phenomena within specific domains of interest. For example, reading comprehension is explained specifically as the process of node activation and strengthening of links between nodes, and generally as the process of integrating the textbase and the situation model (see the CI model in chapter 3, this volume). Scientific reasoning and discovery is explained specifically as the process of frame assignment and generalization, and generally as the process of searching through hypothesis and experiment spaces (see the SDDS model in Chapter 4, this volume). Mathematical reasoning is explained specifically as the process of forming chunks and production rules, and generally as the process of activating declarative and procedural knowledge components in relation to the requirements of specific mathematical tasks (see ACT-R model in Chapter 5, this volume).

None of the models provided a comprehensive catalog of domain-specific content knowledge and skills for large-scale educational tests to include in their assessment of students. The absence of such a catalog owes to the fact that these models describe cognitive processes within domains – they are not necessarily in response to particular tasks, which would require content-specific knowledge to solve. In other words, these models offer conceptual frameworks outlining the key components expected to underlie thinking and problem solving in, for example, reading, scientific reasoning, and mathematical reasoning. As conceptual frameworks, these models delineate key knowledge and skill components within core domains, but they *do not* delineate the domain-specific content knowledge and skills that may be relevant to tackling particular tasks within these domains. This omission occurs not because domain-specific content knowledge and skills are unimportant. Rather, this omission occurs because the models are designed to identify key common components that generalize to all individuals in response to a variety of tasks occurring within specific domains. The CI model, for instance, is designed to elucidate the common components in reading regardless of whether the reading material is expository, narrative, or persuasive.

Using these conceptual frameworks, then, learning scientists select key components and operationalize them for empirical evaluation. For example, the formation and testing of hypotheses using strong and weak methods, as outlined in the SDDS model, can be expected to occur in biological, chemical, physical, and even psychological and cosmological domains. A developmental psychologist interested in investigating how students reason about the ozone hole using the SDDS model as a conceptual framework would first need to identify specific task variables such as a body of data for students to explain (e.g., ozone hole formations over the Antarctic), a set of possible hypotheses that students could use to explain the data (and how to evaluate students' reasoning), a set of possible methods students could use to empirically investigate each of the hypotheses, and a series of permissible inferences based on the results of the experiments. These particular task variables involve domain-specific content knowledge relevant to hypothesis formation and explanation of the ozone hole. However, specific knowledge about the ozone hole would not be included in Klahr and Dunbar's SDDS model, because the model is not exclusively about the ozone hole. Rather, the SDDS model is a conceptual framework to be used as an overarching set of processes for how scientific reasoning and discovery occur within a variety of content domains in science.

HOW CAN THESE COGNITIVE MODELS INFORM
LARGE-SCALE ASSESSMENTS?

The Bad News and Good News

For assessment specialists who may want to use cognitive models in the design and development of large-scale educational tests, what are the implications of cognitive models as conceptual frameworks? The implications are that cognitive models, developed to account for thinking and reasoning in reading, science, and/or mathematics, must first be adapted or translated before they can be used to guide and inform the development of educational test items. In other words, the bad news is that the assumption or belief that cognitive models can be found and used as is, or off-the-rack, directly from published accounts in the learning scientific literature is incorrect. These models are not in a representational form that renders them immediately ready for use in the design and development of large-scale educational assessments. Rather, they must be adapted or translated for specific large-scale assessment applications. How is this to be done? We propose that this is an under-researched question in the field of cognition and assessment today. There is virtually no literature on methods for adapting or translating cognitive models for large-scale assessment purposes. The absence of such a literature might suggest that this is not needed – quite the contrary. It is more plausible that the absence of such a literature suggests that in the excitement of demonstrating the ways in which cognitive research might be integrated into measurement models, an important step has been overlooked or even bypassed. The absence of such methods for adapting and/or translating cognitive models impedes the systematic collection of empirical evidence for designing and developing large-scale educational tests based on learning scientific principles.

That cognitive models are not ready for immediate use and must be adapted or translated for test design should not be surprising to those assessment specialists who already employ Bloom's taxonomy.

Bloom's taxonomy is also a conceptual framework, albeit a simple one, that must be adapted or translated before it is used to inform the design and development of educational test items. For example, in applications of Bloom's taxonomy, particular knowledge and skills may be emphasized in the design and development of test items and others not. Moreover, the taxonomy itself does not show assessment specialists how to develop items. Instead, the taxonomy is used as a guide. The taxonomy's linear hierarchy of knowledge and skills highlights to assessment specialists that a range of cognitive skills can be measured – knowledge, comprehension, application, analysis, synthesis, and evaluation – and that this range reflects variability in depth of understanding. However, this range of cognitive skills does not direct test developers on how these skills should or could be measured. Whether or not test items can be developed to reliably and validly measure specific components of any cognitive model remains an empirical question. Test items developed even from the most elaborate and empirically substantiated cognitive model will still require validation because every instance of a test item reflects an attempt at operationalizing a component of the model; whether this attempt at operationalizing is successful must be evaluated.

Cognitive models provide a conceptual framework for the design and development of educational test items as do other conceptual frameworks, namely, Bloom's taxonomy. However, the good news is that some cognitive models, such as the ones reviewed in this volume, have the added benefit of being specific to core academic domains (e.g., reading, science, or mathematics) and have been empirically substantiated. These are two reasons for why using cognitive models in test design and development is an improvement over the use of Bloom's taxonomy. Consider the development of test items in science. Klahr and Dunbar's SDDS model highlights the key skills of scientific reasoning and discovery: the formation of hypotheses, the testing of hypotheses, and the evaluation of evidence. Furthermore, the SDDS model highlights the strategies or methods of thought associated with increasing levels of mastery. For example, strong methods of search exemplify domain-specific strategies in scientific reasoning. Conversely, weak methods of search exemplify domain-general strategies in scientific reasoning. Strong methods reflect the application of explicit, domain-specific content knowledge and skills within domains. Weak methods reflect the application of general-purpose skills that allow students to transfer or be creative in using multiple approaches to solve novel or ill-defined problems (e.g., insight items). Assessment specialists could use the SDDS model to design items in a series of domain-specific content areas to evaluate students' ability to form hypotheses, test hypotheses, evaluate evidence, and use strong and weak methods of search.

How might this application take form? Consider the specifications of the Biology 30 Diploma Examination, a large-scale educational assessment that is administered to students at the end of their grade-twelve biology course in the Province of Alberta, Canada. A summary of the general content domains and associated outcomes include:

1. **Nervous and Endocrine Systems** (20–25 percent of items). For this content domain, students are expected to "explain how the nervous system controls physiological processes and how the endocrine system contributes to homeostasis" (Alberta Education, 2009, p. 3).

2. **Reproductive Systems and Hormones** (10–15 percent of items). For this content domain, students are expected to "explain how survival of the human species is ensured through reproduction and how human reproduction is regulated by chemical control systems" (Alberta Education, 2009, p. 3).

3. **Differentiation and Development** (5–10 percent of items). For this content domain, students are expected to "explain how cell differentiation and development in the human organism are regulated by a combination of genetic, endocrine, and environmental factors" (Alberta Education, 2009, p. 3).

4. **Cell Division and Mendelian Genetics** (25–30 percent of items). For this content domain, students are expected to "describe the processes of mitosis and meiosis and ... explain the basic rules and processes associated with the transmission of genetic characteristics" (Alberta Education, 2009, p. 3).

5. **Molecular Biology** (10–15 percent of items). For this content domain, students are expected to "explain classical genetics at the molecular level" (Alberta Education, 2009, p. 3).

6. **Population and Community Dynamics** (15–20 percent of items). For this content domain, students are expected to "describe a community as a composite of populations in which individuals contribute to a gene pool that can change over time ... explain the interaction of individuals with one another and with members of other populations; and ... explain, in quantitative terms, the changes in populations over time" (Alberta Education, 2009, p. 3).

In addition to these content domains, students are expected to demonstrate scientific process and communication skills. Process and communication skills include:

1. Formulating questions about observed relationships.

2. Planning investigations about observed relationships using a range of tools to collect and interpret data (evidence).

3. Analyzing data by applying mathematical conceptual models (theories) to assess possible outcomes.

4. Communicating results and inferences using scientific guidelines (see Alberta Education, 2009, p. 4 for specific process, communication skills, and science, technology, and society connections).

In the Biology 30 Diploma Examination, these four processes and communication skills must be demonstrated, more or less, within each of the six content domains mentioned previously. For example, formulating questions about observed relationships is measured in relation to nervous and endocrine systems.

A question that can be asked of these specifications is how they could be related to the SDDS model? To begin, it is important to note that the first three scientific process and communication skills outlined for the Biology 30 Diploma Examination map onto the SDDS model. For example, the first skill, formulating questions about observed relationships, maps onto the *hypothesis formation phase* in the SDDS model. The second skill, planning investigations about observed relationships using a range of tools to collect and interpret data, maps onto both the *experimentation phase* and the *evaluation of evidence phase* in the SDDS model. The third skill, analyzing data by applying mathematical conceptual models to assess possible outcomes, is simply a more specific description of the second skill and maps onto the evaluation of evidence phase in the SDDS model. The fourth skill, communicating results and inferences using scientific guidelines, is not included in the SDDS model given that this last skill has more to do with the conventions of communicating scientific findings than with the scientific process itself.

We see from this brief mapping of specifications against the SDDS model that the key process and communication skills associated with scientific mastery in the Biology 30 Diploma Examination are included in the SDDS model. Let us now consider what is not common between these test specifications and the SDDS model. First, the strong and weak methods of search outlined in the SDDS model are not included in the specifications for the Biology 30 Diploma Examination. Examples of strong methods or domain-specific content knowledge and skills to be assessed in biology might include the following:

1. Laboratory techniques, including how to use test tubes, boiling tubes, Bunsen burners, tripods, and gauze.
2. Microscopy and observation skills, such as using light microscopes, compound microscopes, and electron microscopes,

and mounting specimens for viewing and making biological drawings.

3. Quantitative techniques in biology, including counting cells using a hemocytometer, investigating enzyme activity using a colorimeter, using a photometer to investigate transpiration, bioassay techniques, and datalogging.

4. Fieldwork techniques, such as describing specimens, vegetation, sampling animals, and making environmental measurements (see Adds, Larkcom, Miller, & Sutton, 1999, for a comprehensive list of methods).

Examples of weak methods or domain-general methods to be assessed in biology would include, as outlined in Chapter 4 (in this volume), generate and test, hill climbing, mean-end analysis, planning, and analogy. These methods (i.e., domain-specific and domain-general search skills) are not included in the specifications of the Biology 30 Diploma Examination. That these methods are not explicitly included suggests that although some form of these methods may be measured on the Biology 30 Examination, their direct assessment is likely not taking place. According to the SDDS model, domain-specific and domain-general search skills in science are critical aspects of knowing how to move within and between phases of hypothesis formation, experimentation, and evidence valuation. Without these methods, students could get "stuck" in a phase and not know how to proceed to the next phase. Part of becoming a scientific thinker and cultivating facility with scientific analyses, according to Klahr and Dunbar (1988), includes learning how to use domain-specific and domain-general search skills. These are the methods that allow students to conceptualize questions for investigation, recognize the tools available for testing hypotheses, and evaluate the results from investigations. In other words, the content knowledge and process and communication skills included in the Biology 30 Diploma test specifications are as important as the domain-specific and domain-general search skills with which students must navigate through phases of scientific thinking. The question, then, is how are these more specific search skills being measured with current educational large-scale assessments? If they are not, the SDDS model suggests that they should be formally assessed to ensure students learn how to think flexibly and move between phases of scientific thinking.

CONCLUSION, LIMITATIONS, AND FUTURE DIRECTIONS

The use of cognitive models to guide the design and development of large-scale assessments is a promising new avenue for assessment research. There are many reasons why the use is beneficial to large-scale educational testing efforts. Chief among these reasons is that test items developed from cognitive models may provide better measures of students' knowledge and skills and, therefore, deliver more accurate information about what students have mastered. In other words, cognitively based large-scale educational assessments may lead to stronger test-based inferences than traditional large-scale assessments. Stronger test-based inferences, in turn, should facilitate our capacity to help students struggling with academic material, initiate innovative instructional efforts, and gauge student performance as they strive to compete for knowledge-rich jobs in the twenty-first century. However, there is much work to be done before we can say that the use of cognitive models does, in fact, lead to these positive outcomes.

There are also a number of areas we highlight for further research. One area should focus on how cognitive models could better capture the dynamic and *longitudinal process* of learning. The cognitive models illustrated in Chapters 3, 4, and 5 reflect the knowledge and skills students must possess to exhibit masterful reading, scientific reasoning, and mathematical reasoning, respectively. However, none of these cognitive models presented in Chapters 3, 4, and 5 reflects a longitudinal perspective on learning – how it changes or evolves within students. In other words, none of the models demonstrates a step-by-step process of how cognition changes over time as students become increasingly proficient within a domain. When one considers the cognitive models presented in this volume, and other cognitive models in the learning scientific literature, one realizes that many of these cognitive models illustrate "end points" in cognition at a given point in time. Few models reflect the knowledge and skills students who are struggling with scientific reasoning possess, and how they gradually acquire or stumble on the right path to successfully master scientific knowledge and skills. In this way, cognitive models often show the end points in the learning continuum but not necessarily the "learning progressions" required for getting there. Therefore, it is fair to ask whether cognitive models can be developed to describe students who are struggling to achieve mastery in reading, science, and mathematics, and how they learn to achieve.

A related obstacle is the failure of a single cognitive model to account for the knowledge and skills students from different cultural backgrounds and learning contexts, and/or of different ability levels, employ to solve educational tasks (e.g., Leighton, Cor, & Cui, 2009; see also Jackson, 2005). This failing is slightly different from the one mentioned in the previous paragraph, namely, that cognitive models often fail to demonstrate how cognition changes for a student over time as he or she acquires increasingly more knowledge and skills. However, even from a *cross-sectional perspective*, cognitive models often fail to describe the thinking of students who have creative learning styles or have distinct ability levels. That different cognitive models might be needed to exemplify the knowledge and skills students at distinct ability levels have for solving educational tasks is relatively unsurprising given research on expertise (e.g., Chi, Glaser, & Farr, 1988; Ericsson, 2009). As increasingly more information is assimilated and accommodated by learners, the organization of knowledge and skills change – some become automated, others encapsulated into larger units, and others completely replaced by new knowledge and skills. All the models highlighted in this volume reflect a *one-size-fits-all account* of reading comprehension, scientific reasoning and discovery, and mathematical reasoning. The reason for this one-size-fits-all account is that learning scientists may want to explain what is relatively common among learners and not necessarily what is different. Newell (1973) captures this principle: "To predict [the behaviour of] a subject you must know: (1) his [or her] goals; (2) the structure of the task environment; and (3) *the invariant structure of his [or her] processing mechanisms*" (p. 293, italics added). Focusing on invariant processing mechanisms suggests that we aim to identify what is common among all learners, instead of what is different. However, there may be a need to also identify the divergent strategies students use to tackle educational tasks. For example, we all possess long-term memory and working memory components; these are the invariant aspects of our information processing. However, how these memory components are manipulated by the learner, and on what task features they focus on could depend greatly on individual experiences and, importantly, the repository of information already accumulated in long-term memory. Therefore, cognitive models should be developed and identified for different types of learners, even if it is only at a single point in time.

Cognitive models that show how learning changes over the time and how learners of different ability levels respond to educational test items could impact the design and development of large-scale assessments. In particular, identifying and/or adapting cognitive models that emphasize the development of learning within a domain may increasingly force developers in large-scale assessment programs to consider ways in which alternate, smaller-scale assessments can add information to the snapshot of student performance large-assessments already provide. In Chapters 3, 4, and 5, examples of what these alternate assessments might look like were provided in the form of the small-scale experimental tasks that psychologists often devise to test their cognitive models and theories. Although this volume has not considered what such alternate assessments might look like from a psychometric perspective, one example can be found in the research of Bennett and Gitomer (2008). Bennett and Gitomer are working on Cognitively Based Assessments for, of, and as Learning (CBAL) at the Educational Testing Service. CBAL is being designed as a comprehensive system of assessment that (a) is based on modern scientific conceptions of domain mastery (i.e., cognitive models); (b) measures student learning frequently; (c) uses open-ended tasks; (d) makes use of new technology to deliver frequent assessments; (e) provides not only formative assessments results, but also summative information on student learning; and (f) strives to move away from shallow performance goals to deeper thinking and understanding skills.

Another area for future research focuses on how to avoid falling into the trap of the tyranny of reductionism and the belief that cognitive models are the only types of models that should be considered in understanding student achievement. System models (see von Bertalanffy, 1955; see also more recently Bandura, 2006; Hammond, 2003) illustrate how situational variables and humanistic aspects of learning (e.g., academic and home environments, the learner, and the tasks used to evaluate performance) interact to produce certain outcomes. System models must also be kept close in mind. As attractive as the promise of cognitively based large-scale educational assessments is, we cannot forget the complexity involved in understanding and predicting human behavior and the need to situate academic performance within a broader environmental context.

It is also important to remember, as we outline in Chapter 1, that before judging the utility of cognitive models in the design and development of large-scale educational assessments, proper evidence needs to be collected that these types of assessments are indeed superior to traditional large-scale assessments. We should not be persuaded without this evidence. Controlled studies need to be conducted in which cognitively based large-scale assessments and traditional large-scale assessments are compared and evaluated for the types of test-based inferences and decisions generated about students. Are these inferences and decisions sufficiently distinct to warrant one type of assessment over another? Do they favor one assessment over another? Before such questions can be answered, however, cognitive models in core academic domains need to be identified in the learning scientific literature and presented for evaluation. As this volume has attempted to demonstrate, this is not a straightforward task, because cognitive theories and models are often described in multiple publications and are developed and refined across multiple texts to show their latest iterations. Moreover, some models are not always presented in representational formats that facilitate use. For this reason, we chose to present cognitive models that have diagrammatic representations. It is our expectation that such a representational format should facilitate thinking about cognitive models in relation to educational test design and development. This representational format approximates the form often adopted with Bloom's taxonomy. Questions in relation to these models must then be asked, including: Does this model have sufficient empirical backing? Does the model include an appropriate grain size for the domain of interest and test-item design? Do these knowledge and skill components provide sufficient guides for the generation of test items? Does this model have instructional relevance? As these questions and others begin to be answered in relation to the desirability and feasibility of using particular cognitive models in the design and development of large-scale educational assessments, we will be in a better position to evaluate these new cognitively based large-scale assessments.

To conclude, in Chapter 1 we used the story of "The Emperor's New Clothes" by Hans Christian Andersen to depict the potential trap we may succumb to if we accept a set of ideas that lack empirical proof. As mentioned in our opening chapter, researchers and practitioners (including test developers and administrators) must be wary of the evidence for claims about cognitively based assessments lest we are sold invisible new "clothes." Although it may be true that, in the past two decades, assessment researchers and practitioners have witnessed the intensification of the recommendation that the learning sciences should be integrated into the design and development of large-scale achievement tests, *this recommendation is not currently based on systematic evidence.* Rather, this recommendation is made based on the expectation that these new tests will provide better information about student achievement and learning than current traditional tests. Although the recommendation may be sensible given advances in learning scientific theory, there are still no systematic data or evidence to suggest that assessments based on the learning sciences lead to better information about student achievement and better test-based inferences about student learning than more traditional assessments.

Publications such as the National Research Council's *Knowing What Students Know* (2001) and *Taking Science to School* (2007) provide selective surveys and illustrative examples of cognitive research, but there is no systematic organization of this research into sets of cognitive models within particular domains to develop large-scale educational test items. We need to generate frameworks to summarize and map the learning sciences into a set of guidelines for the design and development of large-scale test items. Then we need to use these frameworks to design test items and develop assessments, and evaluate these assessments against more traditional assessments to determine whether they lead to better inferences about the knowledge and skills students have mastered, better feedback for teachers as they tackle instruction and remediational efforts, and better information for policy makers as they plan educational reforms.

Newell (1973) cautioned that scientists cannot play twenty questions with nature and win. The spirit of his statement indicated that scientists cannot pose questions about nature and expect to produce fruitful answers when the questions are random, disjointed attempts to uncover a phenomenon of interest, particularly when the questions are predicated on weak conceptual frameworks for organizing and directing empirical efforts. In the race to understand how cognition can inform the design and development of large-scale educational assessments, it is our expectation that asking questions about the types, accessibility, and feasibility of cognitive models available in core academic domains is a vital first step toward sketching a framework for how to think, evaluate, and conduct empirically based investigations involving cognitive models and educational assessment. In other words, we need systematic research programs devoted to answering the questions of how cognitively based large-scale assessments can be designed and developed, and whether they do in fact lead to the positive outcomes (including more accurate test-based inferences) we have come to anticipate. The purpose of this volume was to organize relevant diagrammatic cognitive learning models in the domains of reading, science, and mathematics to help inform research into the design, development, and even validation of cognitively based large-scale achievement tests in education. Therefore, there is much work to be done to demonstrate that the marriage between the learning sciences with educational measurement is feasible and, importantly, yields better student information and test-based inferences than current traditional large-scale educational tests.

REFERENCES

Adds, J., Larkcom, E., Miller, R., & Sutton, R. (1999). *Tools, techniques and assessment in biology: A course guide for students and teachers.* Chelteham, UK: Nelson Thornes Publishing.

Ainsworth, S. & Loizou, A. (2003). The effects of self-explaining when learning with text or diagrams. *Cognitive Science, 27,* 669–681.

Anderson, J.R., Bothell, D., Byrne, M.D., Douglass, S., Lebière, C., & Qin, Y. (2004). An integrated theory of the mind. *Psychological Review, 111,* 1036–1060.

Anderson, L.W., Krathwohl, D.R., Airasian, P.W., Cruikshank, K.A., Mayer, R.E., Pintrich, P.R., Raths, J., & Wittrock, C. (Eds.). (2001). *A Taxonomy for learning, teaching, and assessing – A revision of Bloom's taxonomy of educational objectives.* Addison Wesley Longman.

Alberta Education (2009). *Information bulletin: Biology 30, 2009–2010 diploma examinations program.* Author. Retrieved May 21, 2010 from http://education. alberta.ca/media/1116889/10_b30_inforbulle_2009–2010_print.pdf.

Bandura, A. (2006). Toward a psychology of human agency. *Perspectives on Psychological Science, 1*, 164–180.

Bennett, R.E. & Gitomer, D.H. (2008). Transforming K-12 assessment: Integrating accountability testing, formative assessment, and professional support. *ETS Research Memorandum-08-13*, 1–30. Princeton, NJ: Educational Testing Service.

Bloom, B., Englehart, M. Furst, E., Hill, W., & Krathwohl, D. (1956). *Taxonomy of educational objectives: The classification of educational goals. Handbook I: Cognitive domain.* New York: Longmans, Green.

Britton, B.K. & Gülgöz, S. (1991). Using Kinstch's computational model to improve instructional text: effects of repairing inference calls on recall and cognitive structures, *Journal of Educational Psychology, 83*, 329–345.

Chi, M.T.H., Glaser, R., & Farr, M. (Eds.). (1988). *The nature of expertise.* Hillsdale, NJ: Erlbaum.

Embretson, S.E. (2002). Generating abstract reasoning items with cognitive theory. In S.H. Irvine & P.C. Kyllonen (Eds.), *Item generation for test development* (pp. 219–250). Mahwah, NJ: Erlbaum.

Ericsson, K.A. (2009). (Ed.). *Development of professional expertise: Toward measurement of expert performance and design of optimal learning environments.* New York, New York: Cambridge University Press.

Everson, H. (2008). The diagnostic challenge in education: A review of Cognitive Diagnostic Assessment: Theory and applications. *PsycCRITIQUES, 53*(29), no pagination specified.

Ferrara, S. & DeMauro, G.E. (2006). Standardized assessment of individual achievement in K-12. In R. L. Brennan (Ed.), *Educational measurement* (4th ed., pp. 579–621). Westport, CT: National Council on Measurement in Education and American Council on Education.

Ferstl, E.C. & Kintsch, W. (1998). Learning from text: Structural knowledge assessment in the study of discourse comprehension. In S.R. Goldman & H. van Oostendorp (Eds.), *The constructions of mental representations during reading*, (pp. 247–277). Mahwah, NJ: Erlbaum.

Gierl, M.J. & Leighton, J.P. (2007). Directions for future research in cognitive diagnostic assessment (pp. 341–351). In J.P. Leighton & M.J. Gierl (Eds.), *Cognitive diagnostic assessment for education: Theory and applications.* Cambridge, UK: Cambridge University Press.

Graesser, A.C., Singer, M., & Trabasso, T. (1994). Constructing inferences during narrative text comprehension. *Psychological Review, 101*, 371–395.

Greeno, J.G. (1983). Forms of understanding in mathematical problem solving. In S.G. Paris, G.M. Olson, H.W. Stevenson (Eds.), *Learning and motivation in the classroom* (pp. 83–111). Hillsdale, NJ: Erlbaum.

Hammond, D. (2003). *The science of synthesis*. Boulder, CO: University of Colorado Press.

Jackson, N.E. (2005). Are university students' component reading skills related to their text comprehension and academic achievement? *Learning and Individual Differences, 15*, 113–139.

Kilpatrick, J., Swafford, J. & Findell, B. (Ed.). (2001). *Adding It Up: Helping Children Learn Mathematics*. Washington, DC, USA: National Academies Press.

Kintsch, W. (1998). *Comprehension: A paradigm for cognition*. Cambridge, UK: Cambridge University Press.

Kintsch, W. & Kintsch, E. (2005). Comprehension. In S.G. Paris & S.A. Stahl (Eds.), *Children's reading comprehension and assessment* (pp. 71–92). Mahwah, NJ: Erlbaum.

Klahr, D. & Dunbar, K. (1988). Dual search space during scientific reasoning. *Cognitive Science, 12*, 1–48.

Koedinger, K.R. & Anderson, J.R. (1990). Abstract planning and perceptual chunks: Elements of expertise in geometry. *Cognitive Science, 14*, 511–550.

Kuhn, D. (2001). How do people know? *Psychological Science, 12*, 1–8.

(2005). *Education for thinking*. Cambridge, MA: Harvard University Press.

Larkin, J. & Simon, H. (1987). Why a diagram is (sometimes) worth 10,000 words. *Cognitive Science, 11*, 65–99.

Leighton, J.P., Cui, Y., & Cor, M.K. (2009). Testing expert-based and student-based cognitive models: An application of the attribute hierarchy method and hierarchical consistency index. *Applied Measurement in Education, 22*, 229–254.

Leighton, J.P. & Gierl, M.J. (2007a). Defining and evaluating models of cognition used in educational measurement to make inferences about examinees' thinking processes. *Educational Measurement: Issues and Practice, 26*, 3–16.

(2007b). (Eds.). *Cognitive diagnostic assessment for education: Theories and applications*. New York: Cambridge University Press.

Mislevy, R.J. (2006). Cognitive psychology and educational assessment. In R. L. Brennan (Ed.), *Educational measurement* (4th ed., pp. 257–305). Westport, CT: National Council on Measurement in Education and American Council on Education.

Mislevy, R.J., Behrens, J.T., Bennett, R.E., Demark, S.F., Frezzo, D.C., Levy, R., Robinson, D.H., Rutstein, D.W., Shute, V.J., Stanley, K., & Winters, F.I. (2010). On the roles of external knowledge representations in assessment design. *Journal of Technology, Learning, and Assessment, 8*(2). http://escholarship.bc.edu/jtla/vol8/2.

National Research Council. (2001). *Knowing what students know: The science and design of educational assessment.* Washington, DC: National Academy Press.

Newell, A. (1973). You can't play 20 questions with nature and win: Projective comments on the papers of this symposium. In W. G. Chase (Ed.), *Visual information processing* (pp. 283–310). New York: Academic Press.

Ryle, G. (1949). *The concept of mind.* Chicago, IL: University of Chicago Press.

Schmeiser, C.B. & Welch, C.J. (2006). Test development. In R. L. Brennan (Ed.), *Educational measurement* (4th ed., pp. 307–353). Westport, CT: National Council on Measurement in Education and American Council on Education.

Stanovich, K.E. (2009). *What intelligence tests miss: The psychology of rational thought.* New Haven, CT: Yale University Press.

Tubau, E. (2008). Enhancing probabilistic reasoning: The role of causal graphs, statistical format and numerical skills. *Learning and Individual Differences, 18,* 187–196.

Tufte, E.R. (1983). *The visual display of quantitative information.* Cheshire, Connecticut: Graphics Press.

Tversky, B. (2002). Some ways that graphics communicate. In N. Allen (Editor), *Words and images: New steps in an old dance* (pp. 57–74). Westport, CT: Ablex.

Von Bertalanffy, L. (1955). The quest for a general system theory. *Main Currents in Modern Thought, 11* (4), 75–83.

7

Cognitively Based Statistical Methods – Technical Illustrations

Research focused on the application of cognitive principles to assessment practices is thriving in educational measurement, particularly in the area of cognitively based statistical methods. Since the publication of key articles, chapters, and books two decades ago (e.g. Frederiksen, Glaser, Lesgold, & Shafto, 1990; Nichols, 1994; Nichols, Chipman, & Brennan, 1995; Ronning, Glover, Conoley, & Witt, 1990; Snow & Lohman, 1989), there has been clear recognition that inferences about examinees' knowledge and skills require detailed information on the organization, representation, and production of attributes from a cognitive model. The form that these models may take, their learning scientific foundations, and their applicability to the design and development of large-scale educational assessment are topics in this book. The desire to integrate cognition with assessment has also spawned a range of ambitious research activities designed to identify and evaluate examinees' knowledge and skills using new statistical methods. Many recent examples can be cited to document these focused research efforts. For example, an American Educational Research Association (AERA) special interest group, *Cognition and Assessment*, was formed in 2007 to provide a platform for scholars presenting cutting-edge research that combines the fields of cognitive psychology, cognitive science, educational psychology, educational assessment, and statistics to solve complex assessment problems using a multi-disciplinary approach. A special issue of the *Journal of Educational Measurement* was published in 2007 devoted to cognitively based statistical methods. Also in 2007,

Cambridge University Press published *Cognitive Diagnostic Assessment for Education: Theory and Applications*, co-edited by J. Leighton and M. Gierl (2007b), which summarized what was known about the diagnostic potential of cognitively based educational tests. In 2008, the journal *Measurement: Interdisciplinary Research and Perspectives* devoted an entire issue to the topic of cognitively based statistical methods ("Unique Characteristics of Diagnostic Classification Models: A Comprehensive Review of the Current State-of-the-Art" by André Rupp and Jonathan Templin). This feature article elicited lively responses resulting in more than ten published and online commentaries.

The enthusiasm for cognition and assessment also extends beyond the borders of North America and outside the discipline of educational measurement. For example, *Zeitschift für Psychologie*, the main psychological journal in German-speaking countries, prepared a special issue in 2008 on how advances in cognition and assessment could affect methods for computer-based testing. In 2009, the journal *Language Assessment Quarterly* dedicated a special issue to the implications of cognitively based measurement for language testing, which focused on the identification and evaluation of knowledge and skills required for listening and reading English as a second language. In short, there is intense activity in the area of cognitively based assessment.

The purpose of Chapter 7 is twofold. First, we provide a non-technical review of the cognitively based statistical methods featured prominently in many recent publications on cognition and assessment. This review is intended to provide our readers with an up-to-date but non-technical summary of the most current procedures, including available software, for combining cognitive variables with statistical methods in large-scale educational testing. Second, we present and critique three recent applications of these cognitively based statistical methods in the areas of reading comprehension, computing science, and mathematics. It is important to note that in our presentation and critique of these three applications, we do not use the criteria or dimensions we have used in previous chapters to evaluate cognitive models. The reason for not using the criteria of granularity, measurability, and instructional relevance to evaluate these applications is that these criteria were developed primarily to evaluate cognitive models and not to evaluate statistical methods. Many applications of cognitively based statistical methods focus on describing and justifying the mathematical assumptions required to apply these methods. Hence, we think it would be unwarranted to evaluate the cognitive variables in these applications using our criteria given that the objective of these applications has been to explore psychometric infrastructures and not to explain the cognitive variables being modeled (see Leighton, 2009, for a critique). However, it is our hope that the concepts, ideas, and arguments presented in this volume encourage psychometricians to seek out evidence for the cognitive variables and cognitive models included in statistical applications, because this evidence will eventually be essential to generating strong validity arguments for the use of cognitively based assessments. We see this review as providing a fitting end to our book, because it allows our readers to consider the role that cognitive variables can play in understanding the knowledge and skills required to solve items in reading, science, and mathematics using current statistical methodologies, as well as some key limitations when these methods are applied to cognitive assessments.

REVIEW OF COGNITIVELY BASED STATISTICAL METHODS

Thissen and Steinberg (1986) published a useful and often-cited manuscript in educational measurement, titled "A Taxonomy of Item Response Models." The purpose of their paper was to introduce a classification approach for organizing the existing literature on item-response theory (IRT) modeling, to clarify the relationships among these statistical methods,[1] and to identify gaps that could lead to the

---

[1] Statistical methods are often referred to as statistical "models" in the educational measurement literature. Statistical models should not be confused with *cognitive*

development of new methods. A comparable taxonomy for cognitively based statistical methods is warranted because the number of methods continues to grow. One way to organize these methods is from general to specific where, for instance, a general latent-class model is specified and then constraints are placed on the model to produce extensions often described as "families" that can be applied to data from cognitive assessments (Henson, Templin, & Willse, 2008; von Davier, 2005; see also Maris, 1995). Another way to organize the literature is to identify specific statistical methods and then characterize the methods according to key features. The latter approach, used by Fu and Li (2007), Rupp and Templin (2008), and Lee and Sawaki (2009), is adopted here. Our review serves the following purposes. First, it outlines the key features, initially identified by Rupp and Templin and then Lee and Sawaki, necessary for organizing the statistical methods. Second, it incorporates a summary recently provided by Rupp (2009) that highlights the available software for operationalizing these methods. Taken together, our review should help researchers and practitioners identify potentially useful methods, compare and contrast some of their important features, and select the most appropriate software for implementing these methods. We do, however, encourage the reader to consult the original sources for a complete description of each taxonomy.

Table 7.1 contains our summary of twelve cognitively based statistical methods applied frequently in the literature on cognition and assessment along with three features that help characterize each method. The methods include the rule-space methodology (RSM; Tatsuoka, 1983, 1995), the attribute hierarchy method (AHM; Leighton et al., 2004; Gierl, Cui, & Hunka, 2008a), the deterministic input noisy and gate

---

models. Statistical models consist of a set of mathematical expressions and/or functions, including variables, with the purpose of simulating the response of the organism being modeled. In contrast, cognitive models need not involve mathematical language and often include learning scientific concepts, theoretical principles, and experimental facts. The terms statistical method and statistical model are used interchangeably in the present chapter.

TABLE 7.1. *Review of twelve cognitively based statistical methods*

Model	Observed item response scale	Cognitive skill relationship	Software
1. Rule Space Model (RSM)	Dichotomous	Non-Compensatory	K. Tatsuoka & C. Tatsuoka, 2009 (1)
2. Attribute Hierarchy Method (AHM)	Dichotomous	Non-Compensatory	Cui, Gierl, & Leighton, 2009, (2)
3. Deterministic Input Noisy and Gate (DINA)	Dichotomous	Non-Compensatory	de la Torre, 2009˙ (3); Templin, Henson, Douglas, & Hoffman, 2009 (6)
4. Noisy Input Deterministic and Gate (NIDA)	Dichotomous	Non-Compensatory	Templin et al., 2009 (6)
5. Higher-Order Deterministic Input Noisy and Gate (HO-DINA)	Dichotomous	Non-Compensatory	de la Torre, 2009 (3); Templin et al., 2009 (6)
6. Deterministic Input Noisy or Gate (DINO)	Dichotomous	Compensatory	Templin et al., 2009 (6)
7. Noisy Input Deterministic or Gate (NIDO)	Dichotomous	Compensatory	Templin et al., 2009 (6)
8. Non-compensatory Reparameterized Unified Model (NC-RUM)	Dichotomous/Polytomous	Non-Compensatory	Bolt, Chen, DiBello, Hartz, Henson, Roussos, Stout, & Templin, 2009 (4); Templin et al., 2009 (6)
9. Compensatory Reparameterized Unified Model (C-RUM)	Dichotomous/Polytomous	Compensatory	Bolt et al., 2009 (4); Templin et al., 2009 (6)
10. General Diagnostic Model (GDM)	Dichotomous/Polytomous	Compensatory	von Davier & Xu, 2009 (5); Templin et al., 2009 (6)

Model	Observed item response scale	Cognitive skill relationship	Software
11. Loglinear Cognitive Diagnosis Model (LCDM)	Dichotomous/ Polytomous	Compensatory	Templin et al., 2009 (6)
12. Bayesian Network (BN)	Dichotomous/ Polytomous	Non-Compensatory/ Compensatory	Almond & Shute, 2009 (7)

Note: The software column contains the citation and its order of presentation (in parentheses) from the Rupp (2009) symposium.

*The reader is also referred to de la Torre, J. (2008, July). *The generalized DINA model*. Paper presented at the annual International Meeting of the Psychometric Society (IMPS), Durham, NH.

model (DINA, Junker & Sijtsma, 2001), noisy input deterministic and gate model (NIDA, Junker & Sijtsma, 2001), the higher-order DINA model (HO-DINA, de la Torre & Douglas, 2004), the deterministic input noisy or gate model (DINO, Templin & Henson, 2006), the noisy input deterministic or gate model (NIDO, Templin & Henson, 2006), the non-compensatory reparameterized unified model (NC-RUM, Hartz, 2002; Roussos et al., 2007), the compensatory reparameterized unified model (C-RUM, Templin, 2006), the general diagnostic model (GDM; von Davier, 2007), the loglinear cognitive diagnosis model (LCDM, Henson et al., 2008), and Bayesian networks (BN; Pearl, 1988; Yan, Mislevy, & Almond, 2003). Three features that characterize these methods include observed item-response scale (dichotomous/ polytomous), relationship among cognitive skills (compensatory/ non-compensatory), and computer software.

The first feature, observed item-response scale, which could also be described as item format or item type, specifies whether the examinees' observed item responses are scored dichotomously (i.e., 0 or 1 as on a multiple-choice item) or polytomously (e.g., 1, 2, 3, 4, or 5 as on a 5-point Likert scale). This feature is related to the permissible item formats and resulting data structures that can be analyzed. Methods that accommodate dichotomous scales can only be used with exams containing items that are scored 0 or 1, whereas methods that accommodate polytomous scales can be used with exams containing diverse item formats (e.g., multiple choice and constructed response).

The second feature, relationship among cognitive skills, specifies the learning scientific or psychological nature of these attributes and their interactions. A compensatory (sometimes described as disjunctive) structure exists when the examinee executes or implements one or some *but not all* of the knowledge and skills required to solve the item, but still produces a correct response. This outcome can occur when the strength of one or some combination of cognitive skills is believed to compensate for weakness in one or some of the remaining skills required to solve the item. The end result is that the examinee need not master all of the cognitive skills to produce a correct response to a particular item. Conversely, a non-compensatory (or conjunctive) structure exists when the examinee must execute all of the knowledge and skills required to solve the item to produce a correct response. Typically, the cognitive skills are ordered in a hierarchical manner such that the lower-level (i.e., basic) skills must be mastered before the higher-level (i.e., advanced) skills can be performed. The end result is that the examinee must master all of the cognitive skills to produce a correct response to a particular item.

The third feature, available software, shows the viability of using the method in an applied testing situation. That is, a method can only be operationalized when computer software is readily available to estimate the item and ability parameters and/or classify the examinee into diagnostic categories. Until recently, many of the cognitively based statistical methods in the present review were of limited use because researchers and practitioners did not have software access. This problem was addressed in 2009 at a symposium titled "Software for Calibrating Diagnostic Classification Models: An Overview of the Current State-of-the-Art," where a host of computer programs were described, illustrated, and made accessible (Rupp, 2009; see also Rupp,

Templin, & Henson, 2010, for a summary of this work). We present the citations in Table 7.1 from the symposium for each cognitively based statistical method so the reader can access the computer program if desired.[2]

Of the methods shown in Table 7.1, all twelve can be applied to dichotomously scored data, but only five can be used with poly-tomously scored data. Six of the twelve methods are applicable to non-compensatory cognitive skill structures, five methods with compensatory structures, and one method with both structures. Software is now available to operationalize each of the methods – some programs can even implement multiple methods. For instance, Templin, Henson, Douglas, and Hoffman (2009) presented software written in Mplus and SAS that can be used with the DINA, NIDA, DINO, NIDO, NC-RUM, and C-RUM (J. Templin, personal communication, May 12, 2010).

THREE APPLICATIONS OF COGNITIVELY BASED STATISTICAL METHODS

Next, we present recent applications for three of the cognitively based statistical methods cited in Table 7.1 – the non-compensatory repa-rameterized unified model (NC-RUM), Bayesian networks (BN), and the attribute hierarchy method (AHM) – to the content areas of reading, computing science, and mathematics, respectively. Our goal is to illustrate how these methods are currently used to analyze examinees' knowledge and skills, as measured on large-scale educa-tional tests, in three different achievement domains. We conclude by presenting a critique of these applications from a cognitive modeling perspective.

---

[2] The proceedings from the symposium are available online at http://www.education. umd.edu/EDMS/fac/Rupp/AERA-SIG%20Software%20Symposium%20 (Handout%20 Package).pdf

Evaluating Reading Comprehension Using the Non-Compensatory Reparameterized Unified Model

Jang (2009) applied the non-compensatory reparameterized unified model (NC-RUM; Hartz, 2002; Roussos et al., 2007) to a subset of reading comprehension items that were based on the Test of English as Foreign Languages (TOEFL) to generate cognitive diagnostic inferences about examinees. The NC-RUM is an IRT-based method that uses examinees' item-response probabilities linked to a pre-specified cognitive skill structure outlined in a Q-matrix to determine examinees' mastery of each skill. The Q-matrix, of order k-by-p, where k is the number of cognitive skills and p is the number of items, identifies skill-by-item combinations in the assessment. The Q-matrix is significant in a cognitively based statistical method like the NC-RUM because it serves as a type of cognitive-test specification that identifies each skill-by-item interaction (Leighton & Gierl, 2007a). The Q-matrix does not, however, order skills or specify the relationships among the skills, as one would expect with a cognitive model (see chapters 3, 4, and 5 for examples of ordered relationships among knowledge and skills). Jang conducted her study in three phases. In Phase 1, nine primary reading comprehension skills were identified using protocol and/or verbal analysis, and then validated using expert judgments. In Phase 2, cognitively based statistical analyses were conducted on a sample of reading comprehension items using the NC-RUM to estimate the examinees' probability of mastery. These probabilities were used to develop diagnostic score reports. In Phase 3, the diagnostic score reports were evaluated by potential users, including students and teachers, for their information value and instructional worth. Our summary focuses on the results from Phases 1 and 2 of Jang's (2009) study.

Phase 1: Identify and validate primary skills. A cognitive-test specification must be generated in the form of a Q-matrix to implement the NC-RUM. The Q-matrix defines each skill-by-item interaction in the assessment. Jang (2009) identified nine primary reading comprehension skills by first conducting protocol and/or verbal analysis on the verbal reports produced by eleven ESL students and then validating the skills using the judgments from five raters. The ESL students were asked to verbalize their thought processes and strategies as they solved a subset of reading comprehension items sampled from a *LanguEdge* reading comprehension test. *LanguEdge* courseware is an instructional tool developed by the Educational Testing Service for ESL students. The courseware includes test items from two TOEFL forms – hence, Jang considered the *LanguEdge* reading comprehension items to be an adequate proxy for the TOEFL reading comprehension items. The *LanguEdge* test consists of three twenty-five-minute sections, where each section contains one passage and a set of items. The nine primary skills identified from the sample of *LanguEdge* items are presented in Table 7.2. Five raters then evaluated the reading comprehension skills identified by Jang according to their importance and completeness for solving the reading comprehension items. According to Jang, "the nine skills showed a moderate level of agreement" (p. 40) for their importance and completeness among the five raters. The nine skills were used by Jang to construct a Q-matrix by specifying the skill-by-item interaction on two parallel forms of a *LanguEdge* reading comprehension test.

Phase 2: Cognitively based statistical analyses. Statistical analyses were conducted using the Q-matrix from the two *LanguEdge* reading comprehension forms. The dichotomously scored responses were analyzed using multiple-choice and constructed-response items administered to a sample of 2,703 examinees. The NC-RUM specifies an item-response function[3] as

---

[3] The NC-RUM model is expressed mathematically in this example to illustrate the nature of the statistical methods employed in cognitively based assessment research. Although the remaining examples will not include mathematical expressions of statistical methods and only describe them conceptually, readers interested in the mathematical expressions of the statistical methods described in the remaining examples are referred to Table 7.1, where the original sources of the methods are summarized.

TABLE 7.2. *Nine primary reading comprehension skills identified and validated by Jang (2009)*

---

1. CDV involves deducing the meaning of a word or a phrase by searching and analyzing text and by using contextual clues appearing in the text.
2. CIV requires determining word meaning out of context with recourse to background knowledge.
3. SSL requires comprehending relations between parts of text through lexical and grammatical cohesion devices within and across successive sentences without logical problems.
4. TWI is reading expeditiously across sentences within a paragraph for literal meaning of portions of text.
5. TIM is reading selectively a paragraph or across paragraphs to recognize salient ideas paraphrased based on implicit information in text.
6. INF involves skimming through paragraphs and making propositional inferences about arguments or a writer's purpose with recourse to implicitly stated information or prior knowledge.
7. NEG is reading carefully or expeditiously to locate relevant information in text and to determine which information is true or not true.
8. SUM is analyzing and evaluating relative importance of information in the text by distinguishing major ideas from supporting details.
9. MCF is recognizing major contrasts and arguments in the text whose rhetorical structure contains the relationships such as compare/contrast, cause/effect, or alternative arguments and map them into a mental framework.

$$P(X_{ij} = 1|\alpha_j, \theta_j) = \pi_i^* \prod_{k=1}^{k} r_{ik}^{*(1-\alpha_{jk})X_{qik}} P_{c_i}(\theta_i)$$

where the ability parameters, α_j and θ_j, refer to the skill mastery parameters that are both specified and unspecified (i.e., residual) in the Q-matrix, respectively; π_i^* is the probability that an examinee who has mastered all of the skills specified in the Q-matrix for item i will, in fact, apply the skills when solving the item; r_{ik}^* is an indicator of the diagnostic quality of item i for skill k and it can be used to evaluate model-data fit; and c_i is an indicator of the degree to which the item-response function depends on skills other than those specified in the Q-matrix – again, a measure of model-data fit. The software *Arpeggio* (see Table 7.1, Bolt et al., 2009) is used to estimate the parameters with the hierarchical Bayesian Markov Chain Monte Carlo method. This method is an intensive estimation technique, where the program simulates Markov chains of posterior distributions for all parameters using the observed item-response data until the chains converge on the desired distributions.

Jang (2009) evaluated the fit of the Q-matrix to the examinees' response data by reviewing the r_{ik}^* and c_i parameters. r_{ik}^*, an indicator of diagnostic quality, is optimal when close to 0, meaning better fit to the data. c_i, an indicator of the completeness of the Q-matrix, is also optimal when close to 0, and again means better fit to the data. Jang reported that the initial Q-matrix specification resulted in too many large r_{ik}^* and c_i values. Hence, the Q-matrix was re-specified, the c_i parameters constrained, and the NC-RUM re-estimated. The result was adequate fit between the Q-matrix and the observed response data as the predicted score distributions approximated the observed score distributions; the predicted statistics were comparable to the observed statistics; and the examinees' posterior probability of mastery (i.e., diagnostic scores) were highly correlated with total test score, particularly for those examinees in the middle of the score distribution.

Because the Q-matrix fit the observed data, the posterior probability of mastery was computed for each item and every examinee. The item probability indicates how reliably each item classifies examinees into their skill-based mastery levels. The examinee probability indicates the likelihood that an examinee has mastered a specific skill, where a higher value indicates that the examinee is more likely to possess the cognitive skill. Jang reported three mastery levels: "non-master" (posterior probability of mastery < 0.4), "undetermined" (0.4 ≤ posterior probability of mastery ≤ 0.6), and "master" (posterior probability of mastery > 0.6). The examinees' posterior probability of mastery were then used to create a diagnostic score report called *DiagnOsis* (see Jang, 2009, appendix). These reports yield detailed information on each examinee's skill profile and "skill mastery standing." This diagnostic information is directly linked to Jang's nine primary skill descriptions, is produced for each student, and yields diagnostic information in a format that is easily understood.

Assessing Learning Progressions in Computing Science Using Bayesian Networks

West and colleagues (2009) used Bayesian networks (BN; Pearl, 1988; Yan et al., 2003) to assess the computer network problem-solving skill of IP addressing[4] and to classify examinees into four different mastery skill levels. A Bayesian network (BN) is a statistical method that combines probability and graphical theory to identify the probabilistic relationships among variables by specifying the recursive conditional distributions that structure a joint distribution. The variables can possess either a compensatory or non-compensatory relationship. BNs use indicators of competency, where the indicators and their relationships are defined. The indicators and their relationships serve as the cognitive-skill specifications. BNs, drawing on probability theory, use the relationships specified among the cognitive skills to estimate the strength of these relationships (Mislevy & Levy, 2007). West et al. (2009) present a "worked example" for assessing learning in the skill of IP addressing. Their example is developed in two parts. In Part 1, they describe how expert judgments were used to identify four skill levels required to make inferences about how examinees learn IP addressing. In Part 2, they present the results from their cognitively based statistical analyses. BNs produce output that yield probabilistic inferences for judging the quality of the test items for measuring learning as well as the skill level of the examinees as they progress from novice to advanced levels of performance.

Part 1: Identify skill levels. Indicators of skilled performance must be identified and the relationship among these indicators specified to

---

[4] An Internet Protocol (IP) address is a numeric label assigned to networked computers. The IP address allows computers in the network to communicate with one another.

implement BNs. The indicators of skilled performance in IP addressing were outlined in the Cisco Networking Academy[5] curriculum using statements about examinees' knowledge, skills, and abilities (KSAs). The KSAs highlighted key learning outcomes for each curricular area and also guided the development of items for the end-of-chapter tests. The KSAs were arranged into mastery categories by having content experts match the KSAs at four skill levels (see Table 7.3), with items from end-of-chapter exams to identify those items at each skill level that could serve as indicators for learning IP addressing. The items for each skill level were also selected to represent a hierarchy of ordered cognitive skills, meaning that items at lower levels were expected to measure the most basic IP addressing skills and, hence, be relatively easy for examinees, whereas items at the higher levels were expected to measure more advanced skills producing relatively difficult items. In other words, the cognitive skills in this study were assumed to have a non-compensatory relationship. Thirty-four items were used to measure the KSAs at four different skill levels. Examinees who wrote these items were also expected to produce well-defined skill profiles at each level, where, for instance, those examinees at the "Basic" skill level would have a higher probability of mastering the basic items, and examinees at the "Intermediate" skill level would have a higher probability of answering the intermediate items correctly. Preliminary analyses revealed that the average item-difficulty values increased for each level, save one item. This item was subsequently dropped from the study.

After identifying items at the four skill levels, data from a cross-sectional sample of 3,827 examinees were analyzed to evaluate the progression of learning from the "Novice" to "Advanced" skill level. Cross-sectional data were used because every examinee did not

---

[5] The Cisco Networking Academy is a global education program focused on networking technologies in the information technology industry. The program offers courses in physical networking and protocols, routing, LAN switching, and wide-area networking.

TABLE 7.3. *Knowledge, skills, and abilities at four skill levels for IP addressing described in West et al. (2009)*

Skill Level 1 – Novice (Knowledge/Skills)
- Student can navigate the operating system to get to the appropriate screen to configure the address.
- Student knows that four things need to be configured: IP address, subnet mask, default gateway and DNS server.
- Student can enter and save information.
- Student can use a web browser to test whether or not network is working.
- Student can verify that the correct information was entered and correct any errors.
- Student knows that DNS translates names to IP addresses.
- Student understands why a DNS server IP address must be configured.

Skill Level 2 – Basic (Knows Fundamental Concepts)
- Student understands that an IP address corresponds to a source or destination host on the network.
- Student understands that an IP address has two parts, one indicating the individual unique host and one indicating the network that the host resides on.
- Student understands how the subnet mask indicates the network and host portions of the address.
- Student understands the concept of local –vs- remote networks.
- Student understands the purpose of a default gateway and why it must be specified.
- Student knows that IP address information can be assigned dynamically.
- Student can explain the difference between a broadcast traffic pattern and a unicast traffic pattern.

Skill Level 3 – Intermediate (Knows More Advanced Concepts)
- Student understands the difference between physical and logical connectivity.
- Student can explain the process of encapsulation.
- Student understands the difference between Layer 2 and Layer 3 networks and addressing.
- Student understands that a local IP network corresponds to a local IP broadcast domain (both the terms and the functionality).
- Student knows how a device uses the subnet mask to determine which addresses are on the local Layer 3 broadcast domain and which addresses are not.
- Student understands the concept of subnets and how the subnet mask determines the network address.
- Student understands why the default gateway IP address must be on the same local broadcast domain as the host.
- Student understands ARP and how Layer 3 to Layer 2 address translation is accomplished.
- Student knows how to interpret a network diagram in order to determine the local and remote networks.
- Student understands how DHCP dynamically assigns IP addresses.

Level 4 –Advanced (Can Apply Knowledge and Skills in Context)

- Student can use the subnet mask to determine what other devices are on the same local network as the configured host.
- Student can use a network diagram to find the local network where the configured host is located.
- Student can use a network diagram to find the other networks attached to the local default gateway.
- Student can use the PING utility to test connectivity to the gateway and to remote devices.
- Student can recognize the symptoms that occur when the IP address or subnet mask is incorrect.
- Student can recognize the symptoms that occur if an incorrect default gateway is configured.
- Student can recognize the symptoms that occur if an incorrect DNS server (or no DNS server) is specified.
- Student knows why DNS affects the operation of other applications and protocols, like email or file sharing.
- Student can use NSlookup output to determine if DNS is functioning correctly.
- Student can configure a DHCP pool to give out a range of IP addresses.
- Student knows the purpose of private and public IP address spaces and when to use either one.
- Student understands what NAT is and why it is needed.

---

complete all end-of-chapter test items. Rather, different numbers of examinees wrote different end-of-chapter tests during a month-long assessment session.

Part 2: Cognitively based statistical analyses. Cognitively based statistical analyses were conducted using data from thirty-three end-of-chapter multiple-choice items judged by content experts to represent a hierarchy of ordered cognitive skills in IP addressing. Dichotomously scored item responses from a cross-sectional sample of 3,827 examinees were analyzed. The structure for the BN analysis was first evaluated by conducting a latent class analysis on the examinee response data to identify the optimal number of skill levels. Five potential skill-level structures were evaluated, each ranging from two to six skill levels. The analyses revealed that a four -skill-level structure provided the best fit to the observed data and corresponded to increasing levels of performance from "Novice" to "Advanced." These results were used to create a four-skill-level BN. The software *Netica* (Norsys Software, 2007; see also Table 7.1, Almond & Shute, 2009) was used for the BN analyses.

The fit and utility of the four skill levels for predicting examinees' responses were evaluated using conditional probabilities with the BN method. The odds of answering each item correctly were computed for each skill level, and then the odds ratio was computed to compare the adjacent skill levels. The majority of items discriminated between levels, revealing that the items could be used to differentiate between the four skill levels. The posterior distribution for each skill indicator was then used to compute the probability of skill-level membership for each examinee. Again, the majority of examinees had interpretable probability values, indicating that examinees could be placed into one of the four skill levels.

Taken together, the results from this study demonstrate how BNs can yield probabilistic information to promote inferences about learning IP addressing. The results also provide researchers and practitioners with resources for measuring student learning. For example, West et al. (2009) demonstrated that their items differentiated examinees among four skill levels and that these items could be used in future studies to measure IP addressing performance ranging from "Novice" to "Advanced." These classification results can be used by students and teachers not only to describe a student's current competency level, but also to identify the knowledge and skills that should be taught and mastered if the student wants to move to the next skill level.

Evaluating Mathematics Performance Using the Attribute Hierarchy Method

Gierl, Wang, and Zhou (2008b) applied the attribute hierarchy method (AHM; Leighton et al., 2004; Gierl et al., 2008a) to a subset of SAT ratios and algebra items to generate cognitive diagnostic inferences about examinees. The AHM is a psychometric method for classifying examinees' test-item responses into a set of attribute patterns associated with a cognitive hierarchy of knowledge and skills. An attribute is a description of the knowledge and skills needed to perform a task. These attributes are first identified and then ordered to form a hierarchy of non-compensatory knowledge and skills. Gierl et al. (2008b) conducted their study in two steps. In Step 1, an attribute hierarchy was developed by asking content experts to review a sample of SAT ratios and algebra items, identify their salient attributes, and order the attributes into a hierarchy. Then, the attribute hierarchy was validated by having a sample of students think aloud as they solved each item. In Step 2, cognitively based statistical analyses were conducted on the SAT ratios and algebra hierarchy by evaluating the fit between the expected response patterns generated by the attribute hierarchy and the observed response patterns produced from a sample of examinees who wrote the items. Attribute probabilities were also computed for the examinee sample so diagnostic score reports could be generated.

Step 1: Develop and validate algebra-attribute hierarchy. An attribute hierarchy must be specified to implement the AHM. Gierl et al. (2008b) conducted a task analysis on a sample of nine SAT ratios and algebra items to identify the knowledge and skills assumed to underlie performance and then to order these knowledge and skills in the form of a hierarchy. The task analysis conducted by Gierl and his team required that each team member write each test item to identify the mathematical concepts, operations, procedures, and strategies used to solve the items and then categorize these cognitive attributes, producing a logically ordered hierarchical sequence from simple to complex. Their hierarchy for the knowledge and skills in the areas of ratio and algebra is presented in Figure 7.1. The test-item number used to operationalize the knowledge and skills from the task analysis are summarized at the right side of each attribute along with their difficulty level calculated from a random sample of 5,000 students who wrote

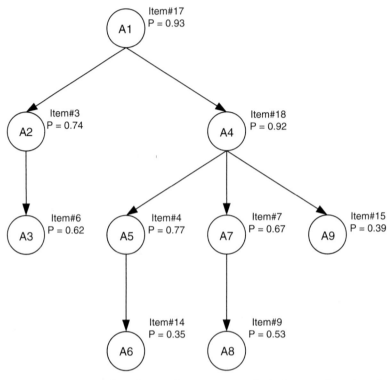

FIGURE 7.1. An attribute hierarchy in ratios and algebra used to describe examinee performance on a sample of SAT mathematics items.

these items. The hierarchy contains two independent branches that share a common prerequisite – attribute A1. The first branch includes two additional attributes, A2 and A3, and the second branch includes a sub-hierarchy with attributes A4 through A9. Three independent branches comprise the sub-hierarchy: attributes A4, A5, A6; attributes A4, A7, A8; and attributes A4, A9. The attributes presented in Figure 7.1 are described in Table 7.4.

Next, the SAT ratios and algebra hierarchy were validated by having a sample of twenty-one high school students think aloud as they solved each item. From the transcribed audiotapes of each session, cognitive flow charts were created to represent students' knowledge

TABLE 7.4. *Knowledge and skills required to solve the items in the ratios and algebra hierarchy as identified and validated by Gierl et al. (2008b)*

Attribute A1 represents the most basic arithmetic operation skills.

Attribute A2 includes knowledge about the properties of factors.

Attribute A3 involves the skills of applying the rules of factoring.

Attribute A4 includes the skills required for substituting values into algebraic expressions.

Attribute A5 represents the skills of mapping a graph of a familiar function with its corresponding function.

Attribute A6 deals with the abstract properties of functions, such as recognizing the graphical representation of the relationship between independent and dependent variables.

Attribute A7 requires the skills to substitute numbers into algebraic expressions.

Attribute A8 represents the skills of advanced substitution. Algebraic expressions, rather than numbers, need to be substituted into another algebraic expression.

Attribute A9 is related to skills associated with rule understanding and application.

and skills reported in the think-aloud protocols. These flowcharts were used to evaluate the item attributes and their hierarchical ordering created initially by Gierl and his team. Two raters compared the student think-aloud flow chart data to the SAT ratios and algebra hierarchy shown in Figure 7.1. Results from the rater analysis revealed that the attribute hierarchy provided a strong approximation to the actual student data: The verbal reports did not result in any structural changes to the hierarchy but did result in more concise descriptions of each attribute in Table 7.4.

Step 2: Cognitively based statistical analyses. Cognitively based statistical analyses were conducted on the data generated from the SAT ratios and algebra hierarchy. Dichotomously scored item responses from a random sample of 5,000 students who wrote the nine SAT items specified in Figure 7.1 were analyzed. The fit of the attribute hierarchy to the examinee response data was evaluated with the Hierarchy Consistency Index (HCI_i; Cui & Leighton, 2009). The software *Mathematica* (see Table 7.1, Cui, Gierl, & Leighton, 2009) was used for all AHM analyses. The HCI_i, which ranges from -1 to $+1$, assesses the degree to which the expected response data, specified based on the attribute hierarchy, are consistent with observed response patterns produced when the examinees respond to the SAT test items. An HCI_i greater than 0.70 indicates good model-data fit. Using data from the 5,000 student sample, the mean HCI_i was high for the SAT ratios and algebra hierarchy at 0.80, indicating good to strong model-data fit.

Because the model fit the data, attribute-mastery probabilities were computed. Attribute-mastery probabilities provide examinees with specific information about their attribute-level performance. To compute these probabilities, a neural network is used (Gierl et al., 2008a; see also Rumelhart, Hinton, & Williams, 1986a, 1986b). The input to train the neural network is the expected response vectors, which are derived from the SAT ratios and algebra hierarchy (see Gierl et al., 2008b, pp. 34–36). For each expected response vector there is a specific combination of examinee attributes such that the relationship between the vectors and the attributes is established by presenting each pattern to the network repeatedly until it learns the associations. These associations are represented as a set of weight matrices that can be used to transform any observed examinee response pattern to its associate attribute vector using a 0 to 1 scaling (McClelland, 1998). These scaled outcomes, described as attribute-mastery probabilities, serve as a type of attribute score that can be interpreted as probabilistic values, where a higher value indicates that the examinee has a higher likelihood of possessing the attribute.

The attribute-mastery probabilities were used to create individualized diagnostic score reports (see Gierl et al., 2008b, p. 40 for an example; see also Gierl, Alves, & Taylor-Majeau, 2010). These reports yield detailed information about the knowledge and skills measured by the test items and the degree to which each examinee has mastered these cognitive skills. Three performance levels were used to report on attribute mastery: "non-mastery" (attribute probability < 0.35), "partial mastery" ($0.35 \leq$ attribute probability ≤ 0.70), and "mastery" (attribute probability > 0.70). This diagnostic information is directly linked to the knowledge and skill descriptions associated with the attribute hierarchy, is individualized for each student, and is easily presented and interpreted.

Limitations across the Three Studies from a Cognitive Modeling Perspective

Important limitations should be noted in our three illustrative examples, particularly as they relate to the specificity of the knowledge and skills and the inclusion of the cognitive variables in the statistical methods. Across all three studies, the knowledge and skills differ in their content, source, and number (see Tables 7.2–7.4); that is, each application extracted different types of knowledge and skills from different sources and at different grain sizes. Grain size refers to both the depth and breadth of the knowledge and skills measured. To promote specific cognitive inferences, knowledge and skills must be specified at an "appropriate" grain size so they can magnify the knowledge and skills that underlie test performance. Unfortunately, the factors required to identify an appropriate grain size are poorly defined, particularly when assessment proceeds without an empirically based cognitive model (see Chapters 1–5). The challenges with selecting an appropriate grain size become even more daunting when methods such as NC-RUM, BN, and the AHM are used, because the knowledge and skills can easily be decomposed into more specific components. By defining cognitive skills at a finer grain size, the specificity of the cognitive inferences increases, but the number of items required to measure these additional skills also increases, leading to a longer exam. West et al. (2009) used knowledge, skills, and abilities (i.e., KSAs) outlined in a curriculum to identify competencies for IP addressing. This approach resulted in a large number of knowledge and skills (i.e., thirty-six KSAs across the four skill levels). Conversely, Jang (2009) and Gierl et al. (2008b) reviewed a sample of existing test items to identify the most salient knowledge and skills and then attempted to verify these cognitive components using protocol and/or verbal analysis. Their approach resulted in a relatively small number of knowledge and skills (i.e., nine cognitive attributes for reading comprehension and mathematics, respectively). The variation across these studies demonstrates that grain size is a factor that permits different types and levels of cognitive inferences. The validity of the cognitive inferences in all three studies rests largely on the judgments of content experts.

Judgments from content experts are used extensively in large-scale educational testing, from the initial stages of item development to the final stages of item validation. Typically, content experts develop items by anticipating the knowledge and skills that examinees will use to answer the items correctly in each content area (see Chapter 2, this volume). However, developing items for cognitively based assessments poses some unique challenges, in part because these types of tests are based on specific, sometimes ordered, knowledge and skills that guide inferences about how examinees' solve test items. Whereas the perception of content experts on how examinees solve items may have some predictive utility, a more principled approach to assessment design and development would draw on empirically based cognitive models. Cognitive models based on examinees from a target population of interest would include relevant knowledge and skills to be used in developing test items and guiding the cognitively based statistical analyses. Ideally, cognitive models used in assessment design would have empirical support in the learning scientific literature (see Chapters 3, 4, and 5).

All three studies we reviewed in this chapter used judgments from content experts to identify the primary knowledge and skills, but only Jang (2009) and Gierl et al. (2008b) attempted to verify these judgments by also analyzing examinees' verbal reports using protocol and/or verbal analysis. The verification of knowledge and skills in these two studies was limited to a small number of students using only a sample of test items. Hence, the usefulness of the protocol and/or verbal analysis results is limited to the student and item sample and, hence, it provides no information on how the findings may generalize to students at different achievement levels, in different gender or ethnic groups, or at different points in the learning cycle. Neither West et al. (2009) nor Jang (2009) and Gierl et al. (2008b) cited research from the learning sciences to support the development or validation of the knowledge and skills used in their cognitively based statistical analyses.

Without a well-defined cognitive model as a starting point for the design and development of an assessment, retrofitting becomes the method of choice. Retrofitting was used in all three examples in this chapter. Retrofitting can be characterized as the application of a new statistical method to examinees' item-response data collected from an existing testing system that, typically, uses traditional test-development procedures and practices. When data from an existing testing program are retrofit to an assessment, the Q-matrix is generated *post-hoc*, typically by conducting content reviews of items that already exist on the test. These existing items are then used to measure the knowledge and skills specified in the *post-hoc* Q-matrix. Although common in large-scale educational testing, retrofitting severely restricts our test-score inferences for at least two reasons. First, the primary skill ratings, skill levels, or attribute hierarchies, as illustrated in this chapter, are based on limited learning scientific evidence – single content reviews and small verbal report studies. To better validate the knowledge and skills, researchers must draw on outcomes from the learning sciences as well as supporting studies that focus on examinee content-specific performances using a host of quantitative, qualitative, and mixed methods. The three studies we reviewed in this chapter offer limited data to fully validate the knowledge and skills used in their applications. Hence, the validity and generalizability of the results from these studies are not well-established, meaning that the inferences we can draw about examinees' knowledge and skills must be considered tentatively.

Second, the knowledge and skills required to perform well in a domain should be identified during test design and prior to item development. In our three sample studies, no new items were developed to measure examinees' knowledge and skills. Yet this sequence of events – where the cognitive model is first identified and the test items are then developed – is needed because the type of knowledge and skills, their grain size, and their relationships within a model should guide the development of test items and, subsequently, the analyses of examinees' item-response data and interpretation of test performance. In other words, when the knowledge and skills specified in the cognitive model are used to create items, the developer is able to control the attributes measured by each item. Furthermore, controlling the attributes measured by each item leads to a more informed selection of the cognitively based statistical method used to analyze the data and, presumably, more specific and valid inferences about the examinees' cognitive proficiencies. These important benefits are not realized with a retrofitting approach, because only the knowledge and skills associated with existing test items are measured. Moreover, the distribution of items is likely to be uneven across the knowledge and skills measured on the test because no new items have been developed. This uneven distribution of items will likely diminish the usefulness of the assessment because some knowledge and skills will be associated with only small numbers of items, leading to uneven informational profiles for test-based inferences.

Assessing model-data fit provides one procedure for evaluating the accuracy of a retrofitting approach. The researchers in our three studies used different methods to monitor the fit of the knowledge and skills specified with the observed response data. In each case, the data were judged to fit the cognitive structure analyzed with their statistical method. Jang (2009) evaluated and subsequently adjusted the fit of the Q-matrix to the examinee response data by reviewing two parameters: r_{ik}^*, an indicator of diagnostic quality, and c_i, an indicator of the completeness of the Q-matrix. West et al. (2009) computed different measures and indicators of model-data fit by drawing on the order of the item-difficulty values to validate the hierarchical item structure as well as the results from a latent-class analysis to guide the choice of BN skill structure. Gierl et al. (2008b) used the Hierarchy Consistency

Index to compare examinees' expected and observed response patterns. Unfortunately, the number of items measuring the knowledge and skills varied dramatically across the three studies, resulting in either a small (e.g., Gierl, Wang, et al.) or highly variable (e.g., Jang and West et al.) skill-to-item ratio that may not adversely affect model-data fit, but most certainly lowers the reliability of the diagnostic scores and, in turn, the accuracy of the test-score inferences (Gierl, Cui, & Zhou, 2009).

CONCLUSION AND SUMMARY

This chapter identified twelve cognitively based statistical methods used in many recent publications on cognition and assessment. The methods were cataloged according to three key features: observed item-response scale, cognitive skill relationship, and software. This presentation provides researchers and practitioners with a concise summary of the statistical methods that can be employed to evaluate the knowledge and skills used by examinees' to solve items on large-scale educational tests. It also provided a brief overview of how these methods compare and contrast. We then presented recent applications for three of the cognitively based statistical methods in the areas of reading comprehension, computing science, and mathematics. Our summary illustrates how cognitive variables are typically conceptualized, identified, analyzed, and reported. We also highlighted some important limitations in how knowledge and skills are often measured on large-scale educational tests relative to the cognitive modeling perspective described in the previous chapters of this book.

REFERENCES

Almond, R. & Shute, A. (2009, April). Calibration of Bayesian network-based diagnostic assessment. In A. Rupp (Chair), *Software for calibrating diagnostic classification models: An overview of the current state-of-the-art.* Symposium conducted at the meeting of the American Educational Research Association, San Diego, CA.

Bolt, D., Chen, H., DiBello, L., Hartz, S., Henson, R., Roussos, L., Stout, W., & Templin, J. (April 2009). Cognitive diagnostic psychometric modelling: Fitting the fusion model with the Arpeggio system software. In A. Rupp (Chair), *Software for calibrating diagnostic classification models: An overview of the current state-of-the-art*. Symposium conducted at the meeting of the American Educational Research Association, San Diego, CA.

Cui, Y., Gierl, M.J., & Leighton, J.P. (2009, April). Estimating the attribute hierarchy method with Mathematica. In A. Rupp (Chair), *Software for calibrating diagnostic classification models: An overview of the current state-of-the-art*. Symposium conducted at the meeting of the American Educational Research Association, San Diego, CA.

Cui, Y. & Leighton, J.P. (2009). The hierarchy consistency index: Evaluating person fit for cognitive diagnostic assessment. *Journal of Educational Measurement, 46*, 429–449.

de la Torre, J. (2008, July). *The generalized DINA model*. Paper presented at the annual International Meeting of the Psychometric Society (IMPS), Durham, NH.

(2009, April). Estimation code for the G-DINA model. In A. Rupp (Chair), *Software for calibrating diagnostic classification models: An overview of the current state-of-the-art*. Symposium conducted at the meeting of the American Educational Research Association, San Diego, CA.

de la Torre, J. & Douglas, J.A. (2004). Higher-order latent trait models for cognitive diagnosis. *Psychometrika, 69*, 333–353.

Frederiksen, N., Glaser, R.L., Lesgold, A.M., & Shafto, M.G. (1990). *Diagnostic monitoring of skills and knowledge acquisition*. Hillsdale, NJ: Erlbaum.

Fu, J. & Li, Y. (2007, April). *Cognitively diagnostic psychometric models: An integrated review*. Paper presented at the annual meeting of the National Council on Measurement in Education, Chicago, IL.

Gierl, M.J., Cui, Y., & Hunka, S. (2008a). Using connectionist models to evaluate examinees' response patterns on tests. *Journal of Modern Applied Statistical Methods, 7*, 234–245.

Gierl, M.J., Cui, Y., & Zhou, J. (2009). Reliability of attribute-based scoring in cognitive diagnostic assessment. *Journal of Educational Measurement, 46*, 293–313.

Gierl, M.J., Wang, C., & Zhou, J. (2008b). Using the attribute hierarchy method to make diagnostic inferences about examinees' cognitive skills in algebra on the SAT©. *Journal of Technology, Learning, and Assessment, 6* (6). Retrieved [date] from http://www.jtla.org.

Gierl, M.J., Alves, C., & Taylor-Majeau, R. (2010). Using the Attribute Hierarchy Method to make diagnostic inferences about examinees' skills in mathematics: An operational implementation of cognitive diagnostic assessment. *International Journal of Testing, 10*, 318–341.

Hartz, S. (2002). *A Bayesian framework for the unified model for assessing cognitive abilities: Blending theory with practicality*. Unpublished doctoral dissertation, University of Illinois at Urbana-Champaign, Urbana-Champaign, IL.

Henson, R.A., Templin, J.L., & Willse, J.T. (2008). *Defining a family of cognitive diagnostic model using log-linear models with latent variables. Psychometrika, 74*, 191–210.

Jang, E.E. (2009). Cognitive diagnostic assessment of L2 reading comprehension ability: Validity arguments for fusion model application to *LanguEdge* assessment. *Language Testing, 26*, 31–73.

Junker, B.W. & Sijtsma, K. (2001). Cognitive assessment models with few assumptions, and connections with nonparametric item response theory. *Applied Psychological Measurement, 25*, 258–272.

Lee, Y.W. & Sawaki, Y. (2009). Cognitive diagnosis approaches to language assessment: An overview. *Language Assessment Quarterly, 6*, 172–189.

Leighton, J.P. (2009). Where's the psychology?: A commentary on "Unique Characteristics of Diagnostic Classification Models: A Comprehensive Review of the Current State-of-the-Art." *Measurement: Interdisciplinary Research and Perspectives, 6(4)*, 272–275.

Leighton, J.P. & Gierl, M.J. (2007a). Defining and evaluating models of cognition used in educational measurement to make inferences about examinees' thinking processes. *Educational Measurement: Issues and Practice, 26*, 3–16.

(Eds.). (2007b). *Cognitive diagnostic assessment for education: Theory and applications*. Cambridge, UK: Cambridge University Press.

Leighton, J.P., Gierl, M.J., & Hunka, S. (2004). The attribute hierarchy method for cognitive assessment: A variation on Tatsuoka's rule-space approach. *Journal of Educational Measurement, 41*, 205–236.

Maris, E. (1995). Psychometric latent response models. *Psychometrika, 60*, 523–547.

McClelland, J.L. (1998). Connectionist models and Bayesian inference. In M. Oaksford & N. Chater (Eds.), *Rational models of cognition* (pp. 21–53). Oxford: Oxford University Press.

Mislevy, R.J. & Levy, R. (2007). Bayesian psychometric modeling from an evidence-centered design perspective. In C. R. Rao & S. Sinharay (Eds.), *Handbook of statistics, Vol. 26* (pp. 839–865). Amsterdam, The Netherlands: Elsevier.

Nichols, P.D. (1994). A framework for developing cognitively diagnostic assessments. *Review of Educational Research, 64*, 575–603.

Nichols, P.D., Chipman, S.F., & Brennan, R.L. (1995). *Cognitively diagnostic assessment.* Hillsdale, NJ: Erlbaum.

Norsys Software (2007). *Netica manual.* Http://www.norsys.com.

Pearl, J. (1988). *Probabilistic reasoning in intelligent systems: Networks of plausible inference.* San Mateo, CA: Kaufmann.

Ronning, R., Glover, J., Conoley, J.C., & Witt, J. (1990). *The influence of cognitive psychology on testing and measurement: The Buros-Nebraska symposium on measurement and testing (Vol. 3.).* Hillsdale, NJ: Erlbaum.

Roussos, L., DiBello, L.V., Stout, W., Hartz, S., Henson, R.A., & Templin, J.H. (2007). The fusion model skills diagnosis system. In J. P. Leighton, & Gierl, M. J. (Eds.), *Cognitive diagnostic assessment for education: Theory and applications* (pp. 275–318). Cambridge, UK: Cambridge University Press.

Rumelhart, D.E., Hinton, G.E., & Williams, R.J. (1986a). Learning representations by back-propagating errors. *Nature, 323,* 533–536.

(1986b). *Parallel distributed processing* (Vol. 1). Cambridge, MA: MIT Press.

Rupp, A. A. (2009, April). *Software for calibrating diagnostic classification models: An overview of the current state-of-the-art.* Symposium conducted at the meeting of the American Educational Research Association, San Diego, CA.

Rupp, A. A. & Templin, J. (2008). Unique characteristics of diagnostic classification models: A comprehensive review of the current state-of-the-art. *Measurement: Interdisciplinary Research and Perspectives, 6,* 219–262.

Rupp, A.A., Templin, J.L., & Henson, R.A. (2010). *Diagnostic measurement: Theory, methods, and applications.* New York: The Guilford Press.

Snow, R.E. & Lohman, D.F. (1989). Implications of cognitive psychology for educational measurement. In R. L. Linn (Ed.), *Educational measurement* (3rd ed., pp. 263–331). New York: American Council on Education, Macmillan.

Tatsuoka, K.K. (1983). Rule space: An approach for dealing with misconceptions based on item response theory. *Journal of Educational Measurement, 20,* 345–354.

(1995). Architecture of knowledge structures and cognitive diagnosis: A statistical pattern recognition and classification approach. In P.D. Nichols, S.F. Chipman, & R.L. Brennan (Eds.), *Cognitively diagnostic assessment* (pp. 327–359). Hillsdale, NJ: Erlbaum.

Tatsuoka, K.K. & Tatsuoka, C. (2009, April). The rule space methodology: The Q matrix theory, rule space classification space and POSET model. In A. Rupp (Chair), *Software for calibrating diagnostic classification models: An overview of the current state-of-the-art.* Symposium conducted at the meeting of the American Educational Research Association, San Diego, CA.

Templin, J.L. (2006). *CDM user's guide*. Unpublished manuscript.

Templin, J.L. & Henson, R.A. (2006). Measurement of psychological disorders using cognitive diagnosis models. *Psychological Methods, 11*, 287–305.

Templin, J.L, Henson, R.A., Douglas, J., & Hoffman, L. (2009, April). Estimating log-linear diagnostic classification models with Mplus and SAS. In A. Rupp (Chair), *Software for calibrating diagnostic classification models: An overview of the current state-of-the-art*. Symposium conducted at the meeting of the American Educational Research Association, San Diego, CA.

Thissen, D. & Steinberg, L. (1986). A taxonomy of item response models. *Psychometrika, 51*, 567–577.

von Davier, M. (2005). *A general diagnostic model applied to language testing data* (ETS Research Report No. RR-05–16). Princeton, NJ: Educational Testing Service.

(2007). *Hierarchical general diagnostic models* (Research Report No. RR-07–19). Princeton, NJ: Educational Testing Service.

von Davier, M. & Xu, X. (2009, April). Estimating latent structure models (including diagnostic classification models) with mdltm: A software for multidimensional discrete latent traits models. In A. Rupp (Chair), *Software for calibrating diagnostic classification models: An overview of the current state-of-the-art*. Symposium conducted at the meeting of the American Educational Research Association, San Diego, CA.

West, P., Rutstein, D.W., Mislevy, R.J., Liu, J., Levy, R., DiCerbo, K.E ., Crawford, A., Choi, Y., & Behrens, J.T. (2009, June). *A bayes net approach to modeling learning progressions and task performances*. Paper presented at the Learning Progression in Science Conference, Iowa City, IA.

Yan, D., Mislevy, R.J., & Almond, R.G. (2003). *Design and analysis in a cognitive assessment* (ETS Research Report No. RR-03–32). Princeton, NJ: Educational Testing Service.

INDEX